THE SEPARATION OF COMMERCIAL AND INVESTMENT BANKING

The Glass–Steagall Act Revisited and Reconsidered

The Separation of Commercial and Investment Banking

The Glass–Steagall Act Revisited and Reconsidered

George J. Benston
Associate Dean, Research and Faculty Department
John H. Harland Professor of Finance, Accounting and
Economics, Emory University, Atlanta, Georgia

New York   Oxford
Oxford University Press
1990

Oxford Univeristy Press

Oxford   New York   Toronto
Delhi   Bombay   Calcutta   Madras   Karachi
Petaling Jaya   Singapore   Hong Kong   Tokyo
Nairobi   Dar es Salaam   Cape Town
Melbourne   Auckland

and associated companies in
Berlin   Ibadan

First published in 1990 by The Macmillan Press Ltd.
Houndmills, Basingstoke, Hampshire RG21 2XS
and London

Library of Congress Cataloging-in-Publication Data

Benston, George J.
    The separation of commercial and investment banking.

    Includes bibliographical references.
    1. Banks and banking—United States—History.
2. Investment banking—United States—History.
3. United States.   Banking Act of 1933—History.
4. Banking law—United States.   5. Securities—
United States.   I. Title.
HG2461.B46   1990   332.1′0973   90–6946
ISBN 0–19–520830–7

2 4 6 8 9 7 5 3 1

Printed in Great Britain

To my wife, Alice: my love, best friend, and teacher – my emotional and intellectual partner

Acknowledgements: Peter Aranson, Roger Mehle, Thomas Huertas, Brian Gendreau, and George Kauf were most generous with incisive criticism and valuable suggestions, for which they deserve great thanks and no blame for what remains.

Contents

List of Tables

1 Introduction

I A VERY BRIEF HISTORY OF THE ACT

In 1933 the US economy had declined to record depths. A quarter of the formerly working population was unemployed. The nation's banking system was a mess. Over 11,000 banks had failed or had to merge, reducing the number by 40 per cent, from 25,000 to 14,000. The governors of several states had closed their states' banks and in March President Roosevelt closed all the banks in the country. Congressional hearings conducted in early 1933 seemed to show that the presumed leaders of American enterprise – the bankers and brokers – were guilty of disreputable and apparently dishonest dealings and gross misuses of the public's trust.

The Banking Act of 1933 was probably the newly-elected Roosevelt administration's most important response to the perceived shambles of the nation's financial and economic system. But the Act did not change the most important weaknesses of the American banking system – unit banking within states and the prohibition of nationwide banking. This structure is considered the principal reason for the failure of so many US banks, some 90 per cent of which were unit banks with under $2 million in assets (White, 1983). (In contrast, Canada, which had nationwide banking, suffered no bank failures and only a few of the over 11,000 US banks that failed or merged were branch banks.) Instead, the Act established new approaches to financial regulation – particularly the institution of deposit insurance and the legal separation of most aspects of commercial and investment banking (the principal exception being allowing commercial banks to underwrite most government-issued bonds). Representative Henry Steagall authored the deposit insurance provisions; Senator Carter Glass was the chief proponent of the separation of commercial and investment banking.

For several years before 1933 Senator Glass had wanted to restrict or forbid commercial banks from dealing in and holding corporate securities. He strongly believed that bank involvement with securities was detrimental to the Federal Reserve system, contrary to the rules of good banking, and responsible for stock market speculation, the Crash of 1929, bank failures, and the Great Depression. It is generally accepted that he was unable to achieve the goal of separating commercial and investment banking until revelations concerning National City Bank were brought forth in the Senate Committee on Banking and Currency's Stock Exchange Practices Hearings.[1] Seligman (1982, p. 29) (and other historians) reports that as a consequence of press accounts of the hearings

> bankers in general became the object of near-hysterical public rage. Surveying the press, the *Literary Digest* recorded an unforgiving mood: 'Apologies, even resignations, do not satisfy listening editors.' The mood in Congress rivaled that of the editors. 'The best way to restore confidence in our banks,' argued Senator Burton Wheeler, 'is to take these crooked presidents out of the banks and treat them the same as they treated Al Capone when Capone avoided payment of his tax.' Carter Glass more than agreed.

'Stock dealings which had made bankers rich and respected in the era of affluence,' Kennedy (1973, p. 104) points out, 'now glared as scarlet sins in the age of depression. Disillusionment with speculators and securities merchants carried over from investment bankers to commercial bankers; the two were often the same, and an embittered public did not care to make fine distinctions.' The Banking Act of 1933 was passed and quickly signed into law.

Several attempts since 1933 by commercial bankers, and at times regulators, to repeal or draft exceptions to those sections of the law that mandate separation of commercial and investment banking – usually referred to alone as 'The Glass–Steagall Act' – generally have not been successful. As a result, the United States and Japan (which was forced to adopt laws similar to the US banking statutes after the Second World War), alone among the world's important financial nations, legally require this separation. (Japanese banks can engage in many securities activities, however, including underwriting and dealing in commercial paper and ownership of up to 5 per cent of non-bank enterprises.) This book explores the reasons for the Act's passage and analyses arguments for and against its continuation.

---

[1] See Perkins (1971) and Kelly (1985a) for excellent concise histories on which this narrative is based. See also Willis and Chapman (1934, p. 101), who state that getting 'the bill [the eventual Banking Act of 1933] adopted in either house was difficult if not impossible . . . [until] the revelations developed by another subcommittee [the Stock Exchange Practices Hearings], concerning undesirable or dangerous practices on the part of investment bankers, gave impetus to the demand for the Glass measure.'

II A BRIEF HISTORY AND OVERVIEW OF THE BOOK

History of the Project

The motivation for this book originated at a 1984 conference I put together and directed for the American Assembly on 'The Future of American Financial Services'. That conference brought together some sixty leading scholars, bankers, and regulators for three days of structured, intensive discussions about the financial services industry and its regulation. In the course of those meetings, I discussed the Glass–Steagall Act's separation of commercial and investment banking with two very able and experienced lawyers, one of whom was then a regulator and the other a senior congressional staffer. Both said, in effect: 'Everyone knows that the Glass–Steagall Act was passed because of the abuses by banks in the late 1920s and early 1930s. If the law were repealed, we might go back to the failures and conflicts of interest that wracked the country before and during the Great Depression.' I responded to the congressional staffer: 'But you were born after 1933,' and to the regulator: 'You were just a few years old in 1933. Neither of you could know from your own experience or even casual observation what actually happened before the Glass–Steagall Act was passed.' They replied: 'But *everybody* knows, it's common knowledge.' To which I said: 'You are both lawyers – give me some citations to the evidence; what is everyone relying on?' The regulator answered: 'Look at Vincent Carosso's excellent book on investment banking, and I recall seeing some descriptions in a recently published book by Joel Seligman, *The Transformation of Wall Street*.' The staffer said that she had seen references to hearings run by Senator Glass and Ferdinand Pecora. That was the beginning of the quest for knowledge that resulted in the writing of this book.

I have tried to track down all of the sources that form the basis of our beliefs about the activities of commercial bankers when they were permitted to engage in securities activities. For this purpose I reviewed the works of historians and economists who have written about the Glass–Steagall Act, primarily (in chronological order of their publication) Peach (1941), Carosso (1970a), Perkins (1971), Kennedy (1973), and Seligman (1982). I examined articles on various aspects of the Act, and their citations to sources and other articles led to additional material. Testimony by the principal proponents of the Act's continuance, the Investment Company Institute and the

Securities Industry Association, often refer to the conditions that gave rise to the legislation. Their descriptions commonly are based on senators' opinions, testimony given at hearings, and the reported findings of congressional inquiries. Some of the writers on the activities of commercial banks before passage of the Glass–Steagall Act, however, rely on secondary sources, such as Pecora's (1939) account of the hearings he conducted (*Wall Street Under Oath: The Story of Our Modern Money Changers*), or just give an unspecified reference to the Pecora Hearings (1933 and 1934), which contain over 11,000 pages.

The principal sources of information about the pre-Glass–Steagall Act period (reviewed in Chapter 2) are primarily congressional hearings and reports. They are the basic building blocks of this enquiry. I traced the conclusions that historians and others drew about the activities of commercial banks when the banks were permitted to engage in securities activities to the testimony given at hearings and data presented in congressional reports. While I take these sources as primary, several important factors limit their value as evidence. The congressmen and their staffs structured the hearings, decided which witnesses to call, and conducted the questioning. Witnesses could not confront their accusers. Nor could people with contrary views call rebuttal witnesses. Thus, there is reason to believe that congressional hearings, then as now, do not provide a complete or unbiased record of events. Indeed, the hearings that preceded the Glass–Steagall Act appear biased towards findings that support the separation of commercial and investment banking. Senator Glass passionately believed that commercial banks should not engage in securities activities. He considered such activities to be a perversion of the banking system, which he helped create with the establishment of the Federal Reserve System in 1913. The 1933–4 Stock Exchange Practices Hearings were directed towards uncovering evidence of wrongdoing, not toward providing a balanced picture of financial practices.

Other sources of information include newspaper accounts, memoirs, interviews and analysis of data. Newspapers can provide insights, but usually little more. Memoirs also can be useful, but they suffer from self-serving bias. Interviews can yield greater insights, since the interviewer asks the questions and can challenge the interviewee's responses. Economists prefer analyses of data because these are impersonal, can be structured to test hypotheses (e.g. banks that had securities affiliates failed more often than those that did not, other things being equal), and can be subjected to formal tests to find out whether the failure rates differ from those that might arise merely from chance (statistical significance). My enquiry does not include direct examination of newspapers and memoirs nor the conducting (or even reporting) of interviews. The basic materials used are congressional hearings and reports and data that report on market and company transactions. I subject these materials to economic reasoning (theory) directed towards delineating and measuring the benefits and costs of alternatives.

Overview of the Book

Most of this book examines and evaluates the evidence and other factors leading to the adoption of the Glass–Steagall Act's separation of commercial and investment banking. The rest of this chapter describes the Act's generally accepted rationale. Chapter 2 reviews the principal sources of information and their contents about pre-Glass–Steagall conditions. Since these sources often are misquoted and misinterpreted and form the basis of many misperceptions about the conditions preceding the Act, it was appropriate to delineate and describe them. Chapter 3 examines the allegations, speculations and data on the relationship between commercial banks' securities services and holdings and risks to the banking system and individual banks. The experience of the financial crisis associated with the Great Depression should provide valuable evidence on the validity of arguments for the passage and continuation of the Glass–Steagall Act.

Chapter 4 explores allegations of conflicts of interest and other abuses. This chapter is relatively long, since it includes a review of the sources of data, and critical analyses of the charges of abuse levied against the National City and Chase National Banks and their securities affiliates, and against commercial-bank-sponsored trusts and investment companies. Chapter 5 examines the belief that the provision of securities services is inherently an improper commercial banking activity. There I offer extensive quotations from an often cited bill of particulars against commercial bank involvement with securities delivered by an important supporter of the separation, Senator Bulkley. Next I report data on the actual performance of banks with respect to securities underwriting and sponsorship of investment trusts to discern the extent to which these possible problems actually had occurred.

Chapter 6 provides alternative explanations (to the safety and soundness and abuses arguments) for the passage of the Glass–Steagall Act. The legal separation of commercial and investment banking may be seen as an example of opportunistic, rent-seeking behaviour by firms that wanted legal constraints put on their competitors. Alternatively, the legislation may have grown out of political necessity – it was the best banks could get in a bad situation.

The next four chapters examine the principal arguments favouring continuation of the Glass–Steagall Act, without concern for whether or not the conditions said to have lead to the original passage of the Act actually occurred. Chapter 7 considers the argument that banks are supported by a federal 'safety net'; consequently, the risks banks can take should be constrained. This chapter reviews evidence on whether the risks that banks face would increase significantly were they permitted to re-enter the securities business. Chapter 8 explores the argument that banks would have an unfair advantage over other suppliers of securities services because they have access to lower cost funds. Chapter 9 briefly examines concerns that an excessive concentration of power and less than competitive performance would result were banks given the right to offer securities services. Chapter 10 delineates the expected advantages and disadvantages of universal banking (which could be the ultimate result of repeal of the Glass–Steagall Act) compared to specialised banking (the present system or even greater specialisation).

The book ends with a return to the initial question, presenting a brief legislative history and analysis of the forces that resulted in the Act's passage, based on the findings of the preceding work, particularly up to Chapter 7. These chapters find an almost complete lack of evidence supporting the separation of commercial and investment banking. Therefore, one is led to question further how the Glass–Steagall Act came to be enacted. The final chapter provides an answer and perhaps some insights into whether and when the Act will be repealed.

III THE PROVISIONS OF THE GLASS-STEAGALL ACT

The 'Glass–Steagall' Act has come to mean only those sections of the Banking Act of 1933 that refer to banks' securities operations –

sections 16, 20, 21, and 32.[1] These four sections of the Act, as amended and interpreted by the Comptroller of the Currency, the Federal Reserve Board and the courts, govern commercial banks' *domestic* securities operations in various ways.

Sections 16 and 21 refer to the direct operations of commercial banks. Section 16, as amended by the Banking Act of 1935, generally prohibits Federal Reserve member banks[2] from purchasing securities for their own account. But a national bank (chartered by the Comptroller of the Currency) may purchase and hold investment securities (defined as bonds, notes, or debentures regarded by the Comptroller as investment securities) up to 10 per cent of its capital and surplus.[3] Sections 16 and 21 also forbid deposit-taking institutions from both accepting deposits and engaging in the business of 'issuing, underwriting, selling, or distributing, at wholesale or retail, or through syndicate participation, stock, bonds, debentures, notes or other securities', with some important exceptions. These exceptions include US government obligations, obligations issued by government agencies,[4] college and university dormitory bonds, and the general obligations of states and political subdivisions. Municipal revenue bonds (other than those used to finance higher education and teaching hospitals), which are now of greater importance than general obligations, are not included in the exceptions, in spite of the attempts of commercial banks to have Congress amend the Act.[5] In 1985, however, the Federal Reserve Board decided that commercial banks could act as advisers and agents in the private placement of commercial paper.[6]

Section 16 permits commercial banks to purchase and sell securities directly, without recourse, solely on the order of and for the account of customers. In the early 1970s, the Comptroller of the

---

[1] 12 USC (1982) §§ 24, 335, 377, 388. See Natter (1988) for an excellent concise description of the Act and its current interpretation, on which much of the following recitation is based. Also, see Fischer *et al*. (1984) for a review of legislation since 1933, and Rogowski (1978, pp. 162–3) for a listing and reviews of the legislative history.

[2] Section 5 of the Banking Act of 1933 subjects state-chartered Federal Reserve members to the provisions of section 16.

[3] 12 USC (1982) § 24(7).

[4] Such agencies include the Federal Home Loan Banks, the Federal National Mortgage Association, the Inter-American Development Bank, the World Bank, and the Tennessee Valley Authority.

[5] See Rogowski (1978).

[6] Federal Reserve System, 'Statement Concerning Applicability of the Glass–Steagall Act to the Commercial Paper Activities of Bankers Trust Company', 4 June 1985.

Currency approved Citibank's plan to offer the public units in collective investment trusts that the bank organised. But in 1971 the US Supreme Court ruled that sections 16 and 21 prohibit banks from offering a product that is similar to mutual funds.[1] In an often quoted decision discussed at length in section IV of this chapter and in Chapters 2, 3, 4 and 5, the Court found that the Act was intended to prevent banks from endangering themselves, the banking system, and the public from unsafe and unsound practices and conflicts of interest. Nevertheless in 1985 and 1986 the Comptroller of the Currency decided that the Act allowed national banks to purchase and sell mutual shares for its customers as their agent and sell units in unit investment trusts.[2] In 1987, the Comptroller also concluded that a national bank may offer to the public, through a subsidiary, brokerage services and investment advice, while acting as an adviser to a mutual fund or unit investment trust.[3] Since 1985 the regulators have allowed banks to offer discount brokerage services through subsidiaries, and these more permissive rules have been upheld by the courts.[4] Thus, more recent court decisions and regulatory agency rulings have tended to soften the 1971 Supreme Court's apparently strict interpretation of the Act's prohibitions.

Sections 20 and 32 refer to commercial bank affiliations.[5] Section 20 forbids member banks from affiliating with a company 'engaged principally' in the 'issue, flotation, underwriting, public sale, or distribution at wholesale or retail or through syndicate participation of stocks, bonds, debentures, notes, or other securities'. In June 1988 the US Supreme Court (by denying certiorari) upheld a lower court's ruling accepting the Federal Reserve Board's April 1987 approval for member banks to affiliate with companies underwriting commercial

---

[1] *Investment Company Institute v. Camp*, 401 US 617 (1971).
[2] OCC, Legal Advisory Services, Interpretative Letter No. 332, 8 March 1985 and OCC, Office of the Chief Counsel, Interpretative Letter No. 363, 23 May 23 1986.
[3] OCC, Interpretative Letter No. 403, 9 December 1987.
[4] The Comptroller of the Currency's ruling was upheld in *Securities Industry Association v. Comptroller of the Currency*, 758 F.2d 739 (DC Cir. 1985), *aff'd* 577 F.Supp. 252 (DDC 1983), *aff'd in part and rev'd in part sub nom. In Clarke v. Securities Industry Association*, 107 S. Ct 750 (1987), the Supreme Court denied certiorari on the DC Court of Appeals' ruling allowing discount brokerage, but reversed the Appeals Court's ruling that the subsidiary was subject to geographic branching restrictions. A similar Federal Reserve Board ruling also was upheld by the courts in *Securities Industry Association v. Board of Governors*, 807 F.2d 1052 (DC Cir.), *cert. denied*, 107 S. Ct 3228 (1986).
[5] An affiliation exists if a common set of stockholders controls 50 per cent or more of both the commercial bank and investment company.

paper, municipal revenue bonds, and securities backed by mortgages and consumer debts, as long as the affiliate does not principally engage in those activities.[1] 'Principally engaged' was defined by the Federal Reserve as activities contributing more than from 5 to 10 per cent of the affiliate's total revenue. In 1987, the DC Court of Appeals affirmed the Federal Reserve Board's 1985 ruling allowing a bank holding company to acquire a subsidiary that provided both brokerage services and investment advice to institutional customers.[2] In 1984 and 1986 the Court held that affiliates of member banks can offer retail discount brokerage service (which excludes investment advice), on the grounds that these activities do not involve an underwriting of securities, and that 'public sale' refers to an underwriting.[3]

Section 32 prohibits a member bank from having interlocking directorships or close officer or employee relationships with a firm 'principally engaged' in securities underwriting and distribution. Section 32 applies even if there is no common ownership or corporate affiliation between the commercial bank and the investment company.

Sections 20 and 32 do not apply to non-member banks and savings and loan associations. They are legally free to affiliate with securities firms.[4] Thus the law applies unevenly to essentially similar institutions. Furthermore, securities brokers' cash management accounts, which are functionally identical to cheque accounts, have been judged not to be deposits as specified in the Act.

Commercial banks are not forbidden from underwriting and dealing in securities outside of the United States.[5] The larger money centre banks, against whom the prohibitions of the Glass–Steagall Act were directed, are particularly active in these markets. Five of

---

[1] *Securities Industry Association v. Board of Governors of the Federal Reserve System*, 839 F.2d 47, *cert. denied* – US – 108 S. Ct 2830 (1988).

[2] 'National Westminster Bank PLC', *Federal Reserve Bulletin*, No. 72 (August 1986), pp. 584–96, affirmed by the DC Court of Appeals (*Securities Industry Association v. Board of Governors of the Federal Reserve System*, 821 F.2d 810 (DC Cir., 1987), *cert. denied* – US – 108 S. Ct 697 (1988).

[3] *Securities Industry Association v. Board of Governors*, 450 US 46 (1984). The case involved the acquisition of BankAmerica Corporation of Charles Schwab Discount Brokers.

[4] The FDIC's ruling to this effect ('Statement of Policy on the Applicability of the Glass–Steagall Act to Securities Activities of Subsidiaries of Insured Non-Member Banks', FDIC News Release PR–72–82, 1982) was challenged in the courts and upheld: *Investment Company Institute v. FDIC*, 815 F.2d 1540, *cert. denied*, 108 S. Ct 143 (1987).

[5] *See Appendices to the Statement by Paul A. Volcker* (1986), Appendix B and Attachments I and II.

the top 30 leading underwriters in the Eurobond market in 1985 were affiliates of US Banks, with 11 per cent of the total market.[1] These affiliates include 11 of the top 50 underwriters of Euronotes.[2] Citicorp, for example, has membership in some 17 major foreign stock exchanges, and it offers investment banking services in over 35 countries. In 1988, it arranged for its London securities subsidiary to cooperate with a US securities firm to make markets in securities in the United States. The Chase Manhattan Bank advertises that it 'has offices in almost twice as many countries as . . . ten [major listed] investment banks combined'.[3] Furthermore, commercial banks' trust departments can trade securities through their securities subsidiaries or affiliates for pension plans and other trust accounts.[4]

In summary, commercial banks can offer some aspects of investment advisory services, brokerage activities, securities underwriting, mutual fund activities, investment and trading activities, asset securitisation, joint ventures, and commodities dealing, and they can offer deposit instruments that are similar to securities. The specific activities that are and are not allowed are too complex to be outlined here; an excellent summary, from Isaac and Fein (1988), is given in the Appendix. Investment bankers and securities brokers similarly can provide loans and money market management accounts that are very similar to deposits. Although the separation is rather imperfect, the distinction between investment and commercial banking is still very important and quite restricting, particularly to commercial banks.

IV   THE GENERALLY ACCEPTED RATIONALE FOR THE SEPARATION OF COMMERCIAL AND INVESTMENT BANKING

The generally accepted rationale for the Glass–Steagall Act is well expressed in the brief filed by the First National City Bank (1970) in support of the Comptroller of the Currency (William Camp), who had given the bank permission to offer commingled investment

---

[1] *Appendices to the Statement by Paul A. Volcker* (1986), table II-C-2.
[2] *Appendices to the Statement by Paul A. Volcker* (1986), table II-C-3.
[3] Chase Manhattan Bank, 'If You're Doing a Merger or Acquisition on Foreign Soil, Make Sure Your Bank Knows the Turf', advertisement in *The Wall Street Journal*, 21 May, 1987, pp. 12–13.
[4] See Kaufman and Mote (1988) for additional examples.

accounts. For this case (*Investment Company Institute v. Camp*, 401 US 617, 1971), which the Supreme Court decided in favour of the Investment Company Institute, FNCB's attorneys described the rationale for the Act thus (First National City Bank, 1970, pp. 40–2):

> The Glass–Steagall Act was enacted to remedy the speculative abuses that infected commercial banking prior to the collapse of the stock market and the financial panic of 1929–1933. Many banks, especially national banks, not only invested heavily in speculative securities but entered the business of investment banking in the traditional sense of the term by buying original issues for public resale.[34] . . . Apart from the special problems confined to affiliation[1] . . . three well-defined evils were found to flow from the combination of investment and commercial banking.
>
> (1) Banks were investing their own assets in securities with consequent risk to commercial and savings deposits. The concern of Congress to block this evil is clearly stated in the report of the Senate Banking and Currency Committee on an immediate forerunner of the Glass–Steagall Act.[36]
>
> (2) Unsound loans were made in order to shore up the price of securities or the financial position of companies in which a bank had invested its own assets. *See* 'Relation of Banks with the Securities Market', *S. Res. 71, Hearings 1063–4.*
>
> (3) A commercial bank's financial interest in the ownership, price, or distribution of securities inevitably tempted bank officials to press their banking customers into investing in securities which the bank itself was under pressure to sell because of its own pecuniary stake in the transaction.[37]
>
> The provisions of the Glass–Steagall Act were directed at these abuses.

The footnotes to this document are of interest, for they indicate the primary sources of the belief by an important opponent of the Glass–Steagall Act separation, the First National City Bank, that the law was based on the actual events of the day. Footnote 34 states: 'The background of the Glass–Steagall Act is exhaustively portrayed in Hearings Pursuant to S. Res. 71 Before a Subcommittee of the

---

[1] The 'special problems' alluded to are a list of seven activities of securities affiliates listed in S. Res. 71 Hearings [Glass Subcommittee Hearings 1931], p. 1057. These are not described in the Hearings as 'problems'.

Senate Committee on Banking and Currency, 71st Cong., 3rd Sess. (1931) [and] Hearings on S. 4115 before the Senate Committee on Banking and Currency, 72 Cong., 1st Sess. (1932).'

Footnote 36 references 'S. Rep. No. 77, 73d Cong., 1st Sess. 8 (1933) [which] stated: "The outstanding development in the commercial banking system during the prepanic period was the appearance of excessive security loans, and over investment in securities of all kinds. . . . [A] very fruitful cause of bank failures, especially within the past three years, has been the fact that the funds of various institutions have been extensively 'tied up' in long-term investments." '

Footnote 37 quotes a speech by Senator Bulkley, a floor leader for the Act (*Congressional Record*, 1932, p. 9912): 'The banker ought to be regarded as the financial confidant and mentor of his depositors. . . . Obviously, the banker who has nothing to sell to his depositors is much better qualified to advise disinterestedly and to regard diligently the safety of depositors than the banker who uses the list of depositors in his savings department to distribute circulars concerning the advantages of this, that or the other investment.'

The former chairman of the Federal Reserve Board, Paul Volcker, provides a more recent example of a continuing belief in the commonly received causes that require maintaining the legislation. An article prepared for, referred to, and given as an appendix to his 1986 congressional testimony (Fein, 1986, p. A–5) lists these problems and abuses thought to have been present at the time of and presumably solved by the Glass–Steagall separation of commercial and investment banking:

Congressional hearings on the securities practices of banks disclosed that bank affiliates had underwritten and sold unsound and speculative securities, published deliberately misleading prospectuses, manipulated the price of particular securities, misappropriated corporate opportunities to bank officers, engaged in insider lending practices and unsound transactions with affiliates.[60] Evidence also pointed to cases where banks had made unsound loans to assist their affiliates and to protect the securities underwritten by the affiliates. Confusion by the public as to whether they were dealing with a bank or its securities affiliate and loss of confidence in the banking system were also cited as adverse consequences of the securities affiliate system. (Footnote 60 is to *Stock Exchange Practices* [Pecora Hearings], 1933.)

V SUMMARY OF THE RATIONALE FOR THE LEGISLATION AND OUTLINE OF THE PRESENT INQUIRY

The original (and, in large measure, continuing) reasons and arguments for legally separating commercial and investment banking include:

1 *Risk of losses (safety and soundness)* (Chapter 3): Banks that engaged in underwriting and holding corporate securities and municipal revenue bonds presented significant risk of loss to depositors and the federal government that had to come to their rescue; they also were more subject to failure with a resulting loss of public confidence in the banking system and greater risk of financial system collapse.

2 *Conflicts of interest and other abuses* (Chapter 4): Banks that offer investment banking services and mutual funds were subject to conflicts of interest and other abuses, thereby resulting in harm to their customers, including borrowers, depositors, and correspondent banks.

3 *Improper banking activity* (Chapter 5): Even if there were no actual abuses, securities-related activities are contrary to the way banking ought to be conducted.

4 *Producer desired constraints on competition* (Chapter 6): Some securities brokers and underwriters and some bankers want to bar those banks that would offer securities and underwriting services from entering their markets.

5 *The Federal 'safety net' should not be extended more than necessary* (Chapter 7): Federally provided deposit insurance and access to discount window borrowings at the Federal Reserve permit and even encourage banks to take greater risks than are socially optimal. Securities activities are risky and should not be permitted to banks that are protected with the federal 'safety net'.

6 *Unfair competition* (Chapter 8): In any event, banks get subsidised federal deposit insurance which gives them access to 'cheap' deposit funds. Thus they have market power and can engage in cross-subsidisation that gives them an unfair competitive advantage over non-bank competitors (e.g. securities brokers and underwriters) were they permitted to offer investment banking services.

7 *Concentration of power and less-than-competitive performance*
   (Chapter 9): Commercial banks' competitive advantages would
   result in their domination or takeover of securities brokerage and
   underwriting firms if they were permitted to offer investment
   banking services or hold corporate equities. The result would be
   an unacceptable concentration of power and less-than-competitive performance.
8 *Universal v. Specialised Banking* (Chapter 10): If the Glass–Steagall Act were repealed, the US banking system would come to
   resemble the German universal system, which would be detrimental to bank clients and the economy.

The rest of this book examines the empirical and logical validity of
each of these eight reasons for separating commercial and investment
banking. I begin with a description of the sources of information
about the events and relationships that proponents and opponents
of the Glass–Steagall Act appear to accept as having occurred and as
having 'required' the legal separation of commercial and investment
banking.

2 Sources and Contents of Information: Pre-Glass–Steagall

It is important for two reasons to identify all the sources of information on which historians, economists, legal scholars and others rely. First, we must satisfy readers' concerns that something significant was not left out. Second, some sources that have been cited actually do not contain information that speaks to the issues in question.

I have been able to identify seven specific sources of information (other than primary economic data from the period and studies of these data) on the safety and soundness of banks and on the abuses said to have been prevalent or at least present in the period before passage of the 1933 Glass–Steagall Act. At various times witnesses before congressional committees, the Supreme Court in its landmark 1971 decision, *Investment Company Institute v. Camp*[1] (which forbade commercial banks from offering common trust funds to the public), and historians, economists, and other writers on the subject have cited each of these sources (and, I believe, only these sources) to support concerns about safety and soundness and abusive practices. Although some of the specific information that these sources provide may not have been available to Congress at the time the Glass–Steagall Act was enacted, the sources are explicitly referred to or implicitly relied on as major reasons for continuing the separation of commercial and investment banking.

The seven specific information sources are: (1) the 1932 hearings on foreign bond sales held before the Senate Committee on Finance; (2) the 1931 and 1932 hearings held by Senator Glass before a Subcommittee of the Senate Committee on Banking and Currency (the basis for the Glass–Steagall Act) (hereafter referred to as the Glass Subcommittee Hearings); (3) the 1932 report of the Glass Subcommittee hearings (here called the Glass Subcommittee Report); (4) charges and observations made on the floor of the US

---

[1] 401 US 617 (1971).

Senate and House in May 1932 and May 1933 (the *Congressional Record*); (5) the 1933 and 1934 Stock Exchange Practices (SEP) Hearings of the Senate Committee on Banking and Currency run by Ferdinand Pecora (hereafter referred to as the Pecora Hearings); (6) the 1934 report of the SEP Committee (called the SEP Report);[1] and (7) the 1940 report *Investment Trusts and Investment Companies* by the Securities and Exchange Commission to a subcommittee of the Senate Committee on Banking and Currency (hereafter referred to as the SEC Study). In addition, published scholarly articles and reports provide useful analyses, usually of financial data. These studies yield insights into the performance of commercial and investment bankers and the factors related to the failures and financial condition of banks and the banking system. To my knowledge, there is no additional information on conflicts of interest and similar abuses.[2]

1   Hearings on Foreign Bond Sales (1931 and 1932)

In December 1931 and January 1932, the US Senate Finance Committee held hearings investigating 'the sale, flotation, and allocation by banks, banking institutions, corporations, or individuals of foreign bonds or securities in the United States'. The Committee heard from the senior officers of the major commercial banks and investment houses and the Department of Commerce. These investment bankers presented data for the record on the foreign securities that they offered, including the amounts of each issue, the rates of interest paid, maturities, and profits recorded. The questioning was directed towards obtaining information; in general, it was not confrontational in tone. The only significant criticism of the underwriters appears in a series of articles from the *New York American*, which were placed into the record of the hearings. These articles criticised bankers and the Department of State for allowing the public to buy bonds (particularly those of South American countries) that had depreciated considerably in market value.

---

[1] Pecora's book based on the hearings (*Wall Street Under Oath: The Story of Our Modern Money Changers*, 1939) is often cited as a source of evidence on abuses. But it references only the Pecora Hearings and the SEP Report as interpreted by the author.

[2] I examined the materials available in the Congressional Archives and in several university libraries and was unable to find any more information than that published in the congressional hearings and reports.

2 Glass Subcommittee Hearings (1931 and 1932)

The 1931 hearings (published in seven parts) were conducted by Senator Glass pursuant to Senate Resolution 71, 'a resolution to make a complete survey of the national and Federal reserve banking systems'. Between 19 January and 2 March 1931 the subcommittee heard from and questioned (at times sharply) twenty-seven witnesses – bankers, regulators and other government officials, and academics. The first four parts of the published hearings present this testimony. Part 5 presents letters and documents that are not relevant to the issues considered here.

Part 6 contains the answers to four questionnaires sent by the subcommittee to each Federal Reserve bank as well as tables of data submitted by the banks. The first questionnaire requested statements of opinion and data on 'the eligibility and acceptability of paper'. The second asked about 'the discount rate policy'. The third requested information on 'open market operations', including the reserve banks' relations with United States securities dealers. The last questionnaire concerned 'bankers' acceptances'. The emphasis of the questions was on the use of Federal Reserve credit to support securities transactions. No questions were asked about commercial banks' securities affiliates, direct securities holdings, or securities-related services provided to customers (e.g. underwriting and transactions).

Part 7 reports the responses to six questionnaires sent to money brokers, bank examiners, and commercial banks, and descriptive and speculative material on banks' securities affiliates. The questions asked money brokers to refer only to loans they made to securities brokers. The bank examiners were asked only about banks' security loans and the examiners' valuations of banks' investments. One questionnaire to commercial banks concerned securities loans, including loans to affiliated institutions. The second asked descriptive questions about the banks' securities affiliates, and asked for data on securities transactions between the bank and its affiliates, the amount of affiliate indebtedness to its parent, and the affiliates' financial data, portfolios, and participations.

The final part of Part 7 (pp. 1052–68) is devoted to banks' securities affiliates; it is the most important and frequently cited portion of the hearings. The first three sections of this part describe the history, organisation, and functions of securities affiliates (which includes real estate holdings). The last section gives data, reports, and speculations about the operations and risks related to securities affiliates.

The 1932 hearings were held between 23 and 30 March 1932, and are published in two parts. Unlike the general inquiry of the 1931 hearings, these concentrated on S. 4115, a bill that became the Banking Act of 1933 (the Glass–Steagall Act). The Glass Subcommittee heard from thirty bankers representing their banks and/or banking associations, four banking regulators and one professor. Almost all testified against the provision of the bill that would separate securities affiliates from their commercial banks, with the notable exceptions of J. W. Pole, Comptroller of the Currency, and Eugene Meyer, Governor of the Federal Reserve Board.

The Glass Subcommittee Hearings (1931 and 1932) include no testimony, data, studies, or speculations by witnesses on specific conflicts of interest or abuses related to commercial banks' securities activities, whether directly or through affiliates.

3   The Glass Subcommittee Report (1932)

The report primarily addresses the relationship of bank lending to credit expansion and stock market speculation. No material is given on bank insolvencies and security affiliates. There is no mention of conflicts of interest or abuses.

4   The Congressional Record (1932 and 1933)

Several commentators and the Supreme Court cite and quote the statements of several senators, particularly Senators Glass, Bulkley, and Walcott, as if the senators were referring to documents, hearings, or other sources of data, or relating instances or allegations of wrongdoing. In every specific comment that I could trace, however, the senators only give their unsupported opinions. These occasionally misrepresented the record; more often they only expressed their expectations of abuses that might happen rather than citing studies or giving reports of actual occurrences.

5   The Pecora Hearings (1933 and 1934)

These hearings are the only source of information on abuses relating to commercial banks' securities affiliates and operations, other than those relating to commercial bank sponsorship and management of investment trusts. The testimony covers over 11,000 pages. I was unable to find any testimony relating to the safety and soundness, competition, or concentration of power questions.

6   The SEP Report (1934)

The SEP (Stock Exchange Practices) Report contains seven chapters covering 394 pages. The material that is relevant to the present issue is in 'Commercial Banking Practices' (Chapter III). This material relates only to 'abuses'. (Chapter V summarises a related 'abuse' issue, income-tax avoidance. Chapter IV considers safety and soundness issues.) None of the text in Chapter III, however, speaks to commercial banks' securities affiliates or operations. Chapter VI discusses investment trusts, but none of these trusts was related to commercial banks.

7   The SEC Report (1939a and b, 1940, and 1942)

Part 3 of the SEC *Investment Trusts and Investment Companies* (1940 and 1942) study presents descriptions and analyses of investment trusts operated by commercial banks that the Investment Company Institute (1987 and 1988) cites to support its allegations of abuses by banks. Parts 1 and 2 (1939a) contain descriptive historical and statistical data. A supplementary report, *Commingled or Common Trust Funds Administered by Banks and Trust Companies (1939b)*, presents information about bank-managed common trust funds.

3 Evidence on the Risk of Losses

I ALLEGATIONS OF RISKS CAUSED BY BANKS' SECURITIES OPERATIONS

In *Investment Company Institute v. Camp*[1] the Supreme Court ruled that the Glass–Steagall Act foreclosed commercial banks from offering commingled investment accounts. The Court explained that the Act 'reflected a determination that policies of competition, convenience, or expertise which might otherwise support the entry of commercial banks into the investment banking business were outweighed by the "hazards" and "financial dangers" that arose when commercial banks engage in the activities proscribed by the Act'.[2] Congress, the Court said, 'was concerned that commercial banks . . . had both aggravated and been damaged by stock market decline partly because of their direct and indirect involvement in the trading and ownership of speculative securities'.[3] Furthermore, the Court believed that '[t]he failure of the Bank of United States in 1930 was widely attributed to that bank's activities with respect to its numerous securities affiliates'.[4]

---

[1] 401 US 617 (1971).

[2] Ibid., p. 629, footnote omitted. This footnote (19) gives three references. One refers to the Glass Subcommittee Hearings (1931) p. 365. There is nothing on that page (which gives the testimony of Owen D. Young, Chairman of the Board, General Electric Co.) that supports the Court's statement. Nor is there anything in Young's testimony about the 'hazards' or 'financial dangers' of banks' security affiliates, operations, or investments. The second reference cites remarks of Senator Bulkley. While he is critical of investment affiliates, he does not speak about 'hazards' or 'financial dangers'. Instead, he reviews the history of affiliates and speaks of his belief that they tend to produce and sell securities excessively and encourage collateral-security loans. The third reference is to S. Rep. No. 77, p. 18. That page only contains the last four sections of the proposed bill that would require member banks to get the Federal Reserve Board's permission to engage in securities transactions; these proposals are followed by the closing paragraph stating that the suggested changes are 'unavoidable and all are thought urgent for the purpose of correcting or eliminating actual hazards'.

[3] Ibid. at 629, excluding footnote 18, which refers to S. Rep. No. 77, pp. 6, 8, 10. These references are valid.

[4] Ibid. at 629, excluding footnote 17, which refers to the Glass Subcommittee Hearings (1931).

20

In a 1981 decision the Court reaffirmed its belief that Congress enacted the Glass–Steagall prohibitions to protect banks and the banking system from losses:[1]

> It is familiar history that the Glass–Steagall Act was enacted in 1933 to protect bank depositors from any repetition of the widespread bank closings that occurred during the Great Depression. Congress was persuaded that speculative activities, partially attributable to the connection between commercial banking and investment banking, had contributed to the rash of bank failures. The legislative history reveals that securities firms associated with banks had engaged in perilous underwriting operations, stock speculation, and maintaining a market for the banks' own stock, often with the banks' resources.

Advocates of the separation, particularly the Investment Company Institute and the Securities Industry Association, similarly assert an assumed causal relationship between the collapse of the banking system in the early 1930s and the separation of commercial and investment banking. For example, the Investment Company Institute (1979, pp. 3–4) states that the Glass Subcommittee Hearings (1931) 'uncovered widespread abuses, and led Congress to conclude that bank entry into the securities business had contributed significantly to the Great Crash and the ensuing depression [footnotes omitted]'. The Securities Industry Association (1985, p. 20) reproduced the Supreme Court's words just quoted in support of its own position.

Some scholarly articles also point to an assumed causal relationship between the collapse of the banking system and banks' securities activities as a reason for the passage of the Glass–Steagall Act and its continuation. A note in the *Virginia Law Review* represents this position:[2]

> Congress also found that bank ownership of securities affiliates had contributed to public distrust of banking. When the market

---

[1] *Board of Governors of the Federal Reserve System v. Camp*, 450 US 46, 48 (1981).
[2] Although it is 'only' a student note, Sam Scott Miller, vice president and general counsel of Paine Webber Incorporated and adjunct professor at Yale Law School, cited this article to me as a 'must read'. It is forty-seven pages in length, very thorough, and representative of a number of articles written by professors and others that conclude that passage of the Glass–Steagall Act was desirable. (See, for example, Karmel, 1980; and Orbe, 1983.)

collapsed, the securities affiliates had been left holding large unsold inventories of worthless securities. The resulting failure of these affiliates undermined public confidence in the parent commercial bank and in commercial banks generally. Even if a particular bank attempted to save its reputation by rescuing its floundering affiliate, the bank simply imperiled its own solvency. [Note, 1983, p. 1308; footnotes referring to the responses to the subcommittee questionnaires in the Glass Subcommittee Hearings (1931) omitted.]

A US Department of the Treasury *Issues Paper* similarly references the Glass Subcommittee Hearings (1931) and states that '[t]he Subcommittee concluded that these loan abuses [loans to affiliates] resulted in commercial banks assuming undue risks. The Subcommittee also found that in declining markets, banks placed even more funds at risk in order to protect security affiliates whose collapse might threaten the bank's own viability, or diminish public confidence in the bank' (US Department of the Treasury, 1975, p. 81).

Finally, it is interesting to examine a 'legal and economic analysis' of 'the securities activities of commercial banks' written by two lawyers and two economists. Fischer *et al.* (1984, p. 504) assert that:

the primary purpose of the Glass–Steagall Act was to protect the banking system from the abuses believed to inhere in the combination of commercial and investment banking. The Pecora hearings in 1933 revealed a multitude of instances in which securities activities engaged in by banks of their affiliates appeared to compromise the safety of the banks.[169] The practice of lending to firms whose securities had been underwritten by the bank's affiliate and the purchasing of hard-to-sell securities by bank investment departments from affiliates clearly placed depositors' funds in jeopardy.[170]

Fischer *et al.*'s footnote 169 cites the SEP (Stock Exchange Practices) Report (1934); their footnote 170 cites the Glass Subcommittee Report (1932). Neither of these documents contains any evidence about the allegations made.

Some important scholarly writings, however, do not mention concerns about safety and soundness. In particular, Peach (1941), the basic scholarly work that many commentators rely on, almost totally ignores this concern. Indeed, virtually the only mention appears in the next to last sentence of the book: 'By abolishing affiliates in 1933 Congress removed at least one source of potential danger to the quality of bank assets, and no more practicable solution of the problem can be safely proposed' (p. 179). Carosso (1970a) and Seligman (1982), two other important historians of the Glass–Steagall Act, also do not express or report concern for bank safety and soundness.

II SPECULATIONS ABOUT RISKS LISTED IN PART 7, CHAPTER IV OF THE GLASS SUBCOMMITTEE HEARINGS (1931)

This important, oft-cited document, entitled 'Relations of Security Affiliates to Banks', concludes: 'From the viewpoint of banking regulation, the operations of the security affiliates can be of interest only in so far as they affect the activities and soundness of the banks with which they are affiliated' (Glass Subcommittee Hearings, 1931, p. 1065). The preceding material consists of a list of speculations about how a securities affiliate *might* affect its parent, and *vice versa*, as indicated by this introduction to the list (ibid., p. 1063): 'Reasoning a priori, a number of ways in which the operations of a security affiliate can affect the position of the parent bank may be distinguished'.

Eleven concerns then appear. Most speak of the possibility that a bank's resources would be depleted because its securities operations are conducted in a separate affiliate, rather than within the bank together with there being transfers between the two entities made on other than arm's-length-determined terms (items 1, 2, 3, 4, 5, 6, 9, and 10 listed below). Five of the possibilities also refer to possible losses from securities transactions that might endanger the bank's solvency (3, 4, 6, 9, and 10). Two are concerned with fluctuations in a bank's stock prices (7 and 8) and one with a conflict of interest (11). Examination of the actual wording given in the Hearings (ibid., pp. 1063–4) should be useful, because this document is cited as 'evidence' of the necessity of maintaining the Glass–Steagall Act.

(1) The security affiliate may borrow money from the parent bank. . . .

(2) The affiliate may sell securities to the bank or another of its affiliates under repurchase agreements.

(3) The bank is closely connected in the public mind with its affiliates, and should the latter suffer large losses it is practically unthinkable that they would be allowed to fail. . . . the knowledge that the affiliate has suffered large losses may in itself be sufficient to cause unfavorable rumors, however unjustified, to spread about the bank.

(4) The bank, to relieve the affiliate of excess holdings, may purchase securities from it. . . .

(5) The bank may lend much more freely to customers on issues sponsored by the security affiliate, in order to facilitate their distribution, than it would otherwise do. Also, it may prove more difficult to insist upon the maintenance of adequate margins on these security loans than on other such advances, in view of the fact that customers are encouraged to make loans by the bank's own affiliate.

(6) The goodwill of the bank with its depositors may be adversely affected to a serious degree when the latter suffer substantial losses on security issues purchased from the affiliate. . . .

(7) Operations by the affiliate in the market for the bank's own stock may cause undesirably wide fluctuations in the latter. . . .

(8) Wide variations in the net asset value, earning power, and dividend-paying ability of security affiliates tend to make bank stock price fluctuations greater than would otherwise be the case.

(9) The existence of the affiliates may induce the bank to make unwise commitments, in the knowledge that in case of need they can be shifted to the affiliates, and thus be removed from the bank's condition statement.

(10) Knowing its access to the resources of the bank in case of need, security affiliates in their turn may tend to assume various commitments less cautiously than do private investment banking houses.

(11) In the case of a trust company or a bank with a trust department, the possession of a security affiliate may adversely affect the independence with which fiduciary activities are exercised.

A bank that conducts securities operations in a legally separate affiliate indeed could present a problem if a bank that is failing transfers resources to its affiliate, thereby reducing the value of bank creditors' (including depositors') claims. This result could occur if the bank loaned funds to its affiliate on less-onerous-than-market terms (possibilities 1 and 2). Or, a bank might purchase securities from its affiliate at greater-than-market prices or sell securities and make loans to facilitate securities purchases from the affiliate at less-than-market prices (possibilities 4 and 5). A bank also might simply transfer resources to an affiliate to keep the affiliate from failing, thereby causing the bank to be in danger of failing (possibilities 3, 6 and 10). These stratagems are similar to those that might be practiced by the owners of any limited liability corporation who wanted to remove resources from the corporation to defraud its creditors. Such practices were and remain illegal, and there is no evidence that they ever were engaged in by banks. Furthermore, regulations such as the Federal Reserve Board's rules 23A and 23B which restrict transfers from banks to their holding companies and its affiliates, could insulate the securities affiliate from the bank.

A related problem arises when the bank and affiliate are owned in different proportions by shareowners. In this situation, resources could be transferred to benefit one group of owners at the expense of the other. But the Hearings (ibid., p. 1056) state that common ownership was the norm; indeed, no alternative form of ownership is even mentioned.[1]

In any event, many of the possibilities (particularly 1 and 2) could be obviated as problems if banks were permitted to conduct securities operations directly. Then there would be no advantage to the bank's owners from transferring resources, directly or indirectly, to its affiliate, as it would only be moving resources within the same legal organisation, which could not disadvantage depositors or other creditors. Indeed, legally separate securities affiliates were established in the United States because the National Banking Act was interpreted as forbidding national banks from conducting securities operations directly. Consequently, national banks established state-chartered entities that were entirely owned by the banks' owners.

Losses from securities operations or investments are no different with respect to the solvency of a bank than are losses from any other

---

[1] The typical method of assuring common ownership was that used by the National City Bank. The shares of its affiliate, the National City Company, were held by six trustees, who were officers of the bank. No shares of the company went into circulation, and the shares of the bank carried proportionate interests in the company. Another method was to print the bank and affiliate shares on opposite sides of the same piece of paper so that one could not be transferred without the other. See Peach (1941, pp. 66–70) for a more complete description.

activity or asset, such as commercial loans. There is no reason to believe that a bank's management would act contrary to share-holders' interests in accepting greater total risk than is desirable simply because the bank deals in securities. In particular, all things being equal, a bank would not make unprofitable or riskier loans to customers simply because they also purchase securities (possibility 5), or risk the goodwill of depositors (possibility 6), cause wide fluctuation in the bank's stock (possibilities 7 and 8), or make unwise commitments (possibilities 9 and 10) without compensating benefits to shareholders.[1] In any event, whether losses from securities actually resulted in or mitigated the failures of banks more than losses from other, permissible activities is an empirical question. Sections III, IV, V and VI of this chapter review the available evidence.

However, a bank might transfer bad securities to an affiliate to improve the bank's financial statement and hence its appeal to depositors and regulators (possibility 9). If the bad securities were transferred at a price greater than their market values, this action would be the same as an additional infusion of equity capital into the bank, which would decrease the probability that it would fail and, thus, benefit depositors.[2]

Transfers of securities between a securities affiliate and trust administered by a bank that are adverse to the interests of the trusts' creators and beneficiaries (possibility 11) was then and is now an illegal violation of a bank's duty as a trust fiduciary. No evidence was presented in the Hearings (1931) that it actually occurred.[3]

The empirical issue, then, on which the Hearings (1931) presents no evidence, is whether or not banks that operated securities affili-ates or engaged in securities activities failed relatively more fre-quently or with greater losses to depositors than did banks not involved in such activities. To examine the evidence that does exist, sections IV and V explore two sources of information. One source

---

[1] Fischer *et al.* (1984), in their review of securities activities and bank safety, argue: 'The practice of lending to firms whose securities had been underwritten by the bank's affiliate and the purchasing of hard-to-sell securities by bank investment departments from affiliates clearly placed depositors' funds in jeopardy.' They support this presum-ably factual account by reference to the Glass Subcommittee Report (1932, p. 8), which does not present any evidence not contained in the Glass Subcommittee Hear-ings (1931 and 1932). As noted, these documents do not contain any evidence of the kind to which Fischer *et al.* refer.

[2] Transfers made at market prices are not different from the sale of assets to indepen-dent third parties.

[3] Allegations and evidence presented in other documents on this possibility are dis-cussed in the fifth section of Chapter 4.

involves the failure of the Bank of United States, which was alleged to have used affiliates to hide losses from depositors and the authorities, thereby misinforming and defrauding them. The second source is an analysis of the failure rates of national banks that actively engaged in securities activities compared with banks that did not.

The Hearings (1931) nevertheless did present some evidence on the risks of underwriting and dealing in securities, which I consider first.

III EVIDENCE ON RISKS GIVEN IN THE GLASS SUBCOMMITTEE HEARINGS

Section 4 of Chapter IV of Part 7 of the Hearings (1931, pp. 1057–58) states:

> An analysis of the portfolios of a typical group of security affiliates indicates that the business of *retailing* securities seldom involves a large measure of risk. The security inventory carried in this connection, while it may include a relatively large number of individual issues, seldom ties up more than a moderate fraction of the resources of the affiliate, and the rate of turnover, even in comparatively inactive periods in the security business, constitutes an additional source of protection for the security company against being tied up with any large volume of securities that can not be marketed without serious loss.
>
> On the other hand, the *wholesale* underwriting of securities does tend at times to leave the security affiliates with big unsold commitments that, in times of rapidly declining prices, may result in large losses of at least a temporary nature. [The Hearings then gives an example of losses in Bethlehem Steel Corporation common stock.]
>
> The portfolios of some of the security affiliates indicate that the profits of years of operation can be more than wiped out through two or three unprofitable commitments of this kind, at least on the basis of quotations prevailing during a depression period [emphasis added].

No data, other than the Bethlehem Steel example, appear in support of these conclusions.

Section 5 describes the operations of eleven 'typical' securities affiliates, based on financial statements submitted to the subcommittee. By mid-1931 the portfolios of two affiliates had depreciated sufficiently to eliminate book equity of the affiliates,[1] the portfolios of two more had depreciated considerably, and the portfolios of three others had depreciated somewhat. Two affiliates were said to have had portfolios that appreciated, no information appears for one affiliate, and the eleventh held only real estate and stock in the bank. There is no mention of unsafe operations. Nor was any other kind of abuse or problem mentioned.

Thus, a major congressional source cited by commentators as a basis for the Glass–Steagall Act yields very little data supporting the belief that securities affiliates or securities operations that banks directly undertook actually resulted in greater risk to depositors. It is possible, however, that banks with affiliates and securities operations suffered greater rates of failure in the period following preparation of the Glass Subcommittee's report. Some additional claims made by commentators with respect to safety and soundness are also considered.

Sections IV, V and VI investigate the validity of three specific claims that are relevant to the mandated separation of commercial and investment banking. Section IV explores whether the operations of the Bank of United States's securities affiliates caused or exacerbated its failure. Section V asks if commercial banks' securities operations resulted in their experiencing higher rate of failure. Section VI asks whether banks' holdings of securities were higher because they had securities affiliates or because they dealt with banks that had securities affiliates and, as a result, these banks experienced higher rates of failure.

These issues do not appear to have been the most important ones concerning bank safety at or in the year the Glass–Steagall Act was enacted or in earlier years. It is clear from the Glass Subcommittee Hearings (1931 and 1932), the Glass Subcommittee Report (1932), and from statements made on the floor of the Senate in 1932 and 1933 that Senator Glass and other congressmen were concerned primarily with commercial banks' presumed support of securities speculation via *loans* made to brokers and investors and with banks' borrowings from the Federal Reserve that presumably were used to

---

[1] The Hearings (1931) do not indicate whether the elimination of book equity resulted in net economic (present value) losses to the stockholders and creditors of the affiliates; no indication is given that any of the eleven banks with securities affiliates (or any of the other banks studied) failed or were in danger of failing.

fuel additional speculation. Senator Glass, in particular, was a strong believer in limiting banks to making short-term, self-liquidating loans (the 'real bills doctrine') and was passionate in his denunciation of securities speculation, which he persistently called 'stock gambling'. Few if any economists today, be they monetarists, Keynesians, or independents, believe that banks' lending to securities brokers and investors was responsible for the 1929 stock market crash or the Great Depression.[1] Nor was bank solvency threatened because of loans made to purchasers of securities.[2]

In any event, the Glass–Steagall Act does not bar banks from making such loans to brokers or to persons who invest in securities. The only relevant issues with respect to bank safety and soundness, therefore, are whether banks that engaged in securities activities had higher failure rates than those that did not, or whether these activities were responsible for the failures of other banks.

IV   THE FAILURE OF THE BANK OF UNITED STATES

The failure of the Bank of United States in 1930 provided ammunition for the passage of the Glass–Steagall Act. It is one of only two examples of unsafe or abusive banking with respect to affiliates mentioned in the congressional debates on the Act in 1932 or 1933. (The other example actually refers to manufacturing companies affiliated with a bank.)[3] The Supreme Court, in *Investment Company*

---

[1] See United States Presidential Task Force on Market Mechanisms (1988), study VIII, 'A Comparison of 1929 and 1987', for evidence and reasoning demonstrating that neither the 1929 stock market crash nor stocks purchased on credit were responsible for the Great Depression, nor were stocks purchased on credit responsible for the 1929 crash. See also Staff of the Board of Governors of the Federal Reserve System (1984, chapter V, 'Margin Regulation and Market Bubbles: A Review of Arguments and Evidence', pp. 135–171), which reviews the literature over the previous twenty-five years and concludes that the hypothesis of lending-fuelled stock market speculation is inconsistent with contemporary finance theory and research findings.

[2] The Staff of the Board of Governors of the Federal Reserve System (1984, p. 90) states: 'During the crash, there were no reports of banks made insolvent due to their extension of securities credit.'

[3] Representative Beedy (Maine) gave that example. He stated that banning affiliates 'is wise. Now, just what does this mean? I call your attention to this because of a situation that arose in my own State'. He then tells of a bank in Portland whose controlling directors 'had set up what might be known as an "affiliate corporation" under the definition in this bill. One affiliate corporation was engaged in the fiber business; another affiliate corporation was engaged in a tooth-paste venture.' The bank then made loans to the affiliates (*Congressional Record*, 1933, p. 3912).

Institute v. Camp (401 US 617 (1971), p. 629), and the Securities Industry Association (1985, p. 18) also give the Bank of United States case as a prime example of securities-driven reprehensible behaviour.

In an appendix, the Glass Subcommittee Hearings (1931, p. 1017) states that '[t]he failure of the Bank of United States in New York City in December, 1930, served to center attention upon the fact that banks may make large loans to affiliated corporations which are not treated objectively, and which, in that particular case became so unwieldy as to have led to the collapse of the institution.'[1] The appendix concludes with the statement that 'sentiment on the subject [of the menace of security affiliates] was aroused among bankers, as well as the general public . . . by the collapse of the Bank of United States, with its 59 different affiliates' (ibid., p. 1068). The Supreme Court cites these quotations in *Investment Company Institute v. Camp*.[2]

In the debate on the Glass–Steagall Act, Senator Walcott cited the collapse of the Bank of United States as his sole example of 'abuse' by affiliates, as follows: 'A very notable case of such abuse of affiliates, which it will now do no harm to mention, is the Bank of the [sic] United States' (Congressional Record, 1933, p. 9905). But he goes on to describe its affiliates *solely* as a vehicle for holding parcels of real estate. He says (ibid.):

---

[1] The US Treasury (1975) *Issues Paper* apparently misreads this statement, for it assumes incorrectly that the affiliates mentioned were securities affiliates. The *Issues Paper* states: 'the failure of the Bank of the [sic] United States in 1930 was often cited by the Subcommittee as an example of the erosion of a commercial bank's soundness which could result from unsound loans made to *security* affiliates' (ibid., p. 81, emphasis added).

[2] 401 US 617 (1971), p. 629, note 17. This note also inappropriately cites pages 116–17 of the Glass Subcommittee Hearings (1931). Those pages report the following testimony of J. H. Case, Chairman of the Board of Directors of the Federal Reserve Bank of New York in response to questions by H. Parker Willis for the Subcommittee:

MR WILLIS   Did you have any information in the Federal reserve bank [sic] of the methods employed by the affiliates of the [sic] United States Bank in the buying up of securities and the speculating in the stock of the bank itself?'
MR CASE   No; not until this examination.
MR WILLIS   You know nothing about it?
MR CASE   No. I remember I did hear a rumor that, in absorbing one of the institutions which they took over in the last year or so, a large number of units of the Bank of the [sic] United States were issued [consisting of shares of bank stock coupled with shares of stock of an affiliated securities corporation]' (ibid., pp. 116–17).

Eventually they [the Bank of United States] were buying real estate at close to the top of the market. The whole thing was getting overloaded and top-heavy; they were pyramiding; they were financing by shoestring operations; and *of course it was inevitable that this great structure of innumerable affiliates should collapse. . . .* I cite that as a *typical case of the excessive abuse of affiliates.* [Emphasised words are the only ones quoted by the Securities Industry Association, 1985, p. 18.]

This could not have happened, in my opinion, if we had examiners who were acting strictly under such provision as are contained in the pending bill. . . . We undertake to control them by strong examination and regulation, but not to put an end to them.

As Senator Walcott indicated, the affiliates of the Bank of United States were used primarily for real estate holdings. The only securities-related affiliates that got the bank into trouble were engaged in purchases of the bank's own stock. The bank failed primarily because it expanded rapidly through acquisitions for which it grossly overpaid.[1] The amounts paid for these acquisitions, either directly or through shares on which high rates of dividends were promised, were more than the bank could afford. Furthermore, the bank's principal officers and owners, B. K. Marcus and Saul Singer, used the bank's assets for their personal gain (for which, among other related crimes, they were sent to prison).

The principals of the bank used its affiliates as a means of removing bad loans from the bank's books so as to avoid criticism by bank examiners and depositors. In this regard, the concerns of the Glass Subcommittee are well taken. But there is nothing in the record to indicate that the failure of the Bank of United States or its use of affiliates was related to securities operations or could have been prevented had the separation of commercial and investment banking the Glass–Steagall Act mandated been in effect.

---

[1] This description and the following conclusion about the Bank of United States are based on Werner (1933) and Lucia (1985).

V   FAILURES OF BANKS THAT CONDUCTED SECURITIES OPERATIONS COMPARED WITH OTHER BANKS

The available evidence contradicts the belief that securities operations were responsible for bank failures during the early 1930s. Eugene White (1986) calculated the proportion of banks with securities operations in 1929 that failed during the years 1930–3. He found that '[w]hile 26.3% of all national banks failed in this period, only 6.5% of the 62 banks which had affiliates in 1929 and 7.6% of the 145 banks which conducted large operations through their bond departments closed their doors' (White, 1986, p. 40). Thus, only fifteen of the 207 national banks (7.2 per cent) that actively dealt in securities failed, a far smaller percentage than that experienced by the national banks that did not conduct both commercial and investment banking.[1]

Securities operations do not appear to have caused these fifteen national bank failures. The largest of these was the First National Bank of Detroit. The assets of its securities affiliate were only 10.7 per cent of its total assets of $180.5 million. Furthermore, the Pecora Hearings' (1934) investigation of the Detroit banking situation does not mention securities activities as a cause of failure. The next largest of the failures, the Federal National Bank of Boston, had total assets of $37.1 million, while the third largest, the Third National Bank of Pittsburgh, had $7.8 million in assets. Thus, almost all the fifteen failed banks with securities operations were relatively small. Their failures could not have been responsible for any but a trivial part of the bad banking situation that characterised the period.

White (1986) examined the issue further by means of a statistical analysis in which national banks with securities operations that failed in 1931 (when most of these banks failed[2]) 'was paired a sample of [nonfailed] banks of similar size from the same locales'[3] (ibid., p. 40).

---

[1] White (1986, p. 40) suggests that '[t]his superior record may be partially explained by the fact that the typical commercial bank involved in investment banking was far larger than average while most of the failures were among the smaller institutions. Larger banks had opportunities for diversification and attaining economies of scale, which if exploited could strengthen their position in the industry.'

[2] White (1986, p. 41) states that '[f]or all other years, only one or two of these banks closed'.

[3] Multinomial logit analysis was used. It is a statistical regression in which the dependent variable is coded '1' or '0' for failed or non-failed, and the residuals are bounded by 1 and 0.

In addition to variables specifying the relative amounts of assets and liabilities that the banks held, dummy variables (coded '1' or '0') were used to measure the effect of a bank's having a securities affiliate or a bond department that dealt in securities. The coefficient of the bond department variable is statistically insignificant (standard error is five times larger than the coefficient) and the coefficient of the securities affiliate variable is statistically significantly (.05 per cent level) negative, indicating that 'the presence of a security affiliate and whatever characteristics were associated with it tended to reduce the likelihood of failure' (ibid., p. 42).

White (1986) conducted some further interesting empirical analyses. He tested the allegation that commercial banks' security affiliates' operations gave rise to large fluctuations in earnings that might endanger the banks solvency.[1] He gathered annual balance sheet and income statement data for the seven years through 1932 on all eighteen national banks with security affiliates on which such data were available. A comparison of the means and standard deviations of returns (measured for banks or affiliates as profits or earnings divided by capital or assets) shows both statistics as higher for affiliates than for banks (ibid., Table 2, p. 44). The covariance of returns between the affiliates' and the banks' profits or earnings is small and statistically insignificant. Thus, banks with security affiliates obtained higher total returns but also experienced higher total variance. White's calculation of the efficient frontier (the optimal combination of return and risk), though, indicates that a slightly higher risk would have been traded for a considerably higher return. He finds that 'if a bank had no securities affiliate, its return [on capital] was 0.084 and the standard deviation was 0.034. If 20% of its capital were devoted to security operations, its portfolio return would rise substantially to 0.102 and its risk increase only slightly to 0.037'[2] (ibid., p. 45). He also found that 'downturns in bank earnings do not appear to have regularly coincided with declines in affiliate earnings' (ibid., p. 44). Thus, while the securities affiliates of the banks studied do not appear to have *reduced* total bank risk, these operations increased their earnings and hence their solvency, which may be an important reason for their lower rates of failure.

White (1986) also tested the allegation that commercial banks'

---

[1] The Glass Subcommittee Hearings (1931, part 7, p. 1064) refers to 'bank stock fluctuations' rather than to solvency, as such.

[2] The average percentage of affiliate capital to total bank and affiliate capital was 10 per cent. The highest percentage was 27.9 per cent.

security affiliates were undercapitalised and dependent on borrowed funds, thereby endangering the banks, which would have had to rescue the affiliates that got into trouble. The test consisted of regressing on the alternative dependent variables, bank capital divided by total bank assets or bank capital divided by loans and investments, independent variables measuring bank size, asset risk, growth, earnings rate, year of data, and affiliate assets divided by combined assets or affiliate capital divided by affiliate assets. He computed six regressions using various combinations of variables. He reports: 'The coefficient on the affiliate to capital ratio was positive and in three cases significant. . . . Security affiliates thus do not in any conventional sense seem to have systematically impaired the capital adequacy of their parent banks' (ibid., p. 48). Although these tests used accounting numbers rather than the more relevant (though unavailable) market values, the metrics employed are those the regulatory authorities use.

White performed a similar analysis with cash items divided by total deposits as the dependent variable to test the hypothesis that affiliates reduced bank liquidity. The affiliate variables' coefficients are insignificant. A variable measuring affiliate indebtedness (affiliate borrowing divided by affiliate cash items) had a significantly (10 per cent level) positive coefficient, 'suggesting that banks increased their liquidity when their affiliates' borrowings rose faster than cash assets' (ibid., p. 50). White concludes: 'National banks' liquidity does not appear to have been weakened by the presence of an affiliated securities business' (ibid.).

VI SECURITIES AFFILIATES AND THE SECURITIES HOLDINGS AND CONSEQUENT FAILURE OF ALLIED OR OTHER BANKS

Senator Glass believed strongly that country banks could not serve local borrowers because the money centre banks 'pushed' securities on them. Many of these securities, he said, became worthless, thereby causing extreme distress to and failure of the country banks. During floor debate in the Senate (*Congressional Record*, 1932, p. 9883), for example, Glass charged:

> It was because of that system of involuntary servitude [correspondent banking] that the great banks in the money centers choked

the portfolios of their correspondent banks from Maine to California with their utterly worthless investment securities, nearly eight billions of them being the investment securities of tottering South American republics and other foreign countries.

He later continued (ibid., p. 9887):

The committee ascertained in a more or less definite way – we think quite a definite way – that one of the greatest contributions to the unprecedented disaster which has caused this almost incurable depression was made by these bank affiliates. They sent their highpressure salesmen and literally filled the bank portfolios of this country with these investment securities.

This description of events perseveres in the congressional testimony of the Securities Industry Association (SIA). Richard Jenrette, Chairman of the SIA Board of Directors, in a review of 'banking history', testified thus: 'And, taking advantage of a correspondent banking system that even today provides the same opportunities for abuse by a bank which is also a securities underwriter, many of these financial giants used the small country banks that trusted them for investment advice as "a good dumping ground for second or third grade securities" ' (Jenrette, 1984, p. 643). An 'issues paper' prepared by the US Department of the Treasury (1975, p. 80) similarly asserted: 'The large banks used their correspondents for the distribution of securities underwritten by security affiliates. The Subcommittee pointed out the pervasive conflict of interest that infected this relationship'.[1]

The Subcommittee nevertheless did not investigate this question nor does the Glass Subcommittee Hearings (1931 or 1932) or the Glass Report (1932) discuss the presumed conflict of interest described. Instead, the Glass Subcommittee Hearings (1931, p. 1032) examined the securities holdings of Federal Reserve member country and city banks. As of year end 1930, the other bonds and stocks component of total investments were 23 per cent for central reserve city banks, 22 per cent for other reserve city banks, and 33 per cent for country banks. The Subcommittee's analysis of the data concludes (ibid., p. 1032):

---

[1] Footnote excluded (number 51), which refers to a rhetorical question raised by Senator Bulkley in congressional debate, in which he does not refer to any example or study.

Country banks, it will be noted, have a larger proportion of their resources in bond investments than do city institutions, whereas the latter are more heavily involved in security loans. This reflects the relatively restricted demand for advances on security collateral in the smaller communities, and the less direct access of country banks to the financial centers, where the need for security loans is keenest. It also reflects the larger proportion of time deposits of the country institutions, as it is generally felt the receipt of such deposits justifies the making of less liquid commitments, including the purchase of securities that may not be readily marketable.

Thus, the Subcommittee acknowledged that country banks' securities holdings are demand rather than supply determined.

The Glass Subcommittee Report (1932, p. 8), nevertheless, draws a conclusion not supported by findings presented in the Hearings (1931 and 1932):

a very fruitful cause of bank failures, especially within the last two years, has been the fact that the funds of various institutions have been so extensively 'tied up' in long-term investments. The growth of the investment portfolio of the bank itself has been greatly emphasized in importance by the organization of allied or affiliated companies under State laws, through which even more extensive advances and investments in the security market could be made.

The Securities Industry Association (1985, p. 17) cites the first sentence (trivially incorrectly – 'three' rather than 'two' years is quoted) in support of its position. The US Department of the Treasury *Issues Paper* (1975, p. 81) also cites this 'finding', introducing it as follows: 'In fact, the Senate Banking and Currency Committee [the Glass Subcommittee Hearings (1931)] found that a major cause of bank failures of commercial banks in the early 1930's had been the extensive investment of bank assets in long-term securities, many of which were acquired from [presumably their own but possibly other banks'] security affiliates.'

The Glass Subcommittee Hearings (1931) found no such thing. No information was adduced about the extent to which banks obtained their long-term investments from bank securities affiliates. No studies were conducted, surveys taken, or data obtained. Although many of the witnesses were asked what they believed were the causes of the large number of bank failures, none identified banks' investments in securities as a cause, regardless of the source of the securities. I could find only a few instances in which the relationship between bank failures and securities investments or other factors were discussed, and these fail to confirm the underlying hypothesis.

The Comptroller of the Currency, J. W. Pole, responding to the question from Senator Glass, 'Mr. Comptroller, what do you conceive to be the general cause of the numerous bank failures for the last five or six years?' (ibid., p. 7), replied:

> Well, 90 per cent of the banks are in the small rural communities. Economic changes have put these small communities within easy distances of the larger commercial centers where the banks are stronger and more efficient in every respect, and as a consequence of this ready access to these centers, the cream of the banking business has gone to those centers, which has had the effect of reducing the opportunities of the small country banks to such an extent that they find it difficult to earn a sufficient amount of money to charge off their losses and to pay a reasonable dividend, and neither can they offer anything like the facilities which the city bank can offer, and with those opportunities removed, the bank its not able to maintain itself.

More specifically, Pole stated: 'I know of no instance where the shrinkage in value of collateral or bank investments as far as national banks are concerned, has been responsible for any bank failure or very, very few of them' (ibid., p. 12).[1]

J. H. Case, chairman of the Board of Directors of the Federal Reserve Bank of New York, pointed to there having been too many banks for the business available (overbanking) as the cause of bank failures (ibid., pp. 109–10). Edmund Platt, vice chairman of the Marine Midland Corporation, identified drops in commodity prices and undiversified operations because of limitations on branching as the cause of bank failures (ibid., pp. 219–24). Professor H. Parker Willis, adviser to Senator Glass, asked B. W. Trafford, vice chairman of the First National Bank of Boston: 'Do you think those investments [bonds] have been a significant cause of bank suspensions in the Northeast or in other parts of the country?' (ibid., p. 243). After

---

[1] Pole mentioned (p. 20) a bank security affiliate that had to write off $57 million in losses, but he does not say that the bank failed.

stating that there were very few failures in New England, Trafford replied (ibid., p. 243):

MR TRAFFORD   The two that I know about were just crooked management; I think a couple more were unintelligent. But there were only five or six.

MR WILLIS   The security movement has had nothing to do with the bank failures in your part of the country at all?

MR TRAFFORD   Not this last year.

Elmer Adams, president of the First National Bank of Fergus Falls, Minnesota exclaimed: 'In the past eight years nine banks have failed in our county. No national bank failed. While the failure of these nine banks was due in part to unwise loans during the land-boom period, there was dishonesty in nearly every one, and ten officials of the banks which failed in the Fergus Falls area were sent to the penitentiary. . . . Practically every one of these little banks which failed was in the farm-land game' (ibid., p. 599). The last witness, C. H. March, member of the Federal Trade Commission (who 'was interested' in Minnesota banks), agreed. In response to Senator Norbeck's question: 'But you attribute the failure of the banks – ', he said: 'I attribute the failure to the condition of the agricultural country' (ibid., p. 629).

Thus, none of the witnesses identified securities activities or securities investment, whether purchased from bank securities affiliates or not, as a cause of bank failures; instead, demographic changes, overbanking, fraud and mismanagement, and poor farming conditions were given as causes. Nor do the statistical data obtained from the questionnaires and presented in the Glass Subcommittee Hearings (1931, part VII, pp. 1033–46) support the contention that losses on securities caused bank failures or even serious financial distress. Specifically, the review of the statistical studies states: '[u]ntil the major deflation period in the bond market in the latter part of 1930 and 1931, losses on bank security investments were reported as being of moderate proportions' (ibid., p. 1042). Aggregate data show losses on stocks, bonds, and other investments to all losses at Federal Reserve member banks in 1929 and 1930 of 32 per cent and 30 per cent. But the analysis continues: '[i]n the great majority of cases, such losses do not include unrealized depreciation'. Therefore, the original cost of the 10 largest bond holdings of 13 banks (8 of which are from New York City) is compared with their market values as of December 1930. These data show market values as percentages of book values ranging from 87 per cent to 122 per cent per bank, with a value-weighted average of 99 per cent. If these data are representative, the aggregate book-value figures do not appear to mis-state bond losses grossly. Hence, losses on securities investments do not appear to have been an important cause of bank failures, although it is possible that bond losses were disproportionately concentrated among failures.

Some additional evidence appears in a study (May, 1934, pp. 538–9), which gives the losses realised from bonds sold (relative to original cost) upon the liquidation of 34 New York state-chartered banks between 1929 and 1933. For the 34 banks, these losses equalled 4.6 per cent of their total assets. Six banks experienced losses of over 20 per cent of total assets. (The largest percentage loss, 45 per cent, was at a bank with $331,000 in assets; the next greatest percentage loss, 31 per cent, was at a bank with $1,213,000 in assets, and the third greatest percentage, 22 per cent, was at a bank with $4,840,000 in assets.) Thus, losses on bonds appear to have been important for a few banks. May (ibid., p. 539) warns, however, that: 'it should be acknowledged that, there being no exchange for sales of, or quotations on commercial loans, it is, of course, impossible to tell the actual realisable value of the commercial loans of these banks during the period in question.'

We may obtain nationwide evidence on this question from a detailed Federal Reserve study of examiners' reports on a sample of 105 member banks whose operations were suspended in 1931.[1] 'All failed national banks with deposits of five million or more were included. The remainder of the banks were apportioned among the twelve Federal reserve districts to give proper representation to each district' (Federal Reserve Committee, 1933, p. 5). The principal cause of the failures was poor and dishonest lending practices, particularly 'lax lending methods', 'slack collection methods', 'unwise loans to directors and officers', and 'lack of credit data' (ibid., table 20). These four criticisms accounted for 68 per cent of the examiners' criticisms of lending policies. Disregard of banking laws and fraud was charged against 60 per cent of the officers or employees of the

---

[1] A sample of 120 member banks whose operations were suspended from 1921 through 1930 was also studied and both samples were compared to thirty-three members banks that did not fail.

suspended banks. The directors of 45 per cent of these banks were criticised for lack of attention to the affairs of their banks.

Bad investments played a much smaller role in the banks' failures. In particular bond depreciation is cited as 'the primary cause of failure in 6 of the 105 banks [6 per cent] selected from the 1931 suspensions, and an important contributing cause of failure in 4 other cases [4 per cent]' (ibid., p. 105). The largest of these banks held $8 million in loans and investments at the time of its last examination. In general, the Federal Reserve Committee (ibid., p. 117) concludes that losses on all securities

> was not large relative to loans and investments, even at the last examination of the sample banks. All but 9 of the banks had depreciation in their securities accounts of less than 10 per cent of loans and investments at their last examination. Of the 9 banks with depreciation of more than 10 per cent of loans and investments only 4 had depreciation of over 15 per cent of loans and investments, and only 2 had depreciation of more than 25 per cent of loans and investments. Two years before their last examination none of the sample banks had depreciation in their securities accounts of more than 10 per cent of loans and investments.

There is no mention in the study about sales (whether forced or not) of investments to correspondents by bank securities affiliates, as Senator Glass claimed. We may infer some evidence on this possibility, however, from the quotations presented and conclusions drawn from examination reports. Seven banks' investment practices are individually discussed. The examination reports complain of excessive bond trading and investment in securities that went down in value, particularly convertibles, real estate, irrigation, and unlisted bonds. The source of the bonds is mentioned for one bank; objections by examiners to purchases from an investment house that one of the bank's directors operated appear in extensive quotations from examiners' reports over several years prior to the bank's failure. (ibid., pp. 135–9.) The Federal Reserve Committee (ibid., p. 123) concludes that '[a] common mistake made by these banks in handling their bond accounts was to place the factor of yield above the factor of safety of principal in selecting issues'.

Finally, the 50 bond issues contributing to the greatest depreciation to the portfolios of the 105 banks were analysed (ibid., table 35, p. 152). Municipals were not included, in part because 'many municipals have no market price and examiners were consequently unable to figure their depreciation' (ibid., p. 153). Among the fifty issues studied, 85.1 per cent of the total depreciation was due to bonds in three groups of industries: public utilities (37.6 per cent), industrials (33.0 per cent), and railroads (14.5 per cent). Both public utilities and rails were regulated by government agencies. The individual industries that accounted for more than 5 per cent of the total depreciation are woollen mills (9.5 per cent), coal (6.6 per cent), and light, heat and power utilities (5.9 per cent). Foreign issues, which Senator Glass singled out as the kind of security 'pushed' by bank securities affiliates, were responsible for 6.5 per cent of the total depreciation, of which 2.9 per cent was attributable to governments, 2.8 per cent to industrials, and 0.8 per cent to rails.

Thus, whether or not banks that failed purchased 'utterly worthless securities of tottering South American Republics and other foreign countries' from the affiliates of their correspondents, as Senator Glass maintained, or from other underwriters and bond dealers, the data reviewed do not support the contention that many banks failed as a result of losses on their bond portfolios.[1] But, even if some banks did fail for this reason, one would have to show both that banks would not have purchased and held investments had they not been offered by their correspondents (directly or through securities affiliates) *and* that the decline in value in alternative assets (such as loans) in the face of the Great Depression would have been less.

VII   CONCLUSIONS

The evidence from the pre-Glass–Steagall period is totally inconsistent with the belief that banks' securities activities or investments caused them to fail or caused the financial system to collapse. Those who claim otherwise (including the Supreme Court) either misread the record, did not look at any actual data, or simply uncritically believed unsupported assertions made by senators and their staffs. Many of the *possible* problems anticipated would affect depositors and bank creditors only if affiliates were used to drain resources from failing banks. This potential problem could be obviated were

---

[1] The record does not support the description drawn by Mehle (1975, note 33), that '[t]he insolvency of many small banks resulted from their holdings of worthless securities sold to them by large city banks'.

banks permitted to offer securities services directly, as any resources shifted between securities and other operations would remain within the bank. In any event, no evidence of actual behaviour that was detrimental to bank creditors was presented or has since become available. Nor was evidence presented before passage of the Act that supports the view that banks that offered securities services, either directly or through affiliates, experienced greater losses or rates of failure than did banks that did not offer these services. Later analysis (White, 1986), however, shows that the securities activities of commercial banks reduced the risk of losses that threatened their safety and soundness.

4 Conflicts of Interest and Abuses

I SOURCES OF DATA

To my knowledge, there are only four sources of data about the abuses that some claim to have been prevalent or at least present in the period before the passage of the 1933 Glass–Steagall Act. These are: (i) charges made in the *Congressional Record* prior to the passages of the Act; (ii) the Pecora Hearings (1933 and 1934); (iii) the SEP (Stock Exchange Practices) Report (1934);[1] and (iv) the SEC Investment Trusts and Investment Companies Study (1940).

The most important source is the hearings that Ferdinand Pecora conducted for the US Senate Committee on Banking and Currency in February 1933, which were instrumental in providing support for the passage of the provisions of the Banking Act of 1933 that separated commercial and investment banking. Kennedy (1973, p. 222) observes that, before the Pecora Hearings, the separation provisions of the Glass bill 'had met with vigorous attack, particularly from Wall Street. The Pecora Hearings changed that attitude. The sensational manner of these hearings, as well as their timing, on the eve of the national moratorium [the March bank holiday], inflamed public resentment. Outrage centred on the securities affiliates, since by 1930 they were sponsoring 54.4 per cent of all new securities issues'.

The hearings (as related to the Glass–Steagall Act) focused first, in late February 1933, on the National City Bank, its securities affiliate, the National City Company and the man principally responsible for the growth of both, Charles E. Mitchell. As Kennedy states (ibid., p. 213), '[s]eparated banking encountered no opposition after March 1933. After the testimony of Charles E. Mitchell before the Banking and Currency Committee, few defended the affiliate'. The hearings then investigated the activities of the private bankers, J. P. Morgan & Co. and associated partnerships, Kuhn Loeb & Co., and

---

[1] Pecora's Book, (*Wall Street Under Oath: The Story of Our Modern Money Changers*, 1939), based on the Hearings is also cited as a source of evidence on abuses. But it references only the Pecora Hearings as the author interpreted them.

Dillon, Read & Co. Seligman (1982, p. 38) concludes that '[t]he public response to the Morgan hearings was directly responsible for the passage of the Banking Act of 1933, which, among other things, required private banks to limit themselves either to receiving deposits or to providing investment services'. Later sessions of the hearings enquired into the conduct of the Chase National Bank, its securities affiliate the Chase Securities Corporation, and most particularly the bank's former president, Albert H. Wiggin. These hearings, together with those concerning the National City Bank as well as the SEP (Stock Exchange Practices) Report (1934) that summarises them, are usually cited as the source of evidence on banking abuses.[1]

II GENERAL AND OFTEN INCORRECT AND MISLEADING ALLEGATIONS OF CONFLICTS OF INTEREST AND ABUSES

The existence of serious abuses by commercial banks' securities affiliates and directly carried out securities activities appears to be accepted by both proponents and opponents of the Glass–Steagall Act, and by many historians and economists. For example, the Investment Company Institute begins a pamphlet opposing bank entry into the mutual funds business thus: 'As a result of widespread misconduct connected with bank securities activities during the 1920s, the Congress in 1933 decided to restore the historic separation between banking and the securities business by enacting the Glass–Steagall Act' (Investment Company Institute, undated, p. 1). An important opponent of the Act also accepts the existence of banks' misconduct before 1933. J. P. Morgan & Co. (1984, pp. 5–6) reports that the Pecora Hearings

> revealed, among other things, that one commercial bank and its affiliate had failed repeatedly to disclose material facts to investors, that the affiliate had engaged in high-pressure tactics, that the affiliate had traded in the stock of the bank and participated in a range of manipulative activities, that the bank had provided the

---

[1] The Pecora Hearings also delved into the failures of commercial banks in Detroit and Cleveland, but these contained no charges about conflicts of interest or other abuses related to securities operations or holdings, with the exception of the charge that a Detroit bank's affiliate sold securities at a profit to the bank's trust accounts. Section V of this chapter discusses this allegation.

affiliate with customers, and that the bank had used the affiliate to relieve the bank of bad loans to the alleged detriment of shareholders. [Footnote reference to Pecora, 1939, pp. 70–123 excluded.]

Having accepted these charges as fact, Morgan (ibid., p. 6) argues that '[m]ost of the abuses revealed by the Pecora Hearings were addressed by the Securities Act of 1933 and the Securities Exchange Act of 1934'.

Other observers also mis-state the record that the Pecora Hearings (1933 and 1934) established. In particular, the 'Issues Paper' prepared by the US Department of the Treasury (1975, p. 79) incorrectly reports: 'In its investigation of the banking system, the Glass Subcommittee [1931] identified multiple abuses that arose primarily through attempts by commercial banks to promote the underwriting operations of affiliates'. As I explained in Chapter 3, the Glass Subcommittee (1931 or 1932) did not identify any such abuses. Indeed, the referenced quotations are but the speculations of Senator Bulkley. The US Department of the Treasury (1975, p. 80) also claims:

> The misuses of these commercial banking operations [loans to and purchases of securities from affiliates] to promote security affiliates also represented serious conflicts of interest between the bank's responsibility to its depositors, shareholders, and customers and its promotion of the affiliate. The Committee found that this conflict promoted neither the interests of the bank nor the security affiliates, but rather those of bank directors and other insiders who stood to profit more from their role in the underwriting affiliate than as directors or bank shareholders.

But the Glass Subcommittee (1931 and 1932) neither asked for nor published any information about the promotion of affiliates, bank directors or other insiders, or bank shareholders. The Subcommittee did get and report information on transactions between security affiliates and the parent bank, but it did not characterise these relationships as giving rise to conflicts of interest, serious or otherwise.

In *Investment Company Institute v. Camp* (401 US 617, 631 (1971)) the US Supreme Court points to abuses that it believes Congress sought to correct in passing the Glass–Steagall Act. In particular, the Court mentions four such abuses. For the first three the Court refers only to remarks made on the floor of Congress by Senator Glass, Representative Fish, and Senator Bulkley. Yet none of the Congressmen cited any instances to support their speculations.

[1] the bank's salesman's interest might impair its ability to function as an impartial source of credit.

[2] Congress was also concerned that bank depositers might suffer losses on investments that they purchased in reliance on the relationship between the bank and its affiliate [ibid. p. 631, footnotes omitted].

[3] Another potential hazard that very much concerned Congress arose from the plain conflict between the promotional interest of the investment banker and the obligation of the commercial banker to render disinterested investment advice [ibid., p. 633].

The Supreme Court characterises the fourth abuse thus: 'Congress had before it evidence that security affiliates might be driven to unload excessive holdings through the trust department of the sponsor bank.' Because of the seriousness of this charge (such an act was and is illegal), I evaluate it in section V of this chapter.

Virtually all the other important commentators on the Glass–Steagall Act rely on the testimony presented at the Pecora Hearings (1933) and its summary in the SEP Report (1934) and presentation by Pecora (1939). In particular, these records and narratives are the basis for the first description by an historian, Peach (1941, chapter V), of abuses alleged to have been committed by or via security affiliates. The other major historians, Carosso (1970a), Kennedy (1973), and Seligman (1982), similarly refer to these sources. Articles such as Saunders (1985b), and Kelly (1985a and 1985b), which find the Glass–Steagall Act separation of commercial and investment banking undesirable, and Fein (1986), which finds the separation prudent, refer to the same set of conflicts of interest and abuses and sources. A typical description is this one given by Litan (1987, p. 27):

hearings orchestrated by the chief counsel of the Glass subcommittee, Ferdinand Pecora, uncovered various abuses involving large banks and their securities affiliates. These hearings revealed that certain banks had made loans to securities purchasers to help support artificially securities prices, dumped 'bad' securities with correspondents or in trust accounts, and used securities affiliates to relieve the banks of their bad loans and to purchase stock in companies to which the banks had loaned money. The hearings also revealed that several leading bankers had evaded income taxes by failing to report substantial sums of income [reference to the Pecora Hearings, 1933 and 1934, in general][1]

The acts specified refer only to two banks – the National City Bank (NCB) and its affiliate, the National City Company (NCC), and the Chase National Bank (CNB) and its affiliate, the Chase Securities Corporation (CSC) – and their leaders at the time the abuses were alleged to have occurred, Charles Mitchell of National City and Albert Wiggin of Chase. This chapter considers each bank and its associated affiliates and leaders separately, as the charges against Chase were not made until after the Glass–Steagall Act was enacted.

III THE CHARGES AGAINST NATIONAL CITY BANK AND MITCHELL

I based the investigation reported in this chapter on Carosso's (1970a) list of charges against the National City Bank, its investment affiliate, and president. His book, *Investment Banking in America: A History*, has been an important source for students and scholars. Where appropriate, I also reference the writings of Seligman (1982), Kennedy (1973), and Peach (1941).

Carosso (1970a, p. 330) describes thus the Pecora Hearings' findings on National City Bank and its president, Charles Mitchell:

The abuses uncovered were so gross that the financial community itself was appalled. The conservative *Commercial & Financial Chronicle*, never an admirer of the Senate investigation, admitted that the revelations were 'far from pleasing to say the least,' and described the testimony of National City officials as 'highly sensational'. . . . Nothing the committee uncovered in the next seventeen months revealed the 'sickening story of exploitation'

---

[1] Litan (1987, p. 27) cites Saunders (1985c, pp. 17–25 – the entire article) as the source of the final sentence about bankers' evading their income tax liabilities. Saunders does not discuss this 'abuse' at all. Instead he describes (p. 18) the Pecora Hearings' other 'findings' in language very similar to that used by Litan.

unfolded during the National City hearings. 'The only thing that some of our great financial institutions overlooked during the years of boom,' observed Heywood Broun, the noted Scripps-Howard columnist, 'was the installation of a roulette-wheel for the convenience of depositors.'

While it may be true that the popular press was shocked and the financial press upset, the question of present concern is whether the hearings actually revealed abuses that the Glass–Steagall Act's provisions were designed to cure.

Carosso reports that '[w]itnesses disclosed a wide variety of abuses and excesses' (ibid., p. 330). He particularly charges the following ten kinds of 'abuses and excesses' (ibid., pp. 330–5):

Charge 1: avoidance, if not evasion, by Mitchell of personal income taxes;

Charge 2: high salaries and bonuses paid to Mitchell and other top executives that were not reported to stockholders;

Charge 3: special lending facilities for officers but not for other employees;

Charge 4: profiting by executives from individual participations in the affiliate's securities floatations;

Charge 5: bonds sold with inadequate or misleading information given to investors;

Charge 6: sales of domestic corporation stock under similar circumstances;

Charge 7: ethically dubious activities, such as stock exchange speculation and participation in pool operations;

Charge 8: steering depositors to the securities affiliate;

Charge 9: trading in the stock of the National City Bank by its securities affiliate; and

Charge 10: use of the affiliate to disguise bad banking practices and to hide losses from the stockholders.

Seligman (1982, pp. 25–9) describes aspects of charges 1, 4, 5, and 8. He adds one more charge:

Charge 11: a loan by National City Bank to the general manager of the Port Authority of New York before National City received the right to issue $66 million in Authority bonds (ibid., p. 29).

Pecora (1939, pp. 89–112, 120–4), Kennedy (1973, pp. 112–25), and Peach (1941, chapter V) also delineate most of charges 1 through 10. In addition, Pecora and Kennedy describe:

Charge 12: the plight of an investor, Mr Edgar D. Brown, who lost $100,000 as a result of churning and bad advice by National City Company employees (Pecora, pp. 84–9; and Kennedy, pp. 115–19).

The first two charges are irrelevant to the issue of the separation of commercial and investment banking, although they are said to have been instrumental for the passage of the Banking Act of 1933. The third is also irrelevant, but some may consider it indicative of the inequitable manner in which banking was conducted. The eleventh similarly is irrelevant to the issue. Therefore, I relegate analysis of the first three and the eleventh charges to an appendix to this chapter and now examine each of the other charges by reference to the 1933 Pecora Hearings. Most of these remaining charges, however, are also not relevant to the Glass–Steagall Act, because they relate to events that were not peculiar to securities activities conducted by commercial banks. These charges are pertinent, nevertheless, as they indicate that commercial banks should have conformed and presently should conform to a less profit-motivated standard of business practice than is expected from investment bankers or others who may engage in securities underwriting and transactions.

Profiting by Executives From Individual Participations in the Affiliate's Securities Flotations (Charge 4)

Carosso (1970a, p. 334) states: 'Large salaries and "stupendous bonuses" were only two roads to private riches. Like the partners in many private investment banking firms, the executives of the National City Co. also profited handsomely from participating individually in the affiliate's flotations.' The reference is to two stock issues that Pecora describes (1939, pp. 124–6) – Boeing Airplane and Transportation Corporation, and United Aircraft. Pecora (ibid., p. 124) states that in October 1928 the National City Company 'bought from it [the newly organised Boeing] for $5,013,000 a large block of . . . stock'. Rather than sell this stock to the public, Pecora says that the National City Co. 'retained a large block for itself, and the remainder of its purchase was allotted . . . to Mr. Mitchell and a select list of officers, directors, key men, and special friends'. The stock was listed nine days later and within five months the National City Co. and the 'insiders' profited greatly. Similarly, Pecora (ibid., p. 126) states in January 1929: 'the National City Company acquired another block of common and preferred stock of the airplane company, now called United Aircraft. . . . Most of this was sold to the public, but once again the 'insiders' kept a block of stock for their own use. . . . [The 13,000 shares] had cost the company $70 per share; it was sold to Mr. Mitchell and a second list of select company officers at $80 per share; and within two days it was selling on the market at $96 per share.' Kennedy (1973, p. 124) also describes this situation: 'In 1928 and 1929 officers bought into particular profitable flotations, such as aircraft stocks, while the same offerings were withheld from the public as 'too speculative.' When issues such as Boeing common and preferred turned downward, a suitable advertising campaign helped the National City men to unload with considerable gains.[1]

Kennedy's charge that Boeing stock was sold with the help of 'a suitable advertising campaign' is incorrect. It appears to be based on the following 'flash' sent to National City Company offices:

Advertisement on Boeing . . . stock is being published today only in the following cities: New York, Chicago, San Francisco, and Seattle, with the statement that all units have been sold privately and the advertisement appears as a matter of record only. The statement we are making to customers regarding our inability to consider orders from them is substantially as follows: We have purchased an interest in this company, and on account of the fact this industry is still somewhat unseasoned, even though we regard this particular company as sound and having a very bright future, we were not quite ready to make a general offering to our customers. It would have been next to impossible to avoid taking orders from the type of investor who should not buy this stock. Therefore, our own family and certain officers and employees of the Boeing Co. and affiliations have taken the entire issue [Pecora Hearings, 1933, p. 2333].

---

[1] Kennedy's footnote reference 53 is omitted. It is to Pecora (1939, pp. 123–6). Pecora does not mention a 'suitable advertising campaign' in these pages, nor does he mention other issues (as is implied by Kennedy's words, 'issues such as'). Seligman does not offer this charge.

Turning next to the circumstances of the stock issue, the testimony (by Joseph Ripley, who managed the issue) reveals that the National City Company purchased 90 per cent of the initial Boeing issue, of which some 30 per cent of the preferred and 17 per cent of the common stock was allotted to 'insiders'. (Pecora Hearings, 1933, pp. 2334–7). Pecora (1939, pp. 125–6) and the Pecora Hearings (pp. 2331, 2335) indicate that the insiders made $1,629,000 and that the National City Company made $2,499,000 from the Boeing issue (60 per cent of the total). The United Aircraft issue was selling for $88 a share when it was sold to the bank's and company's officers and directors for $80 a share. Thus, they made $104,000. The Hearings (ibid., p. 2342) state that the National City Company grossed $1,447,820 on that issue (93.3 per cent of the total). the Hearings also report that the shares went up considerably in price *after* sales were made to the public.

Ripley claimed that the company acted responsibly in not offering the issue directly to the public. He said that 'there was grave doubt, at the time we bought these stocks from the Boeing Airplane & Transport Corporation as to how the market would receive them' (ibid., p. 2336). Furthermore, because National City Bank's vice president Gordon Rentschler and his family were prominent shareholders in United Aircraft, there is reason to believe that the issue was not underpriced. Rentschler and his family would have suffered directly had this occurred. It seems reasonable to expect that he would protect his and his family's position.

Thus, the record does not support Pecora's contention that insiders benefited at the expense of the general public. He could have argued, though, that all the gain (and, presumably the loss had that been the result) should have gone to the National City stockholders. Had the National City Company adopted this form of executive compensation, it could have avoided later criticism, although at the expense of paying its officers higher direct salaries. But this form of compensation would not have allowed the National City Company to use a desirable form of risk-sharing between its owners and employees that theory indicates is beneficial to shareholders.[1] This kind of sharing helps to align managers' and stockholders' interests, because the managers gain if shareholders gain. Hence, they have incentives to make decisions and to take risks that tend to benefit shareholders, for in so doing, they benefit themselves. In any event,

---

[1] See, for example, Jensen and Meckling (1976).

the 'flash' quoted earlier ('our own family . . . have taken the entire issue') indicates that the participation of National City Company officers in the stock issue was not hidden.

Bonds Sold With Inadequate or Misleading Information Given to Investors (Charge 5)

Carosso (1970a, p. 330) describes the hearings as showing that '[i]nvestors were lured into buying issues sponsored by National City Co. and were told few, if any, pertinent facts concerning the quality of the securities recommended'. He points specifically to $8.5 millions of bonds issued by Minas Geraes (now spelled Gerais), a Brazilian state (charge 5.1), $90 millions in Peruvian bonds (charge 5.2), a $15 million Cuban sugar bond issue (charge 5.3),[1] and a $32 million bond issue for the Lautrato Nitrate Company of Chile (charge 5.4). Although other underwriters also sold bonds that defaulted, Carosso and Pecora emphasise that 'people had purchased them [the bonds] largely because of the "faith in the integrity and presumed conservatism of the National City Bank" ' (Carosso, 1970a, p. 331, footnote to Pecora, p. 92). But the Minas Geraes, Peru, and Lautrato Nitrate issues plus that of the Republic of Chile were the only South American issues that the National City Company underwrote that were in default at the time of the hearings (Pecora Hearings, 1933, pp. 2050–1).

Minas Geraes Bonds (Charge 5.1)[2]

From Carosso's description, the sale of these bonds by National City Company seems irresponsible, if not fraudulent. Carosso (1970a, p. 330–1) describes Minas Geraes as a state[3]

[a]   whose authorities a National City official had described earl-

---

[1] Carosso (1970a, p. 330) calls these 'loans'.
[2] Pecora (1939, p. 99) says that the bonds had fallen to around 21–22 at the time of the hearings (which may be one reason for his having examined this particular issue closely). He states: 'The bankers and selling houses had pocketed a profit of approximately $600,000, and the public had lost approximately $13,000,000 (pp. 99–100). He fails to mention that his questioning also brought out that the State defaulted in 1932 because it was unable to obtain the necessary foreign exchange as a result of severe exchange restrictions imposed by the Federal Government of Brazil (Pecora Hearings, 1933, p. 2167).
[3] Footnote reference omitted to *Stock Exchange Practices: Hearings* pt 6, p. 2137. See also Pecora, *Wall Street Under Oath*, pp. 96–100.

ier as being lax, negligent, and entirely uninformed concerning the responsibilities of a long-term borrower.

[b]   Not only was none of this information given the investor, but the prospectus for the issue, prepared by this same official, actually referred favorably to the way the state's finances had been administered. The next year Minas Geraes negotiated a second $8 million loan,

[c]   one-half of which was to be used to bail out the National City Co., which had advanced some $4 million in short-term credits. Instead of disclosing this fact to the public, the prospectus stated only that the funds were 'designed to increase the economic productivity of the State'. When asked why National City had not given investors all the facts, Ronald M. Byrnes, a former vice president of this affiliate, replied:

[d]   'In my opinion there is no investor that I know of who would have had the slightest interest, or whose judgment would have been in the least affected, by the fact that the moneys from this loan were to be used to pay advances which were made for these purposes.'

I now examine each of these statements of alleged fact, identified by letters a to d in square brackets.[1]

[a] The National City Company official (George F. Train, whom the company had sent to Brazil) testified (and Pecora concurred) that his description 'referred to the details concerning the external loans contracted in 1907 and 1911' and in 1916 to a French firm (Pecora Hearings, 1933, p. 2155). Train eventually was permitted to explain that '[t]he French bankers in that case were banking firms which I subsequently found, upon investigation, to have been somewhat sharp in their dealings, and it was my feeling that the State officials of that day, while admittedly careless and lax and lacking in knowledge of the technical details of external financing, had nevertheless been misled in many respects by the French banking houses with whom they had done business' (ibid., p. 2160). Furthermore, Train's letter, from which Carosso's description quoted above was paraphrased, went on to explain: 'The foregoing recital serves to

---

[1] The source of the allegations was difficult to trace, because Carosso only gives a specific reference to the Pecora Hearings, 1933, for the quotation, and Pecora does not give any references.

show the complete ignorance, carelessness, and negligence of the *former* State officials in respect to external long-term borrowing' (ibid., p. 2155, emphasis added). Contrary to the implication given by Carosso, the National City official (Train) was describing the situation that occurred at least ten years before the bond issue and to Minas Geraes administrators who no longer were in power.

[b] The prospectus statement about the way the state's finances were administered, Train said, referred to the State's management since 1916 and to its internal finances '[o]n which the security of the loan rested . . .' (ibid., p. 2156). These administrations, he testified, had 'a succession of budget surpluses, with one or two minor exceptions, which practically continued from 1916 to 1929' (ibid., p. 2156). Although he continued to insist that the statements in the prospectus were correct, after repetitive questions from Pecora, Train admitted that '[i]t would have been more accurate had I said the "State's budget" or "budgetary position" rather than their "finances" ' (ibid., p. 2159).

[c] Although Pecora said that between $3 million and $4 million of the $8 million second loan was used to repay short-term credits, the National City Company witnesses said that National City Bank was owed only $750,000. Train testified that this amount plus an advance of £150,000 from London banking houses were loans intended 'to bridge the gap until the long-term bond issue could be duly authorized and issued' (ibid., p. 2161). No question was raised about the State's ability to repay the National City Bank loan. Hence, the assertion that the loan served to 'bail out' the bank is not correct.[1] Furthermore, Byrnes pointed out that the advances had been used to increase the economic productivity of the State; hence, the statement in the prospectus was correct. (ibid., p. 2136).

[d] The quotation as given apparently is the basis for Carosso's conclusion (1970, p. 330) that '[i]nvestors were lured into buying issues . . . and were told few, if any, pertinent facts concerning the quality of the securities recommended'. Therefore, the balance of

---

[1] Securities were underwritten to repay bridge loans then as now. Investment bankers sometimes arrange for bridge loans (often from the firm's funds) only if the borrower later engages the firm as the underwriter for its securities. This procedure offers the advantage of reducing information and other transactions costs.

Byrnes's statement is of interest. He continued (Pecora Hearings, 1933, p. 2137):

> MR BYRNES . . . But such an investor is interested in the real expenditures of the State, and for what purpose the State is really borrowing. And that is the essential information given. Now, to have quoted the law in full, to have embodied in the prospectus the full legal opinion of our Brazilian counsel and our New York counsel on this thing, would have made such prospectus so inordinately long that there would have been no chance that the investor would have read it, in my opinion.
>
> • • •
>
> SENATOR BROOKHART That proposition would not have taken much space, just to set out the interest of the National City Co. and say that the company itself was going to have in this money, would it?
>
> MR BYRNES It is assumed in all financial practice in every market I know that the fiscal agents and bankers for the Government carry it with short-term advances, just as the Federal Reserve bank carries the United States Government pending the funding operation.

From this testimony neither Carosso nor Pecora are justified in charging the National City Company with fraud or misrepresentation in its offering of Minas Geraes bonds. But Senator Brookhart's suggestion, that information on the State's finances might have provided investors with useful information, appears well taken, particularly considering the criticism later levied against the National City Company. Today underwriters routinely provide this kind of information in conjunction with state, municipal, and foreign bond offerings in the United States. It is not clear, though, whether this information is used by investors or whether underwriters use information overkill as a shield against criticism.

Peruvian Bonds (Charge 5.2)

As a 'notable' example of National City Company's 'pushing low-quality securities on unsuspecting investors', Carosso (1970a, p. 331) points to 'the three Peruvian loans of 1927 and 1928, totalling $90 million, about which the public was never told that National City's own experts had described the credit position of this government as "an adverse moral and political risk" '.[1] The issues defaulted in 1931 and were selling at $7 per $100 face value bond in February 1933. Pecora (1939, p. 101), to whose narrative Carosso refers, states that, although the NCC 'for six years properly declined to aid the Government of Peru in obtaining money from the American investor . . . as the bull market grew greater and greater, the careless "New Era" psychology grew more and more pervasive, [and] the National City suddenly found nebulous reasons to justify a complete change of attitude [in 1927]'. Further, Pecora charges, National City Company mislead investors: 'The prospectus . . . contained an impressive list of the various Peruvian borrowings, but never even mentioned that there had been a default on any of these debts' (ibid., p. 102). Kennedy (1973, pp. 119–20) states that 'Pecora revealed that the company should not have become involved in the first place. National City agents on the scene had warned before each bond flotation . . . that Peru was a bad "moral and political risk" '.

Seligman (1982, pp. 27–8) emphasises the Peruvian bonds in his critique. His description of National City Company's procedures are very damaging to the company. He states that after the first ($15 million, 1927) issue,

[a]   National City telegraphed its Latin American representatives for updated reports. The replies were uniformly unfavorable. In July 1927,

[b]   the overseas manager of the National City Bank [J. H. Durrell] wrote Mitchell: 'As I see it, there are two factors that will long retard the economic importance of Peru. [Its largely

---

[1] Carosso's footnote 40 is omitted. It refers to Pecora (1939, p. 100) and states; 'See also *Stock Exchange Practices: Hearings*, pt. 6, 2082–87, on the way the Institute of International Finance (IIF), a "supposed independent fact finding body", sponsored by New York University, was used to assist sellers of foreign bonds, in this case the National City Co'. All that is contained in these pages is repetitive questions by Pecora to Baker about the IIF and its financing. Baker, president of the National City Company, repeatedly replied that he knew nothing about it. Pecora repeatedly asked Baker about his understanding of this statement given in the IIF's annual report: 'It is obvious that the director and the assistant director, under the customs of academic freedom, can express themselves more completely as individuals than they may in their official capacities as representatives of the institute' (Pecora Hearings, 1933, p. 2084). Baker repeatedly replied: 'I say again, I haven't any idea what the professor had in mind, and I should think the only way I could determine that would be to ask him' (p. 2085). There is no mention in the pages Carosso cites about how the IIF 'was used to assist sellers of foreign bonds.'

Indian population and foreign ownership of its wealth] . . .
The country's political situation is equally uncertain.'

[c] Six months later, National City received another report that
'the balance of international payments is unfavorable to
Peru';

[d] in March 1928, 'the whole taxation system is a hodgepodge'.

[e] The manager of the Lima branch of the bank concluded a
September 1928 cablegram: 'We have assumed (a) no further
loan can be safely issued and (b) integrity Republic's finances
threatened unless floating debt problem solved.' The National
City Company nonetheless cosponsored a December 1927
$50 million Peruvian bond issue, and a $25 million bond
distribution in October 1928.

Thus Seligman gives the impression that National City Company
acted in total disregard of warnings.

In fact, the hearings show the following:

[a] No testimony indicates that 'National City telegraphed its Latin
American representatives for updated reports'.

[b] Both Victor Schoepperle (who was directly in charge of the
Peruvian bond issues) and Ronald M. Byrnes (who supervised the
foreign issues department and to whom Schoepperle reported) testified that they had not seen Durrell's memo until the day of the
hearings (Pecora Hearings, 1933, pp. 2100, 2120). This probably
resulted from Durrell's position in the National City Bank rather
than the company. His job and that of the author of the cablegram
cited by Seligman [e], H. E. Henneman, are described by Schoepperle as follows: 'Mr. Durrell and Mr. Henneman were commercial
banking men who were interested in making observations in Peru
for the purpose of determining the position of their commercial loans
and commercial branch banking operations. . . . Mr. Durrell would
visit branches all around the world, . . . stay a few days, and write
an opinion to Mr. Mitchell' (ibid., p. 2115).

[c] The report said to have been 'received' in January 1928 ('six
months later') is entitled 'Penny Report of 1926', and was authored
by a vice president of the Foundation Co. The beginning of the
sentence reprinted by Seligman reads: 'The present low value of
Peruvian money is due primarily to the fact that', after which follows
the portion quoted: 'the balance of international payments is unfav-

orable to Peru' (ibid., p. 2078). This information about 1926 money exchange values was neither timely nor relevant to the company's decision to be included as an underwriter of an October 1928 bond issue.

[d] The quote about the tax system was taken from a report by Frederick R. Kent, a director of Bankers Trust Co. of New York and an expert on currency stabilisation. The beginning of Kent's partially quoted observation is: 'As I had the feeling that the whole taxation system is a hodgepodge', which is followed by concerns about the efficiency of the tax collection system, not for the amount of taxes collected (ibid., pp. 2108–9). His report concludes (ibid., p. 2116):

> Further, if the program recommended [stabilisation of the currency – it was achieved but not maintained] is carried out there is no reason why the Government and business interests of the country cooperating together can not so strengthen the economic position of Peru that it will be able to meet successfully all the emergencies which naturally arise now and again from years of crop failures or overproduction or from reduced foreign markets due to degrees of world prosperity.

The quotation that Seligman presents thus is not a fair representation of this communication.

[e] The commercial banking officer sent the cablegram and it refers to loans that, Schoepperle testified, were 'solved' by a consolidation of debt that the bond issues made possible (ibid., p. 2113).

Although Seligman's description of the Peruvian bonds 'abuse' is incorrect and misleading, testimony at the hearings largely supports the essence of the charges that he, Carosso, Pecora, and Kennedy made, that the information available to the company did not justify the issuance of long-term bonds. As I note later, Baker (NCC's president) did not know why the bond prospectuses did not disclose Peru's prior poor fiscal record and questionable prospects. (The lead underwriter, J. & W. Seligman & Co., prepared the prospectuses, but NCC approved them.) He referred Pecora's questions to the persons in charge of the issues, Schoepperle and Byrnes.[1] Schoep-

---

[1] Byrnes was not asked about the prospectuses. He generally concurred with Schoepperle's testimony.

perle (and Baker, ibid., p. 2069) said that the Peruvian tobacco monopoly secured the first ($15 million) bond issue, which appeared to provide sufficient funds to service the debt (ibid., p. 2095). He could not explain why the prospectuses for the following issues did not reveal Peru's past history. He had been against lending to Peru, but he changed his position for two reasons. First, a long report dated 3 December, 1925 from C. W. Calvin (National City Company's Lima representative since 1919), who had been against National City's becoming Peru's financial representative, recommended secured lending.[1] More importantly, an interview in February 1927 with Peru's strongman, President Leguia, convinced him that the future would be different. In a somewhat rambling testimony, Schoepperle explained (ibid., p. 2095):

> we thought that we could embark on a program that would clear the financial position in Peru, stabilize the currency, establish a balanced condition in his [Leguia's] budget, help him carry out the public works program already under way, which was showing increased taxing power and increased revenues – it was only in that way that we were willing to embark upon the financing of Peru, and it was on the President's assurance that we be given such an opportunity that we went into that business.

In response to a question by Pecora – 'Peru [still] was a bad moral, economic, and political risk [as you wrote before 1927]?' (Pecora Hearings, 1933, p. 2114), Schoepperle replied (ibid., p. 2115):

> I regret to say that in the light of subsequent developments after 1927 and 1928, the opinion that I had previously expressed earlier, in 1921, 1922, and 1925 was borne out. I thought, like a great many others, that I was in a new era, and I made an honest mistake of judgement.

Pecora established that the National City Company netted $681,000 on the three issues and that Schoepperle received a bonus of $70,000 in 1928 (ibid., p. 2117).[2] Pecora's questions also revealed that substantial portions of the first two loans were used to repay (consoli-

---

[1] The report is printed in Pecora Hearings (1933) pp. 2103–6.
[2] Schoepperle was not asked whether his bonus was related to the Peruvian bond issues, nor did Pecora or the historians mentions this possible relationship.

date) other borrowings, none of which was owed to the National City Bank or National City Company.

Cleveland and Huertas (1985) analysed the Peruvian bond issues extensively. They point out that 'these bonds amounted to only 2 per cent of the total underwriting commitments for foreign bonds made by the National City Company in the years 1921–29' and they had the worst record of any foreign issue underwritten by the company. (ibid., pp. 175–6). These bonds, they report, were graded 'A' by Moody's, an independent rating service, in 1927. In 1928 Moody's reduced the rating to Baa, with the comment that the 'the debt should be adequately protected' (ibid., p. 176). Furthermore, they show that the price of the 1927 issue (the only one discussed) sold above its original issue price until May 1930. Then the bonds fell in price 'as a result of the depression's impact on the Peruvian economy' (ibid., p. 180). This led to a revolution, the deposing of President Leguia, default, and abrogation of foreign debts.

One can read this record and analysis and draw at least two conclusions. First, Pecora and the historians obviously regard this testimony as evidence that the National City Bank misused its reputation to 'push low-quality securities on unsuspecting investors', who were not even informed about the risks they were taking. Profits to the company and bonuses to its officers may have motivated this enterprise. But, except to a small degree, the evidence from the testimony does not support this conclusion. When examined in detail, the testimony indicates that the National City Company did not act abusively towards investors as its accusers argue. A respected investment bank, moreover, was the lead underwriter.

Second, the National City Company had reason to believe that conditions in Peru had improved sufficiently to bring the bond issues to investment grade, as the Moody's rating indicates, and that the returns offered investors were consistent with the risk. Investors must have had information about the exported commodities on which the Peruvian economy depended. The effect of the unexpected world depression on Peru and not *ex ante* bad judgement, furthermore, caused the bonds to become virtually worthless. As Hamilton (1987) shows, the drastic declines in commodity prices experienced after 1929 were entirely unexpected (as indicated by future prices) in previous years. It is not reasonable to expect the National City Company to have predicted future conditions better than market commodity traders at the time it sold the bonds to the public.

The important additional question for present purposes is whether

National City's name on the bond issue made investors less likely to evaluate the issue. That is, would investors have been more cautious if only investment bankers were involved in the underwriting and distribution of the bonds? A test of this hypothesis requires knowledge of the purchasers of the Peruvian bonds. Were they relatively naive depositors who did not purchase securities from nonbank-associated houses or were they sophisticated investors? Chapter 5 provides some indirect evidence on this question from a comparison of the default record of bonds floated by bank affiliates on non-bank underwriters. The evidence presented there indicates that the bonds underwritten by commercial bank affiliates and by banks that also underwrote securities were not inferior, and were more notably superior, to those underwritten by other houses.

Cuban Sugar Bonds (Charge 5.3)

Carosso (1970a, p. 331) follows his condemnation of National City Company's Peruvian loans (quoted above), with: 'The same lack of responsibility was shown in the flotation of a $15 million loan [bond issue] for the Cuban Dominican Sugar Company'. Only Pecora (1939), to whom Carosso refers, mentions these bonds. Pecora charges that when the company floated the bonds in 1924 it 'did not feel in any way called upon to inform the public that the Cuban sugar industry had collapsed in 1920 and had shown only a minor flurry of improvement in later years' (Pecora, 1939, p. 103).

When Pecora made an almost identical statement to Mitchell at the hearings, Mitchell replied: 'bear in mind that Cuban Dominican has a portion of its assets only in Cuba, where these difficulties were occurring, and the properties that they had there were among the best, and the bonded debt, as I recall it, was exceedingly small' (Pecora Hearings, 1933, p. 1799). Furthermore, when asked if he had approved the issue, Mitchell stated: 'Yes; and I thought it was such a good investment that I went away buying the bonds myself and bought stock in the open market and put it away in my box, and it is there today' (ibid., p. 1799). There is nothing in the hearings about disclosures in the prospectus or the price of the bonds over time. Nor is there any reason to believe that the National City Company could have hidden the state of the Cuban economy from the public. This record seems hardly sufficient for a conclusion that the company showed a 'lack of responsibility'.

Lautrato Nitrate Company of Chile Bond Issue (Charge 5.4)

The final example of NCC's 'lack of responsibility' that Carosso (1970a, p. 331) gives is 'a \$32 million bond issue for the Lautrato Nitrate Company of Chile'. Again, he refers to Pecora (1939), who charges that when these bonds were floated in 1929 National City Company 'knew that the future of the Chilean nitrate industry, of which Lautrato company was a part, was greatly jeopardised by the development of synthetic nitrogen. But it neither passed on its information to the public, nor, when the bonds dropped precipitously from 99 to 2½, did it feel any tremors of remorse or responsibility' (Pecora, 1939, pp. 103–4).[1]

The testimony given at the hearings does not support Pecora's characterisation. NCC Vice President Byrnes testified: 'Although we had very great confidence in the acumen and the ability of the Guggenheim organization [which developed the process on which Lautrato Nitrate's operations were based], so-called, in the engineers whom they had then attached to their organization, we did take the final precaution of sending a man to Chile to study the industry' (Pecora Hearings, 1933, p. 2317). That man, an engineer, prepared a study in New York (in which he mentioned the production of synthetic nitrogen) and then went to Chile and sent back cable reports prior to the bond issue date. In these reports he stated (as read by Pecora at the hearings, ibid., pp. 2320–1):

> The unknown factor is obsolescence. By the substantial reduction in the cost of producing Chilean nitrate the industry is placed in advantageous competitive position with synthetic and other pro- duction of fertilizing chemicals. But with the current march of progress, it is impossible to prophesy the conditions which may exist in the Chilean nitrate industry within the 25-year term of new financing. There is, however, every possibility that the Lau- trato Anglo-Chilean management will be able to maintain its lead in the Chilean industry and to continue operations at a rate of earnings which will place the security of the debenture beyond reasonable doubt.

Pecora's characterisation of the company (or of its representatives) as not feeling 'any tremors of remorse or responsibility' because the

---

[1] Neither Kennedy nor Seligman mention this issue.

bonds were selling at 2½ similarly is not supported by the record. The only mention is on page 2309, where Byrnes is asked the market value of the bonds, which he gave. He was not asked for nor did he volunteer a description of his feelings which, in any event, are not relevant to the present issue except as an indication of Pecora's bias.

Sales of Domestic Corporation Stock with Inadequate Information Given to Investors (Charge 6)

Carosso states (1970a, p. 331):

> Methods such as these [referring to the bond flotations] had been employed also in selling stocks of domestic corporations. As bankers of Anaconda Copper, the National City Co. 'promptly sold' to its customers its own sizable holdings in this corporation's stock when the price of copper dropped sharply, while it continued to *tout* these shares to the public. Not satisfied with this, National City bought an additional million shares, which it resold at a profit of some $20 million. [emphasis added]

He continues: 'When asked about these transactions, Mitchell denied that the drop in copper prices had in any way influenced him to sell his company's holdings.'[1] Carosso apparently included this statement to imply that selling shares *after* relevant information became public is evidence of a dishonest or disreputable 'method' of selling stocks. Pecora (1939, p. 94), the cited source for Carosso's description, offers a similar implication, when he writes after noting that the price of Anaconda stock had dropped 'forty or fifty points': 'the public lived in eager hope that soon it would skyrocket again. Why, then, stop selling it, when customers were still buying so merrily?' Unless there is reason to believe that the market for Anaconda stock was remarkably inefficient (such that the price of copper was unknown to market participants), or that the National City Company disseminated false information to mislead investors or withheld

---

[1] Carosso (1970a, p. 331) follows the passage just quoted: 'He explained National City's subsequent purchases in these words: "it became our duty, or so we conceived it, so long as our customers viewed that stock as an investment stock, to buy in the market and to sell additional shares to them. Which we did." ' This quotation (Pecora Hearings, 1933, p. 774) is not in response to anything related to copper prices. It is an explanation of NCC's purchases of shares to meet customer demand.

adverse information (charges that were not made), we can dismiss this implication of wrongdoing without further investigation.

In any event, the record does not provide evidence about the influence of copper prices on National City Company's sales of Anaconda stock, except Mitchell's explanation for variations in the price of the stock reflecting copper consumption and prices: 'a one cent difference in the price of copper [which sold for around $0.20 a pound] means a difference of $1.25 per share in the Anaconda shares' (Pecora Hearings, 1933, p. 780). Nor does the record indicate anything about 'touting' shares. Indeed, Mitchell quoted an analysis by an independent, prestigious firm, Standard Trade & Securities Service (Standard Statistics Co.) dated 26 August 1929 which identified Anaconda as one of only eleven stock issues that its staff unanimously rated as outstanding for long-term holding. NCC conducted its selling operations between 6 August and 1 October 1929. During this period the stock price daily highs started at 122, reached a peak of 133, and ended at 117. The $20 million profit that Carosso mentioned (which he evidently took from Pecora (1939), since this number does not appear in the hearings) is based on National City Company's initial purchase price of the shares, including the shares purchased a year earlier. Thus, as Mitchell insisted at the hearings, the 'profit' reflects a holding rather than a trading gain.[1]

In the passage quoted at the beginning of this subsection, Carosso makes a very serious charge by implying that National City Co. used inside information about Anaconda obtained from its (actually National City Bank's) role as Anaconda's banker. It is this sort of situation that the Glass–Steagall Act provisions were supposed to prevent. The only statements in the record (Pecora Hearings, 1933) that refer to National City Bank in this regard are Mitchell's introductory statement that NCB had relationships with Anaconda since 1885 and that three of the directors of the company also are directors of the bank (Mitchell, Percy A. Rockefeller, and John D. Ryan). The National City Company purchased its initial Anaconda shares (50,000) in March, 1928, from United Metals Selling Co., an affiliate of Anaconda, at $65 per share which, Mitchell testified, was 'within three or four points of the market' (ibid., p. 782). NCC obtained

---

[1] Despite the detailed evidence presented in the hearings about the timing and prices of shares that NCC purchased, Pecora (1939, p. 95) exclaims: 'making a total profit of over $20,000,000 – in two months! It will readily be seen that there exists no real incompatibility between the strict performance of one's duty as a banker, as conceived by Mr. Mitchell, and the making of a handsome profit.'

the additional shares it sold from bond conversions and market purchases, all of which were at current market prices. No claims or statements implying use of inside information from NCB or any other source appear in the record. Furthermore, NCC retained a significant block of Anaconda stock throughout the 1929–31 period, even though the price declined from over $100 to $4 per share. While this decision does not speak well for the company's ability to predict the market, it is consistent with its having acted in good faith in recommending the shares to its customers.[1] This finding should not be surprising, in view of the benefits NCC gained over the years from its reputation as a company that served its customers well.

Anaconda is the only stock issue that Carosso or Pecora mention. The record, therefore, fails to support their charge of improper security sales or Carosso's implication of NCC's use of inside bank information.

Ethically Dubious Activities, Such As Stock Speculation and Participation in Pool Operations (Charge 7)

Carosso (1970a, p. 332) reports:

> From the hearings the public also learned how the National City Co., the nation's largest investment banking house and the affiliate of the world's second largest bank, had engaged in various other ethically dubious activities. It speculated on the stock exchange and participated in pool operations.

He refers only to

> three copper stock pools, which Mitchell insisted on calling 'joint accounts'. However labeled, these operations earned huge profits for the participants, all of whom were either executives of the corporations whose stocks were being manipulated or individuals with access to inside information not available to the public (ibid., p. 332).

---

[1] Mitchell was asked questions about pool operations in which Rockefeller, Ryan and Lee Olwell (a vice president of National City Company) were said (by the committee's attorney) to be members. Mitchell denied any knowledge of their membership in such pools. In any event these pools ceased operations in May 1929; NCC did not begin to offer Anaconda stock until June 1929. Hence, the pool operations are irrelevant to the question at hand.

Carosso's footnote (number 44) appended to this quotation refers to Pecora (1939, pp. 105–9) and the SEP Report (1933, pp. 168–73), which identify the three stock pools as Andes Copper Mining Co., Chile Copper, and Greene Cananea, all subsidiaries of Anaconda Copper Co.[1] The entire testimony on this issue is Mitchell's, and is printed in the Pecora Hearings (1933, pp. 1839–66).

The Andes Copper 'pool' was an agreement between NCC and Anaconda for NCC to purchase up to 200,000 shares of Andes for a joint account that NCC would manage, with profits or losses divided 50–50. Between 13 December 1928 and 18 January 1929 NCC purchased and sold 151,045 shares on the market for a total profit of $335,043, which it divided as agreed. (The record does not report the amount invested in the shares and the variance of the prices.) Mitchell denied that the effect of the trades was to 'maintain certain market prices for the stock' (Pecora Hearings, 1933, pp. 1844–5). Pecora and the senators did not inquire about the purpose of the agreement. Mitchell did say, however, that he would not have the NCC engage in that sort of activity again because of the subsequent 'headache', apparently from investigations such as the one to which he was being subjected (ibid., p. 1846).

Stock of Chile Copper, which soon thereafter merged with Anaconda, was purchased pursuant to an agreement between the chairman of the board of Anaconda, John Ryan, the Guggenheim brothers (Harry and Daniel), and NCC, each of whom had a one-third interest. Between 14 January 1929 and 14 February 1929 140,500 shares were purchased and either sold or kept by the participants. The group made a total realised and unrealised profit of $1.2 million. (The record does not report the amount invested and the extent to which the venture was risky) (Pecora Hearings, pp. 1847–50). Mitchell testified that '[t]he account was formed in order to facilitate the conversion. . . . It was necessary, as I recall it, to maintain that ratio of exchange that was offered' (ibid., p. 1848). No questions were asked and nothing was stated about stock manipulation (except for Mitchell's repeated insistence that the purpose of the account was to stabilise stock prices) or inside information. Ryan, and possibly the Guggenheims, however, clearly were insiders. Ryan managed the account, and he and the Guggenheims personally retained their

---

[1] Kennedy (1973, pp. 120–1) briefly mentions these transactions and provides the same references.

shares of the profits. While NCC might have profited as a result, the gains went to the company and not to Mitchell.

The third alleged pool was a joint account between NCC and Ryan (who gave a share to the president of Anaconda, Cornelius Kelley) to purchase 100,000 shares of Greene-Cananea Copper Co. between 13 December 1928 and 21 March 1929. Mitchell testified that '[t]his was very definitely an account to acquire stock which would give the base for a conversion in due course' (Pecora Hearings, 1933, p. 1853). This occurred in July 1929. The shares were purchased at around $100 per share and sold in August and September 1929 at about $120 per share. Nothing in the record indicates manipulation of stock prices. We might infer the use of inside information because the most senior executives of Anaconda, Ryan and Kelley, participated personally in the accounts. However, the committee did not pursue this possibility at the hearings or mentioned it in the SEP Report (1934). In any event, insider trading was not illegal in 1929 and the Glass–Steagall Act did not address this issue.

Steering Depositors to the Securities Affiliate (Charge 8)

After describing NCC's trades in NCB stock, Carosso (1970a, p. 332) declares: 'While the affiliate engaged in these questionable activities, the bank assisted it by providing clients. Bank officials advised depositors seeking investment counsel to call on the affiliate's security salesmen, all of whom were exhorted to push sales by pep talk and special sales contests'.

Carosso's description of NCC's selling practices is not entirely consistent with the record (he cites Pecora, 1939 and the SEP Report, 1934), as this exchange between Pecora and Hugh Baker, president of the National City Company, shows (Pecora Hearings, 1933, pp. 2018–20):

> [MR PECORA] Were the lists of depositors of the bank and its various branches used as a source from which your company [NCC] gathered names of new prospects?
> [MR BAKER] No, sir.
> [MR PECORA] How do you know that?
> [MR BAKER] I know it because we would never have access to the names of depositors in the National City Bank. It is entirely possible that in some of the smaller branches there might be some discussion of that kind, in which the name might be given,

but as far as a general policy of taking the names of the depositors of the National City Bank, so far as I can recall, that has
never been done. . . .

[MR PECORA]   So that when a depositor of the bank went to the
bank seeking advice on matters of investment the name of that
customer or depositor would be transmitted by the bank's representative to the company?

[MR BAKER]   The probabilities are that it would; yes, sir. . . .

[MR PECORA]   And if that depositor or customer then followed up
that suggestion by calling upon the National City Co. for advice
as to his investments, it would not be an unusual thing for the
National City Co. to suggest investment in securities that the
company was sponsoring, was it?

[MR BAKER]   That is right.

[MR PECORA]   In fact, it was the usual thing, wasn't it?

[MR BAKER]   That is right. . . . [T]he reason that I feel that is the
proper way to do it is because of the facilities which we had in
the National City Co. for a study of investments, and based
upon that we made our recommendations.

Thus, it is true that NCC salesmen were encouraged by memos
and commissions to sell securities. But there is nothing in the record
to indicate (other than by the innuendo of wrongdoing implicit in
Pecora's questions) that customers received advice inconsistent with
their investment goals and means, with the possible exception of
case of Mr. Brown, discussed later. Furthermore, the data in Chapter
4 indicate that NCC's customers did as well or better than they
would have done had they purchased securities from an independent
securities dealer or investment banker.

The National City Bank (and Chase National Bank), moreover,
were restricted to offer deposit services only within New York City.
But National City Company was a nationwide securities firm with
offices in over fifty different cities. The Bank's opportunity to steer
customers to its securities affiliate, therefore, was severely limited
by law. State branching laws similarly restricted other banks.

**Trading in the Stock of the National City Bank by Its Securities
Affiliate (Charge 9)**

Carosso (1970a, p. 332) states:

The National City Co. also traded heavily in the stock of the

National City Bank itself, driving up the price to what Pecora called 'dizzying heights'. In January 1928, when National City officials took the stock off the New York Stock Exchange because they feared that it might be manipulated, it sold for $785. Early in 1929, after a five-for-one split, it was selling for $585 [$2,925 before the split]. No one was more responsible for booming this stock than the National City itself; it was the single largest trader, sometimes buying and selling from 30,000 to 40,000 shares a day.

Seligman (1982, pp. 28–9) similar describes the situation and adds:

At the same time as the company manipulated the bank's stock price, company salesmen were offering special bonuses for hawking the stock. National City Company securities customers were encouraged to sell other securities and switch to the bank's stock. In February 1929, prospective purchasers were offered the opportunity to purchase bank stock for $5.00 below the rapidly rising market price. After the 1929 crash, the bank's stock price fell from its peak of nearly $3000 to just over $100.[1]

Seligman (ibid., p. 28) also points out that 'it was illegal for a national bank to purchase its own stock. . . . The National City Bank's investment affiliate persistently evaded these strictures'. The National City Company (and other banks' affiliates) did trade in the parent bank's securities, which was not illegal. But because the owners of the bank and the affiliate were always the same (the shares had to be traded together), such purchases were contrary to the spirit of the law.

Pecora documented that over the three-and-a-half years ending 31 December 1930 'approximately 1,950,000 shares of the bank's stock, at an approximate cost of $650,000,000 were sold to the public' (Pecora Hearings, 1933, p. 1880). Hugh Baker, president of the National City Company, testified that a major purpose of this activity was to increase the number of shareholders of National City Bank,

---

[1] Kennedy (1973, pp. 120–1) gives a much more carefully and accurately worded description. She cites the Pecora Hearings (1933) rather than only Pecora (1939) and the SEP Report (1934).

and, consequently, of NCC, since the shares of both companies could only be purchased together (ibid., p. 1938):[1]

> [MR BAKER]   It seemed to me that the more stockholders that the National City Bank had in the United States the more business opportunities there would be opened to the bank and the more people there would be interested in the business of the bank.
>
> [MR PECORA]   Well, why was that the concern of the National City Co. as the securities selling organization?
>
> [MR BAKER]   Because those same people with whom we were doing business throughout the United States, and others, and we were constantly increasing our business range, they would be prospective customers of the bank and of the company and of any other facility we had in banking.
>
> [MR PECORA]   In other words, the stockholder of the bank would become a potential customer of the National City Co. for its securities.
>
> [MR BAKER]   If he were an investor; yes.

Baker testified that the number of stockholders increased from 15,854 in 1927, to 18,402 in 1928, 62,868 in 1929, 68,491 in 1930, 79,260 in 1931, and 84,892 in 1932 (ibid., p. 1940).[2]

Baker denied that the Company drove up the price of the stock, whether to 'dizzying heights' or not.[3] Pecora asked him (ibid., p. 1919):

> Now, Mr. Baker, was it the policy of the National City Co. to

---

[1] Baker testified earlier that the bank's stock was taken off the NY Stock Exchange, as Carosso notes, because of concern that it might be manipulated. This concern, Baker said, came from observing relatively large price fluctuations among five sales of fifty shares each when the bank had 750,000 shares outstanding. He said he did not complain to the Stock Exchange about the possible manipulation (ibid., p. 1920).

[2] These might be the numbers of shares outstanding, since Baker later said that the numbers were not adjusted for a stock split in 1928 (ibid., p. 1940). However, Gordon Rentschler, president of the National City Bank, gave similar numbers (ibid., p. 1880).

[3] Rentschler testified that bank employees did not sell the stock. They referred customers who wanted to buy shares to the company and did not receive a commission. (ibid., p. 1885). If commissions were given (and Rentschler doubted that they were), they would have been credited to the branch rather than to the employee (ibid., p. 1886). Baker was later asked the same question and he also denied that bank employees received commissions. During a six month period in 1931 when operations were retracted and the NCC had no representatives in some branches, however, those branches received service allowances (ibid., p. 2017).

seek to exercise any control of the market in the shares of the bank?

[MR BAKER] We tried to keep the price of our bank stock, the City Co. did, in general line with other bank stock, the general market conditions.

[MR PECORA] Did you seek to control the market for that purpose?

[MR BAKER] Oh, no, I should not say so.

[MR PECORA] Wasn't it the –

[MR BAKER] (interposing). We were prepared to make a bid for the stock as well as make an offering for the stock, at anytime. . . .

[MR PECORA] Wasn't it the studied purpose and policy of the company to try to control the market on City Bank stock?

[MR BAKER] I don't think so; no. We could not possibly. There were many, many dealers in bank stocks in New York. I don't know how many thousand shares of bank stocks they were dealing in, but certainly we were only a very small part of the market.

No questions were asked of witnesses nor evidence produced about misinformation or other means of market manipulation, or trading on inside information.

No evidence was presented showing that NCC gave its salesmen special premiums for selling NCB stock.[1] It is true, however, that they were encouraged to sell the stock to as many customers as possible, to tie them closer to the company and the bank.[2] But Baker denied that 'National City Company securities customers were encouraged to sell other securities and switch to the bank's stock', as Seligman (1982, pp. 28–9) charged. Baker said changes were recommended only when, 'in the judgment of our experts, [it] was a desirable exchange to make', and the testimony only refers to 'securities sponsored by the company', not to 'the bank's stock'. (Pecora Hearings, 1933, p. 2021).

In summary, although NCC did strive to distribute NCB (and thus NCC) shares as widely as possible to widen and strengthen its customer base, there is nothing in the record, with the exception of

---

[1] Baker was asked this question, but he said he was unable to answer it (ibid., pp. 2008–9).

[2] A sales letter suggests to salesmen that they get customers to put cash left over from transactions into a few shares of NCB stock (the price per share of which had just declined due to a five-to-one split) (Pecora Hearings, 1933, p. 2020).

Pecora's presumptive questions, indicating manipulation of share prices or attempts to increase the price of the stock.

Use of the Affiliate to Disguise Bad Banking Practices and to Hide Losses from the Stockholders (Charge 10)

This charge is potentially serious with respect to the rationale for the Glass–Steagall Act. As Carosso (1970a, p. 333) puts it:

> Such close ties as existed among these institutions, especially those between the bank and its investment affiliate, disguised bad banking practices and kept mistakes and losses from reaching the attention of the stockholders. A striking example of this deception occurred in 1927; the National City Bank, criticized by federal examiners for having made some poor sugar loans, unloaded some $25 million of these on its affiliate and did so at the expense of the bank's stockholders and without their knowledge.

The bank floated a $50 million stock issue, half of which increased the capital of the National City Company. These funds were transferred from the National City Company to the National City Bank in exchange for its sugar-producer loans. Carosso (p. 333) notes that NCC 'subsequently had to put down its investment' to $1. He also states with clear disapproval: 'When Mitchell was asked why stockholders of National City Co. were not told that part of their money was to be used to "bail out" the bank, he replied: "I hardly think there was any necessity of it" '.

Seligman (1982, p. 28), implying that the bank perpetrated a fraud on its stockholders, incorrectly describes the situation thus: 'In 1928, the company began the sale of bank stock worth $650 million. Just before the sales campaign, the investment affiliate purchased a worthless $25 million National City Bank loan to Cuban sugar firms, with a resulting improvement in the bank's financial statements'.[1]

I examine Seligman's account first, because he presents a very misleading reading of the record. As Carosso more correctly reports, the February 1927 $50 million stock issue increased the assets of NCB by this amount and $25 million of its Cuban loans were transferred to NCC. It is not true that the bank raised $650 million in capital. Nor

---

[1] Kennedy (1973, p. 119) gives a reasonably accurate account of the situation, perhaps because she read the testimony, which she cites.

does anything in the record join the $50 million stock issue with a 1928 'sales campaign'. It appears that Seligman misread the SEP Report (1934, p. 168), since it refers to a 'vigorous, extensive campaign for the sale of the capital stock of the National City Bank', which 'sold approximately 1,950,000 shares of the bank stock at an approximate cost of $650,000,000 to the public'. But this statement is a description of the NCC's role as a stockbroker (see the discussion of charge 9), and it refers to the NCB stock that went through NCC (Pecora Hearings, 1933, p. 1880).

It is true that the National City Bank's financial statements would have appeared worse if, in the absence of the transactions, the bank would have written the sugar loans down or taken them off the books as losses. But, although Pecora (1939, p. 121) called the loans 'practically worthless', Mitchell insisted that in 1927 the loans were slow but good. In his testimony he objected strenuously to Pecora's characterisation of the transaction as a 'bail out' or 'unloading' (Pecora Hearings, 1933, pp. 1828–38, especially 1831–2 and 1835). Mitchell read into the record the history of sugar prices (which were the principal determinant of the value of the investment) from 1922, when the bank first made the loans, through 1933. He pointed out that the price of sugar had risen until 1924, then fallen in 1925 and was rising again when the management transferred the $25 million loans from the NCB to the NCC. The price was in line with the past twenty and thirty year averages. Mitchell estimated that, at the 1927 price level, the loans would be paid off, since the sugar company was expected to earn $6 million a year (ibid., p. 1934). Indeed, the price of sugar remained stable until 1932, when it dropped from about 3.00 cents a pound (from about 3.10 in February 1927) to 0.57 cents and then to 0.125 cents in 1933. That is when the loans were written off. Thus, Mitchell insisted that at the time of the transaction 'that investment was considered by the officers and directors a sound investment for the National City Co' (ibid., p. 1834).

As for informing the shareholders, Mitchell (ibid., p. 1934) explained:

I would not have considered it necessary. That was not an investment of the shareholders of the bank that they did not already have. They had it in the form of obligations that were in the bank in one way and another, and it seemed advisable to the directors that that be taken out and put in the form of a more permanent investment, because it was not sufficiently liquid as a current account to be held in a commercial bank.

Indeed, the bank, in annual reports and special statements from management starting in 1921, had informed shareholders about the status of the loans. In addition, the board of directors owned a significant proportion of the stock at the time, and the issue was a rights offering. Nor did the bank hide the situation from the bank examiners. In fact, the loans had been 'the subject of frequent criticism' (ibid., p. 1835) by the examiners, who objected that the loans were illiquid and were secured by properties being operated at a loss (ibid., p. 1838).

Assuming that stock market participants knew about the Cuban sugar loans and the price of sugar, the stockholders did not lose from the transaction. As I note above, an owner of bank shares had to be a proportional owner of company shares. Because the bank was not in danger of failing in 1927 (or later), shareholders gained from the transaction to the extent that depositors' confidence in the bank increased. This increased confidence would occur, because after the transaction the bank held more liquid and possibly higher valued assets. In any event, the bank did not disguise its practices (bad or not) and, at the time, there may have been no losses to disguise. However, there seems to be no valid reason for the management not having explicitly informed the shareholders about the primary reason for the stock issue.

Investor Brown's $100,000 Loss (Charge 12)

Kennedy (1973, pp. 115–19) and Pecora (1939, pp. 84–9) devote much space to this witness, who claimed to have lost the proceeds of the sale of his business in 1928 as a result of a National City Company salesman's churning and bad advice. When Brown testified he was sick and bankrupt. Kennedy (1973, p. 118) writes that 'his unfortunate story found a sympathetic audience. No agent or official of the National City complex refuted Brown's claims. Nor did any other clients appear to tell how their investment had made them wealthy'. While churning, if it occurred, clearly is not unique to the National City Company and is not a subject of the Glass–Steagall Act, I include this charge here because it gives rise to the belief that commercial banks misused their positions as respected suppliers of financial services.

In spite of an extended search, I could not find any evidence of other investors telling a story of bad treatment at the hands of the National City Company or any other bank affiliate. No other such witness appeared at the hearings. A detailed perusal of the committee records at the National Archives in Washington DC failed to uncover letters or memoranda of complaints.

The senate committee did not permit representatives of the National City Company (or other witnesses) to call rebuttal witnesses. Aside from the disastrous effects of the depression on stock prices, this might be one reason for other witnesses not having come forward 'to tell how their investment had made them wealthy'. Furthermore, Mr Brown was not exactly an unsophisticated investor. Although he was sick and bankrupt at the time of the hearings, he had been a successful businessman with $100,000 to invest (approximately equal to $735,000 in 1989 dollars) when he began investing. Thus, the record is seriously inadequate in providing evidence that National City Company's churned its customers' accounts. In any event, the Glass–Steagall Act does not address churning.

Summary – National City Bank and National City Company

The record does not support most of the allegations made by Pecora's (1939), Carosso's (1970a), Seligman's (1982), and, to a lesser extent, Kennedy's (1973) allegations. From a review of these historians' work, I have identified twelve specific charges against the National City Bank and Company and the chief executive officer, Charles Mitchell. Eight of them are relevant to the Glass–Steagall Act separation of commercial and investment banking. (The appendix to this chapter analyses the other four charges.) With a few exceptions, a record of the Pecora Hearings (1933) does not support the charges. In particular:

- The allegation that NCC executives profited from individual participations in stock flotations at the expense of outside investors finds no support, although one might argue that the NCC's shareholders rather than its officers should have received all the gains. Alternatively, we can view the arrangement as an efficient form of risk sharing and executive compensation that tends to make congruent managers' and stockholders' rewards.
- When we examine the record closely, we find that the National City Company sold neither bonds nor stocks with inadequate

or misleading information given to investors, with the possible exception of more detailed information about Minas Geraes and Peru.

- Nor is there evidence of stock exchange speculation or participation in pool activities, with the exception that the National City shareholders possibly benefited from inside information known to the head of a company with which the bank did business.

- In answer to enquiries National City Bank employees did suggest the services of the National City Company to depositors, but they did not steer depositors to the NCC. Indeed, this allegation does not take into consideration that NCB served depositors only in New York City while the NCC operated offices in fifty cities.

- The NCC did trade heavily in the stock of the NCB, but there is no evidence or reason to believe NCC manipulated or drove up the price of the stock.

- Nor is there much support for the allegation that the bank used its affiliate to hide bad loans. Management transferred a possibly bad Cuban sugar loan from the bank to the company and the bank's financial position and statements were strengthened with the proceeds from a $50 million rights issue. Depositors benefited from this additional investment by the stockholders in the bank. Although the stockholders also probably benefited from the greater confidence of depositors, the National City Bank might be criticised for possibly inadequate disclosure to stockholders about the reason for the rights issue.

It is unfortunate, therefore, that Carosso did not add the words inserted in square brackets to his description of the public reaction to the Pecora Hearings: 'the [alleged] abuses uncovered were [or, rather, appeared to be] so gross that the financial community itself was appalled'. My examination of the record does not support the allegations of abuse.

IV   THE CHARGES AGAINST CHASE NATIONAL BANK AND WIGGIN

Only Carosso (1970a) and Pecora (1939) specify Chase's abuses as a basis for adoption of the Glass–Steagall Act provisions. Other writers cite them as a reason for the Act's continuation.

Carosso (1970a, p. 346, charge numbers added for identification and later reference) describes the situation thus:

> The Chase hearings produced the same 'shocking disclosure of low standards in high places' that had been revealed eight months earlier, when the [Fletcher-Pecora] subcommittee was investigating the affairs of its rival, the National City Co.
>
> For nearly two months the country was treated to another chapter in the recent history of high finance. The errors of the private bankers [e.g. Morgan & Co., Kuhn Loeb, and Dillon, Read & Co.], great as many of them were, came nowhere near those of the Chase Securities Corporation and its respected and admired president, Albert H. Wiggin, who headed the Chase Bank. . . . Like the National City Co., Chase Securities matched, if it did not exceed, its competitor in the number and variety of its 'misdemeanors'.
> [Charge 1]: stock pools,
> [Charge 2]: market manipulations,
> [Charge 3]: 'insiders' profits',
> [Charge 4]: large salaries and substantial bonuses,
> [Charge 5]: excessive trading in the bank's own stock for personal gain [by Wiggin],
> [Charge 6]: short sales [by Wiggin],
> [Charge 7]: 'preferred lists' and other forms of favoritism, and
> [Charge 8]: income tax avoidance were as characteristic of the Chase as they were of the National City and its executives.[1]

Pecora (1939, p. 135, charge numbers added for identification and later reference) similarly claims that

> [m]ost of the characteristic evils which beset the National City organization flourished here [at Chase National Bank] in equally glaring fashion:
> [Charge 13]: the use of affiliate corporations, to do indirectly that which the bank could not legally do directly,
> [Charge 4]: huge, overstuffed salaries,
> [Charge 9]: financing stock market pools,
> [Charge 3]: 'insiders' profits',
> [Charge 10]: dealings in the bank's own stock.

---

[1] Citations omitted to Pecora (1939) ch. vii-viii and to SEP Report (1934) pp. 195–205.

He continues several pages later (ibid., p. 140):

> Just as in the case of the National City, its affiliates gradually led the Chase Bank not only into the field of investment banking proper, but into
> [Charge 1]: market pools,
> [Charge 2]: manipulations, and other kinds of dubious transactions.

Finally, Pecora (1939, pp. 146 and 158) charged Wiggin with receiving:

> [Charge 11]: helpful additions to his regular earnings . . . [from corporations that] received large loans from the Chase National Bank,

and

> [Charge 12]: intermingling his private business with the bank's.

Thus Carosso charges Chase with eight 'misdemeanors' and Pecora levies five additional charges. The first of these listed, 'the use of affiliate corporations, to do indirectly that which the bank could not legally do directly' (charge 13), apparently refers to national banks' use of state chartered affiliates to engage in securities transactions, with Pecora (following Senator Glass's position) believed was illegal *per se*. Since this position was not held seriously by the historians, I do not consider it further. Seven of the remaining twelve items – insiders' profit (charge 3), large salaries (charge 4), stock trading by Wiggin for personal gain (charge 5), short sales by Wiggin (charge 6), income tax avoidance (charge 8), personal director's fees from bank customers (charge 11), and intermingling of Wiggin's private business with the bank's (charge 12) – are not relevant to the concerns of the Glass–Steagall Act's separation of commercial and investment banking. These charges refer to the actions Wiggin took as an individual or as an officer of the Chase National Bank or Chase Securities Company that section 32 of the Glass–Steagall Act, which prohibits interlocks between the officers and directors of commercial banks and securities companies, or other provisions of the Act would not have affected. While the Securities Act of 1933, the Securities Exchange Act of 1934 and other legislation address most of Wiggin's criticised acts, it is important for our understanding of the practices of the time to discern the extent to which some important writers' perceptions of these events conforms to the record (the Pecora Hearings, 1934) to which they refer. Consequently, I analysed them in the Appendix to this chapter.

The remaining five charges – participation in stock pools (charge 1), market manipulations (charge 2), favouritism (charge 7), financing stock market pools (charge 9), and dealings in the banks own stock (charge 10) – are relevant to the Glass–Steagall Act only to the extent that they provide a basis for the belief that we should not permit banks, in contrast to other firms, to underwrite, market, and hold corporate securities because of the banks' past poor record. As a result of other legislation and regulation, all the actions that these charges entail either are now illegal for all market participants (stock pools, market manipulations, and favouritism) or for banks (dealings in own stock), or are still legal and acceptable (financing of stock transactions, if not stock pools).

Stock Pools and Market Manipulations (Charges 1 and 2)

A 'stock pool' is a secret agreement among a small group of investors to purchase or sell short the shares in a corporation with the expectation of running the price up or down as a result of their transactions, of artfully spread rumours, or of the release of inside information. A stock pool need not include such acts as the recording and release of false stock prices established by means of rigged bids, and the planting of false rumours in the financial press. Nevertheless, pools now generally are characterised as a form of unfair market manipulation; at the time, though, stock pools were legal.

Pecora severely criticises Chase Securities' involvement in pools or trading accounts. In spite of Wiggin's repeated denial that one could describe Chase's activities as participation in pools, Pecora asserts that 'Mr. Wiggin's ingenuity could evolve no satisfactory rationale for these pools' (Pecora, 1939, pp. 185–6). In his book, Pecora then quotes his questions and Wiggin's answers thus (ibid., pp. 185–7, omitted material from Pecora Hearings, 1934, pp. 2834–5 in italics):

[MR PECORA] . . . What prompted the chase securities corporation to engage in these trading accounts in the open market, dealing in securities other than the Chase National Bank from 1928 down?

[MR WIGGIN] I think the times. . . .

[SENATOR COUZENS] I assume you mean the speculative atmosphere?

[MR WIGGIN] I think perhaps that covers it. There was a great deal of atmosphere. . . . *There were a great many people who began to think you did a great injustice to everybody if you did not have equity stocks. It even got to be the custom to think that trust funds – it was a pity to limit them so that they could not invest in equity stocks: that we were doing a great injustice to them. In other words, it was the times. . . .*

[MR PECORA] Do you now think that a national bank affiliate should engage in stock-market speculation of the kind that you then had in mind?

[MR WIGGIN] No sir; if for no other reason than respect for public opinion.

[SENATOR COUZENS] Oh. That is a new one! So public opinion does have some effect upon Wall Street?

[MR WIGGIN] I think it has a pretty good effect.

[MR PECORA] What is your own personal judgment?

[MR WIGGIN] I certainly would not do anything today that, if it turned out unfortunately, was going to be criticized. And that is what would happen if we did make a mistake. Therefore I could not take the risk.

Pecora could have demonstrated the detrimental effect of stock pools on investors by showing that they were misled by false information released by the pool operators, one of which was a respected commercial bank. Or, he could have objected to the bank's securities affiliate using inside information that came to it as a consequence of its position. But he made neither these nor similar charges. Instead Pecora's and the senators' questions and statements were concerned entirely with the propriety of banks dealing indirectly in securities on a short-term basis.

For example, Pecora (1939, pp. 183–4) concludes:

It [Chase Securities] was wholly unhampered by any fine-spun distinction between legitimate 'investment' and 'speculation'. To Mr. Wiggin, the distinction was merely between ability and failure to make money. 'An investment that is unsuccessful,' he declared, 'is usually called a speculation' – a pragmatic definition that reflects, faithfully enough, the typical Wall Street philosophy of don't-get-caught.

But this is not the thrust of what Wiggin said. His definition of 'speculation' appears at the end of the following colloquy with Senator Couzens (Pecora Hearings, 1934, p. 2418–9):

> [SENATOR COUZENS] Then you believe in speculation of bank stocks?
> [MR WIGGIN] I believe in the purchase and sale of bank stocks; yes sir.

After Couzens and Pecora repeatedly tried to get Wiggin to state that trading in stock was speculation, Pecora asked:

> [MR PECORA] But what does speculation in stock mean to you? . . .
> [MR WIGGIN] An investment that is unsuccessful is usually called a speculation.
> [MR PECORA] Is that what the term speculation means to you?
> [MR WIGGIN] I think that is about what it means to investors.
> [MR PECORA] What is the difference between speculation in stock and gambling in stock, to your notion?
> [MR WIGGIN] You are asking me questions that there is no definite answer to. It is really a matter of opinion that you are asking me to express.
> [MR PECORA] Let us have your opinion. We understand that you are not on the stand as an expert lexicographer.
> [MR WIGGIN] I think in the newspapers the words 'gambling in stocks' and the words 'speculation in stocks' are given about the same interpretation.

The interchange continued in this vein for another two pages. None of this material allows one to draw the conclusion that Wiggin, Pecora, or Couzens said or implied a philosophy of 'don't get caught'.

The only evidence presented in the hearings or asked for by Pecora or the senators about the effect of Chase Securities Corporation's involvement in stock pools or manipulations (assuming that these occurred; no evidence is presented) on its stockholders is the net profits of the affiliate's operations. The SEP Report (1934. 183) states that '[t]he speculative transactions of the affiliates were as disastrous to the affiliates as to the investing public'. The financial statements presented in Pecora Hearings (1934, pp. 2388–9) show the following as of 30 June 1930:

Aggregate capital paid in since June 1917		$115.3 million
Add net earnings to 30 June 1930		41.1
Total capital earnings		156.4
Paid out in dividends	$ 21.9	
Reserves for losses	120.1	142.0
Total 30 June 1930		14.4

The $120.1 million in reserves increased per year as follows: 1921 ($1.0 million), 1929 ($1.8 million), 1930 ($19.6 million), 1931 ($52.0 million), 1932 ($4.7 million) and 1933 ($41.0 million). Of the total, $71.6 million was attributed to the write-down to market of assets that Chase Securities Corp. still owned.[1] Thus, the losses to stockholders appear to be the consequence of the depression-determined reduction in securities prices and not losses from securities transactions, whether in pools or otherwise. Although one might conclude (as does the report) that the stockholders lost funds because of the stockholdings of the bank's affiliate (whether 'speculative' or not), it does not appear correct to conclude (as do Pecora and Carosso) that the stockholders lost as a result of stock pools, trading or manipulations by the affiliate. Unfortunately, however, the available data do not permit a clear distinction between write-downs on securities held for trading purposes and on securities held for investment.

The only evidence indicating that other investors might have lost as a result of Chase Securities' stock transactions is profits accruing to participants in Sinclair Consolidated Oil Corporation stock syndicates. One syndicate, run by Arthur Cutten and organised by Harry Sinclair (chairman of the board of the corporation), purchased 1,130,000 newly issued shares at $30 per share in October 1928. Harry Sinclair offered these shares to Cutten at a time when the outstanding shares were quoted at $28 (Pecora Hearings, 1934, p. 3066). Sinclair testified that 'at the time these negotiations were being had [sic] the shares of our company in the past 4 years before that time had never sold as high as 30. I do not think that we would have been successful – that is my personal opinion – if the shares had been sold to the stockholders' (ibid., pp. 3274–5). Cutten testified that he believed that Sinclair, Blair & Co. and Chase chose the syndicate (ibid., p. 3070). Its members included the Chase Securities

---

[1] I could not find out the extent to which Chase Securities's losses were consistent with those that similarly diversified operations experienced, or were even more or less than the overall change in market prices.

Corporation for 15 per cent, Shermar Corporation for 7.5 per cent, Blair & Co. for 22.5 per cent, the Cutten Co. Ltd. for 22.5 per cent, H. F. Sinclair for 22.5 per cent, and seven others. Chase National Bank stood ready to advance the participants funds, should these be required; they borrowed and repaid $12 million. When the existence of the syndicate was made public, the price of the Sinclair Consolidate stock increased by $11 to $12 a share and the syndicate sold out the issue for a profit of $12 million, $1.8 million going to Chase Securities and $0.9 to Shermar Corporation (ibid., p. 3093). The price of the Sinclair stock remained at about $38 a share until June 1929, but declined to about $11 a share in October 1933. Thus Chase's shareholders benefited. Considering that the price of the shares did not decline for a year or more, it does not seem that the purchasers of the shares lost as a result of the syndicate. Instead, the stock apparently declined as a result of the general depression-caused decline in securities prices. In any event, the evidence does not support the conclusion that the Chase National Bank, its security affiliate, or its president (Wiggin) engaged in stock price manipulation.

The second syndicate was organised to trade the Sinclair stock to prevent its price from declining. The syndicate had thirty-two members, including Chase Securities Corporation at 6.7 per cent and Shermar Corporation at 3.3 per cent. Although some might criticise the syndicate as having been organised to manipulate the market, Chase's profits were only $27,892 and Shermar's were only $13,946 (ibid., p. 3094). These numbers are consistent with price stabilisation rather than price manipulation.

The instances presented above are the extent of the record on stock manipulation, with the exception of data on trading accounts given in Table 4.1.

Financing of Stock Pools (Charge 9)

The Chase National Bank apparently financed stock pools and stock purchases generally, including the Sinclair pool just described. At the time such activities were legal and accepted practice. No evidence was presented at the hearings about the interest rates charged. Nor did Pecora or the senators allege that the loans were made at terms favourable to the borrowers and at the expense of the bank's shareholders. All of the loans appear to have been repaid by the borrowers. Regardless, the Glass–Steagall Act's provisions separating

Table 4.1 Trading accounts in which Chase Securities Corporation participated other than trading accounts operated in connection with security offerings (1928–32)

Issue	Date of information	Date of settlement	Gain or loss to Chase	Participation by	
				Chase Sec & Harris Forbes	Shermar & Murlyn
Continental Paper Bag bonds	2/28	4/28	996	25.0%	0.0%
Bank of East Prussian Landowners	3/28	5/28	55	50.0%	0.0%
Gen Gas & Elect common	3/28	9/28	98,217	25.0%	20.0%
Twin City Rapid Transit bonds	5/28	2/29	−2,136	25.0%	0.0%
Washington Gas Light common	5/28	6/29	268,569	19.0%	19.0%
Int'l Paper & Power preferred	10/28	7/30	15,510	20.0%	0.0%
Sinclair Consolidated Oil common	10/28	5/29	27,892	note a	note a
Republic of Poland bonds	11/28	1/29	676	20.0%	0.0%
Prairie Oil & Gas common	12/28	2/29	530,930	21,750 shares	note b
Prairie Pipe Line Co.	12/28	2/29	6,693	7,250 shares	note b
Chicago Traction Securities	1/29	9/31	1,448,149	25.0%	25.0%
American Woollen Co stock	1/29	2/31	292,984	17.0%	17.0%
Int'l Paper & Power preferred	6/29	8/29	81,890	10.0%	0.0%
Transcontinental Oil stock	6/29	8/29	209,621	note a	note a
Utility Power & Light class A	6/29	9/30	235,853	note a	note a
Transcontinental Oil common	7/29	11/30	511,688	note a	note a
Utility Equities common	7/29	NG	113,586	note b	0.0%
Chase National Bank stock units	7/29	11/29	225,109	40,000 shares	40,000 shares
Cuba Cane Sugar warrants	8/29	4/30	1,214	note a	note a
Transcontinental Oil common	9/29	3/30	111,385	note a	note a
Int'l Paper & Power bonds	9/29	12/29	85,600	75.0%	0.0%
Vacuum Oil common	9/29	4/30	27,571	note a	note a
Seaboard Airline Ry syndicate	9/29	open		note a	note a
Bethlehem Steel common	10/29	various	1,120,283	10.0%	0.0%
Chase National Bank stock units	1/30	3/30	23,259	2,475 shares	825 shares
Grigsby Grunow common	4/30	11/30	455,703	25.0%	0.0%
St Louis San Francisco Ry stock	4/30	7/31	3,090,623	note c	note c

Canadian Int'l Paper bonds	5/30	1/31	8,063,800	75.0%	0.0%
Mission Securities syndicate	6/30	open		16.7%	8.3%
Republic of China bonds	9/30	7/31	651,728	25.0%	0.0%
International Hydro Electric bonds	11/30	1/31	572	50.0%	0.0%
National Steel Car Lines bonds	1/31	3/31	1,567	33.0%	0.0%
Curtis Publishing preferred	3/31	10/31	600	50.0%	0.0%
McKesson & Robbins bonds	3/31	5/31	1,134,510	note b	0.0%
total net gain			18,834,697		

Notes

a: given only as Chase Securities Corporation and others

b: Chase Securities Corporation and others only listed. Shermar or Murlyn not mentioned

c: Chase Securities Corp. $6,666,667, Murlyn $3,333,333

Where shares are given for Chase Securities or Harris Forbes and Shermar or Murlyn, other brokers also are mentioned.

Source: Pecora Hearings (1933) pp. 2858–9

commercial and investment banking do not prevent a bank from lending to brokers or other investors.

Dealings in the Bank's Own Stock (Charge 10)

The SEP Report (1934) devotes about one-quarter of its pages on 'commercial bank abuses' to 'trading and pool operation in the capital stock of commercial banks by investment affiliates' (pp. 168–83). Sixty per cent of these pages describe Chase Securities Corporation's operations. Pecora (1939, p. 150) points out that 'Mr Wiggin could not be brought to admit that there was the slightest impropriety in the bank's encouragement of and participation in these gigantic pools in its own stock'. Instead Wiggin insisted that the purpose of the trading was 'to keep a steady market in the stock' (Pecora Hearings, 1934, p. 2417). As just quoted, Pecora ridiculed this claim by pointing out that Metpotan, the Chase subsidiary organised to trade in the bank's stock, only made $159,000[1] over the five years 1928–32 on trades of over $860,000,000.

This small profit nevertheless supports Wiggin's explanation that the purpose of Metpotan's trading in Chase National Bank stock was to act as a specialist in making a market for the stock, thereby reducing transactions costs to stockholders, rather than as a trader on inside information who (in effect) transfers wealth among stockholders. The data presented in Table 4.2, drawn from numbers presented in the hearings, are consistent with the market-maker description. In each year the number and dollars of shares purchased closely match the amounts sold. In only two years does the ratio of purchases to sales exceed 1.02 or go below 0.98: in 1929 the ratio for shares was 1.05 and in 1931 the ratio for dollars was 0.92. Thus, whether or not one considers it to be good public policy for a bank (or any corporation) to trade in its own shares (directly or through a subsidiary), the data do not support the conclusion that the trading by Chase's subsidiary, Metpotan, tended to transfer wealth from some shareholders to others. The data are more consistent with the belief that shareholders benefited from lowered transactions costs in trading Chase National Bank stock.

---

[1] Elsewhere in the hearings the amount given is $825,000 (see Table 4.2).

Table 4.2   Transactions in the shares of Chase National Bank and Chase Securities Corporation Stock participated in by the Chase Securities Corporation and Metpotan Securities Corporation

Year	Purchases		Sales		Net (Purch − Sales)		Purchases/Sales	
	Shares	Money*	Shares	Money*	Shares	Money*	Shares	Money*
Stock								
Old								
1928	71,869	45,974	70,758	45,754	1,111	220	1.02	1.00
1929	61,106	66,045	61,623	65,804	−517	241	0.99	1.00
New**								
1929	716,001	150,692	684,709	145,816	31,292	4,876	1.05	1.03
1930	762,593	112,285	769,292	113,913	−6,699	−1,628	0.99	0.99
1931	523,802	31,380	531,619	34,116	−7,817	−2,736	0.99	0.92
1932	310,624	11,090	316,906	11,238	−6,282	−148	0.98	0.99
Total	2,445,995	417,466	2,434,907	416,641	11,088	825	1.00	1.00
Rights								
1928	74,272	3,943	74,275	3,943	−3	0	1.00	1.00
1929	67,230	9,364	67,229	9,364	1	0	1.00	1.00
Totals		430,773		429,948	0	825		1.00

* thousands of dollars
** old stock split 5 for 1

Source: Pecora Hearings (1933), p. 2839

'Preferred Lists' and Other Forms of Favouritism (Charge 7)

It is not clear to me to what Carosso (who listed this 'misdemeanour') refers. He may have had in mind the participation of Chase officers in underwritings and trades engaged in by Chase Securities. In this event their participation should have benefited Chase's shareholders. Their personal participation in the risks Chase Securities undertook tends to increase their incentives to balance risks and returns consistent with the interests of Chase's stockholders. If their compensation were unrelated or only imperfectly related to the outcome of their decisions, these decision makers would have incentives either to accept less risk than is optimal (thereby safeguarding their salaries) or more risk than is optimal (if they receive bonuses based on recorded net profits). One might argue that, in practice, the officers would escape the downside risk by being permitted to get out of 'bad deals'. If this were the case, it also is likely that they would receive salaries and bonuses based only on profits, with no reductions for losses. Indeed, this is usually the situation for accounting-data-based profit sharing plans. Thus, in either event they would avoid the downside risk; stockholders would be no worse off from the officers' participation in securities underwritings.

I was unable to find any other instances that might be labelled as 'favouritism' or any mention of a 'preferred list' in the Pecora Hearings (1934).

Summary – Chase National Bank and its Security Affiliates

Nothing in the record that Carosso or Pecora (the only writers who specifically refer to evidence) cite supports the contention that Chase's securities operations gave rise to abuses. Most of the allegations of abuses concern the activities of Chase's president, Albert Wiggin. But even these do not indicate much in the way of actual wrongdoing. He was well paid. He tried to minimise his income taxes by using personal corporations, some of which were incorporated in Canada. He did appear to merge many of his personal activities with those of the bank. But there is no evidence showing that these activities harmed the bank's other shareholders or its depositors. Indeed, it appears that his activities resulted in greater profits for the other shareholders, because he only benefited when they benefited, and he lost when they lost. The only possible exception to this conclusion is his sale and repurchase of Chase stock before and after the 1929 crash. But there is no evidence (or allegation) of his having based his trades on inside information; furthermore, he later held his stock as its price declined from $155 to $40 per share.

It is not clear whether Wiggin's personal and, until revealed at the hearings, apparently secret participation (through his private corporations) with Chase Securities Corporation's deals resulted in harm or yielded benefits to the Chase National Bank's other share-holders. When revealed by Pecora, they certainly damaged, indeed, destroyed his personal reputation and hurt the reputation of the bank. Still, they are not activities that the Glass–Steagall Act covers.

V UNLOADING EXCESS OR BAD SECURITIES ON BANK TRUST DEPARTMENTS BY SECURITIES AFFILIATES

Glass Subcommittee Hearings

The Glass Subcommittee (1931, Part 7, p. 1064) expressed concern that '[i]n the case of a trust company or a bank with a trust department, the possession of a security affiliate may adversely affect the independence with which fiduciary activities are exercised'. The US Supreme Court cited this speculation in *Investment Company Institute v. Camp* (401 US 617, 633 (1971)) (emphasis added): 'Congress had before it *evidence* that security affiliates might be driven to unload excessive holdings through the trust department of the sponsor bank'[31]. The Supreme Court's footnote 31 refers to the Glass Subcommittee Hearings (1931, pp. 237 and 1064). I quote page 1064 in full in section II of chapter 3; it includes no evidence nor did any other evidence on this issue emerge in the Glass Subcommittee Hearings. Page 237 reports this testimony by B. W. Trafford, vice chairman of the First National Bank of Boston. I reproduce it in full to illustrate how misleading is the Supreme Court's citation of the record:[1]

[MR WILLIS] There has been some feeling that when you had that arrangement, that – in the hands of a bank officer who was not of the highest standards – there was some danger of the exercise

---

[1] We perhaps can excuse the Supreme Court's sloppiness by considering that statements confirming this view appear in the brief that the First National City Bank (1970) filed, portions of which I quote in chapter 1, section IV.

of the fiduciary function in that the security affiliate from time to time unloaded or dumped securities upon the trust company. Have you seen any development of that in New England?

[MR TRAFFORD]   I should say generally not. In our case we are forbidden. We do not do it. Our trust company does not buy from the security affiliate, and we advertise that we do not do that.

[MR WILLIS]   But others do that.

[MR TRAFFORD]   I do not think many of them do.

[MR WILLIS]   Then, there would be no harm in forbidding such a transaction by law?

[MR TRAFFORD]   I would see no objection to it. I do not think they ought to do it. Whether you want to put it into the law or not I do not know.

[MR WILLIS]   Still, if it is very rarely practiced and everyone disapproves of it, a law to that effect would do no harm.

[MR TRAFFORD]   I should not think so. If I could strike my answer off the record, I should say I would be very glad to have it done.

Following the quotation given on page 89 from the Supreme Court's *Investment Company Institute v. Camp* opinion is this sentence:

> Some witnesses at the hearings expressed the view that this practice constituted self-dealing in violation of the trustee's obligation of loyalty, and indeed that it would be improper for a bank's trust department to purchase anything from the bank's security affiliate.[32]

The witnesses cited in the Supreme Court's footnote 32, George Davison, president of the Central Hanover Bank and Trust Co. of New York, and Charles Mitchell, chairman of the National City Bank, also testified that their banks expressly forbade trust accounts from buying securities from or through their securities affiliates (Glass Subcommittee, 1931, pp. 266, 300, 311). Indeed, the National City Bank's annual report includes the following statement: 'In the investment of trust funds, it is the policy of the Trust Company not to purchase securities from the Bank or the National City Company, even when trust instruments contain express authority to do so' (quoted in Citicorp, 1985, pp. 6–7).

Pecora Hearings

The only other evidence on commercial-bank-managed trusts purchasing securities from the bank's investment affiliate that I could find is in the Pecora Hearings (1934, pp. 5293–17), traced through the Stock Exchange Practices *Index to Hearings* (1941). The *Index* refers to the questioning of Ralph Stone, vice chairman, and W. J. Thomas, treasurer, of the Detroit Trust Co. about trust purchases from the First Detroit Co., the bank's security affiliate. Pecora and the senators questioned the propriety of any unit of the bank selling obligations to trusts at more than the cost paid for obligations, regardless of the trusts' provisions or the market price at the time of sale. Stone testified that the trusts purchased obligations from the bank's affiliate only during nine months in 1931, just after the affiliate was organised (ibid., p. 5304). He said that the bank's policy was for the trusts it administered to purchase obligations from the bank's affiliate at cost, unless the trust provisions called for purchases 'at prevailing market prices' (ibid., p. 5297). Some data were put into evidence (the source is not indicated) showing thirty-five obligations presumably sold by the affiliate to the bank-administered trusts, giving the unit costs to the First Detroit Co. and to the Detroit Trust Company's trusts. For twenty-one of these obligations (60 per cent) the spread percentage (cost to the trust less cost to the affiliate divided by cost to the affiliate) is less than 1 per cent, for five obligations (14 per cent) the spread is 1.5 per cent, for five obligations (14 per cent) the spread is 2 to 3 per cent, for three obligations (9 per cent) the spread is 4 to 4.5 per cent, and for one obligation the spread is negative. The record provides no further explanation.

Thus, there is no evidence in the record supporting the assertion that commercial banks' securities affiliates 'dumped', 'unloaded', or even sold securities to the banks' trusts. Indeed, all of the testimony and other evidence states that this practice was against the policy of most, if not all, banks. The only instance to the contrary involved one bank's sales of some obligations over a very limited period at slightly higher than cost, with no indication that its securities affiliate underwrote these obligations. The bank's officers testified that the affiliate sold these obligations at market prices, in accordance with the trusts' instructions.

VI   CONFLICTS OF INTEREST AND ABUSE BY AND THROUGH COMMERCIAL-BANK-SPONSORED TRUSTS AND INVESTMENT COMPANIES

Allegations by the Investment Company Institute (ICI)

Prior to the passage of the Glass–Steagall Act, commercial bank affiliates and investment banks sponsored and managed investment trusts and companies offering investors shares in a portfolio of securities and loans. Today, this product is offered primarily in the form of mutual funds. Most of these are 'open-end'; investments in these funds are repriced daily, and investors purchase and sell a claim on these amounts less the operator's costs and charges. Investors in 'closed-end' funds, which were dominant before the second world war, purchase and sell a share in an investment company which, in turn, invests in the stocks of other companies. The price of the investment company's shares need not directly mirror the prices of the securities owned by the company. The Investment Company Institute is the national trade association representing the interests of some '477 open-end investment companies, their investment advisors and principal underwriters' (Investment Company Institute, 1979, p. 1). It has been militant in opposing the re-entry of commercial banks into the industry, and was the successful plaintiff in the landmark case, *Investment Company Institute v. Camp* (401 US 617 (1971)).

In the late 1930s the Securities and Exchange Commission (SEC) extensively studied the operation of investment trusts and companies (hereinafter called 'investment companies'). It presented its findings to the House of Representatives in 1938, 1939, and 1940 in three parts and in several supplementary reports published in 1939, 1940, and 1942 (hereinafter called the 'SEC Study'). The first two parts present the history of and descriptive statistical data on investment companies. Part 3, covering 2805 pages in seven chapters, concerns abuses and deficiencies in the organisation and operation of investment companies. In congressional hearings considering repeal of or change in the Glass–Steagall Act, the Investment Company Institute cites portions of Part 3 to support its position that the law should not permit commercial banks to offer and manage mutual funds.[1]

---

[1] I was unable to obtain the actual hearings on which the SEC Study was based. It is possible that more could be learned from going to the source, if it exists.

David Silver, president of the Investment Company Institute, repeatedly has testified before Congress that 'many of the abuses of the 1920s resulted *precisely* because of the combination of commercial banking and securities activities' (Silver, 1988, p. 5). He begins his recitation of abuses with this statement: 'Banks were heavily involved in the mutual fund (then known as investment trust) business in the 1920s and early 1930s' (ibid., p. 5). As evidence of that involvement he cites John Flynn's (1930) book, *Investment Trusts Gone Wrong!* Flynn, however, does not present a survey of the relative involvement of commercial banks with investment trusts; he merely makes this observation (as quoted by Silver): 'Investment trust affiliates of banks are well known. . . . Many if not most of the banks have them' (Flynn, 1930, p. 69).

The SEC Study Part 2 (1939a), though, presents extensive data on investment companies, including their sponsors. The Study presents data for all 675 investment companies known to exist on 31 December 1929, including companies that later became defunct or were restructured following the Glass–Steagall Act's required separation of commercial and investment banking (SEC Study, 1939a, p. 27). Of these, 193 (29 per cent) are management investment companies; these companies held 39 per cent of the total assets of the 675 companies. The SEC obtained information on sponsorship for 181 of the 193 management investment companies. Commercial banks and their securities affiliates sponsored twenty-eight such companies. In addition, it identified six investment companies as common trust funds, all of which appear to be managed by commercial banks. The SEC did not discuss sponsorship of the rest of the companies (of which 7 per cent are management-investment holding companies, 8 per cent fixed and semifixed investment trusts, and 56 per cent unclassified). Lists of their names do appear (ibid., pp. 92, 95, and 98), however, and inspection of these lists suggests that none of these companies are commercial-bank related. These data, then, reveal that commercial banks sponsored and managed only 4 per cent of the number of investment companies that held 3 per cent of the industries' total assets.

It also is interesting to note that Flynn (1930) discusses commercial-bank-related investment companies only briefly. In the chapter from which Silver (1988, p. 5) quotes him, Flynn describes an unnamed investment trust organised by officers of a national bank. He objects to the bank's officers instead of the bank (as the public, he says, was lead to believe) owning the voting stock of the trust.

Flynn directs his other major criticism at 'the exploitation of trusts by investment bankers or any persons interested in any venture, who may desire to control the funds of an investment trust' (Flynn, 1930, pp. 190–1). The next-to-the-last section of this book (ibid., pp. 233–8) describes and recommends for small investors the Uniform Trust (also called the Composite or Managed Trust) offered by commercial banks' trust departments.[1] He lists and describes in an appendix 'several investment trusts and investment funds which in varying degrees conform to the standards set up in this book' (ibid., p. 247). This list of seven companies includes four independent companies or trusts and three trust companies (considered commercial banks under the Glass–Steagall Act).[2] Flynn devotes much more space on criticisms of other investment companies, particularly large well-known ones sponsored by investment bankers, for imposing relatively large, often hidden, fees on investors (pp. 78–105). Silver's (1988) citation of Flynn as authoritative is ironic, as Flynn provides no illustrations of poorly or abusively managed investment companies that are entirely owned by banks. To the contrary; he praises bank-sponsored companies and criticises the type that Silver represents.

Evidence from the SEC Study (1940) on Bank-Sponsored Investment Companies

The Investment Company Institute, in the person of its president, argues that the experience of the 1920s demonstrates that it would be imprudent, even dangerous, to allow banks to sponsor mutual funds and distribute their shares to the public (Silver, 1988, pp. 5–8 and 1987, pp. 8–14).[3] He states that 'banks were heavily involved in

---

[1] These trusts are similar to the commingled funds that the Supreme Court's decision in *Investment Company Institute v. Camp*, 401 US 617 (1971) prevented Citibank from offering.

[2] In order of their appearance, the list includes: Massachusetts Investors Trust (an investment company, 'IC'), Irving Investors Management Company (a trust company, 'TC'), City Bank Farmers Trust Company's Uniform Trust (the trust company of the National City Bank, a TC), Brooklyn Trust Company Composite Funds, Series A (a TC), Counselors Securities Trust (an IC), North American Investment Corporation (an IC), and the Wisconsin Investment Company (an IC). Flynn does not identify any investment banks as sponsors.

[3] Silver uses almost the exact same language in his 1987 and 1988 statements. His 1987 statement, however, includes a longer list of abuses and specific citations to the record (which he omits from his 1988 statement). Consequently, I use his 1987 statement as the basis for this investigation.

the mutual fund business in the 1920s, and there were widespread abuses in the operation of bank-sponsored funds (then known as "investment trusts") . . . Many of the widespread abuses stemmed from the bank's role as a commercial lender' (Silver, 1987, p. 9).

Silver then provides the only list of abuses of which I am aware with citations to the SEC Study (1940, 1942). He says (1987, pp. 9–10, footnote references omitted, numbers in parentheses added for identification and later reference):

The abuses included
(1) mutual fund investment in debentures of a troubled company which was financed by the bank;
(2) fund purchases of illiquid loans from the bank; and
(3) fund loans to accommodate 'good customers' of the bank.

In addition, there were instances in which the fund had invested in companies in order to further the bank's commercial interests – for example,

(4) fund purchases of stock in other banks in anticipation of statewide branching; and so that the bank would be in a better position to sell correspondent services to these smaller banks. Other abuses included
(5) fund investment in stock of the bank;
(6) fund loans to the bank, its securities affiliate, bank officers and directors, and companies controlled by insiders;
(7) fund purchases of securities from the bank or its securities affiliate;
(8) fund investments in companies in which insiders had an interest; and
(9) fund purchases of securities being underwritten by the bank's securities affiliate.

Silver footnotes each charge, citing pages in the SEC Study, Part 3 (1940, 1942). The page references given below are to this source.[1] The SEC has not published the transcript of the actual hearings and it is not available to me (or, perhaps, to anyone else). Hence, the available evidence is that which the SEC's staff chose to reproduce and summarise.

---

[1] Page references to chapter 1 and 2 (SEC Study, 1940) are between 1 and 798; page references to chapter 7 (SEC Study, 1942) are between 2485 and 2805.

All the abuses that Silver (1987) lists are charged to three bank-related investment companies, with two exceptions. These concern abuse 6, 'companies controlled by insiders', and abuse 8, 'fund investments in companies in which insiders had an interest', for which Silver refers to page 2716 of the SEC Study. The discussion there is about a loan made to Fox Theatres Corporation by a Bankers Securities Corporation, which is not identified as related to a commercial bank. The insider (William Fox) was a sponsor and important director of Bankers Securities. The discussion describes fees and interest the investment company received and indicates that the company did not incur losses from the transactions.

The three bank-related investment companies are the Chatham Phenix National Bank & Trust Co (NY), the Central Trust Company of Illinois, and the Liberty Bank of Buffalo (NY). Chatham Phenix National Bank is responsible for abuses 1, 5, 6, 7, 8, and 9. The SEC cites the Central Trust Company for abuses, 2, 4, 5, 6, and 7. It cites the Liberty Bank of Buffalo for abuses 3 and 6.

The principal complaints against Chatham Phenix Allied Corporation (the investment company) are trading in the stock of the bank, losses from investments in companies associated with the investment company's directors (the bank is not mentioned), and, after a non-bank purchased the company, investing 87 per cent of its assets in companies controlled by the non-bank.

The investment company associated with the Central Trust Company intermixed its affairs with the bank and with the bank's security affiliate that sponsored it. This intermixing gave rise to conflicts of interest among the different shareholders of the organisations.

The SEC criticised the Liberty Bank of Buffalo primarily for using its associated investment company as a source of loans to its officers and employees who traded in the bank's stock.

The record Silver (1987) cites does not often support the specific abuses he delineates. I consider each alleged abuse by reference to that record; few turn out to have been as he implies.

Fund Investment in Debentures of a Troubled Company Financed by a Bank (Abuse 1)

Silver misleadingly describes this 'abuse'. The section of the SEC Study he cites (pp. 115–42) discusses the partial financing in 1929 of the Empire State Building by Chatham Phenix Allied Corporation, the investment company sponsored in part by the securities affiliate of Chatham Phenix National Bank & Trust Co. The group undertaking construction of the building (all directors of the bank) had raised $37.5 million of the $51.0 million required ($10.0 million from the group, half of which was borrowed from the bank and its affiliate, and $27.5 million from the Metropolitan Life Insurance Company). The group obtained half of the remaining $13.5 million from two of its members (Raskob and du Pont); it borrowed the other half from Chatham Phenix Allied Corporation in the form of debentures secured with a second mortgage on the Empire State building. The debentures carried a 7 per cent coupon and were issued at a 10 per cent discount. They are described by the investment company as 'a prime investment', but, the SEC Study (ibid., p. 127) points out, ' "primeness" . . . was determined by those individuals whose pecuniary interest was directly affected by the sale of these debentures to the investment company'.

Nothing in the record indicates that Empire State, Inc. was a 'troubled company' until 1931 (two years after the fund purchased the group's Empire-State-building-secured debentures), when '[l]easing of space in the building proved exceedingly difficult' (ibid., p. 129). Nor was Empire State, Inc. financed by the bank, although the investors personally did borrow less than 10 per cent of the financing (no more that $5 million of the $51 million) from the bank. Silver thus misleadingly states his charge; indeed, it is almost entirely wrong.[1]

Fund Purchases of Illiquid Loans from the Bank (Abuse 2)

Silver's (1987) citation is to the Central-Illinois Securities Corporation's (SISC), which was formed and managed by the Central Trust Company of Illinois and the Central-Illinois Company, the bank's securities affiliate. SISC purchased brokers' call loans from the bank following the 1929 stock market crash, in the amount of $13.5 million. The loans were repaid. In addition, $4.5 million in 'loans [were] made [by the bank or its affiliate] to affiliated interests or to enterprises in which affiliated interests were involved [not further described]' (ibid., p. 150). As of 31 December 1935 about 27 per cent ($1.2 million) of these loans were written off (ibid., pp. 150–1).

---

[1] In 1931 the Atlas Corporation, which acquired control of the Chatham Phenix Allied Corporation, exchanged shares of the Chatham Phenix National Bank for the debentures. At that time the bank stock had a market value of $1.6 million (ibid., p. 129).

The basis for Silver's (1987) charge apparently is this statement (ibid., p. 151):

> A characteristic of most of the loans, excepting the loans to brokers, taken over by the investment company from the bank and its security affiliate, was their illiquidity. In large measure the same attribute characterized loans in which the investment company was induced to participate directly with the bank and its security affiliate.

The loans described were secured with collateral that the bank held. The bank, its securities affiliate, and the investment company sustained losses on some of these loans. Nothing in the record, however, indicates that illiquidity (a feature of most loans) or the bank's or its affiliate's self-dealing caused the losses, although a 27 per cent write off could indicate self-dealing.

Fund Loans to Accommodate 'Good Customers' of the Bank
(Abuse 3)

Silver's (1987) citation is to loans that the Liberty Share Corporation made to customers of the Liberty Bank of Buffalo, which established and managed the investment company (ibid., p. 2658, note 44). Note 44 describes a $19,648 loan made by the Liberty Share Corporation to the president of the Great Belt National Bank, with which the Liberty Bank did business. The Liberty Bank could not take the loan, which was collateralised with bank stock, because it 'had on loan an excess amount of the collateral of the Great Belt National Bank'. The SEC Study quotes testimony to the effect that the bank and the affiliate transferred some loans back and forth. The Study makes no mention of losses to the investment company or to the bank on these loans, or of the terms of the loans.

Hence, while the Study reports an intermingling of the business of the bank and the investment company it managed, it does not indicate whether the transfers were a disadvantage or advantage to the stockholders of either organisation. Such intermingling among companies with different ownerships (as well as loans to related parties by banks that have no securities operations) nevertheless are subject to possible abuse. But when the stockholders of the related companies are the same, as was the situation for commercial banks and their securities affiliates and as would be the situation were banks allowed to conduct securities operations directly or through subsidiaries, there can be no abuse.

Fund Purchases of Stock in Other Banks in Anticipation of State-wide Branching and to Facilitate Sale of Correspondent Services to Smaller Banks (Abuse 4)

Central-Illinois Securities Corporation invested in local bank stocks on behalf of its sponsoring bank. Its investment of $2 million resulted in a loss of 76 per cent when bank stock prices collapsed (ibid., p. 167). The SEC Study does not indicate whether the general decline in bank stock prices or particularly bad purchases made to accommodate the bank accounted for this loss. The stock price decline explanation seems more likely, because the investment company also incurred a 71 per cent loss in its $447,000 investment in Chase National Bank stock (ibid., p. 168). I could find nothing in the Study about sales of correspondent services to smaller banks except this testimony by Phillip R. Clarke, president of the Central Republic Bank and Trust Company (ibid., p. 167):

> the Central Trust Company . . . [did] what was more or less fashionable in Chicago at that time, in anticipation of branch banking. The large Loop [downtown Chicago] banks were going to the outlying banks and acquiring either through some larger source or picking up in the open market from time to time a sufficient ownership in those banks to establish a sort of correspondent relationship between the large downtown banks and the outlying banks.

Thus, the record fails to support about half of Silver's (1987) charges.

Fund Investment in the Stock of the Bank (Abuse 5)

The directors of Chatham Phenix Allied Corporation (all directors of the bank) authorised it to 'make purchases and sales [of bank stock] for the purpose of supporting the stock at levels on a parity with comparable bank stocks' (ibid., p. 131). Between October 1929 and November 1931 the corporation purchased $6.9 million in bank stock and sold $6.8 million, for a net loss of $88,000, or 1.3 per cent of purchases (ibid., p. 131). The Central-Illinois Securities Corporation purchased stock in its sponsor-bank and its successor in an attempt to support the market price of the stock. After the bank became insolvent and closed in 1932, the investment company incurred a loss of $2.5 million, a third of its accumulated losses through 1935 (pp. 162–5). Thus, the record supports Silver's (1987) charge. The essential question is whether the stockholders in the Central-Illinois Securities Corporation knew that their funds were being invested in the bank's stock. If they did not know, these dealings both potentially and actually harmed them. I could find in the SEC Study no indication of disclosures that the investment company made.

Funds Loans to the Bank, its Securities Affiliate, Bank Officers and Directors, and Companies Controlled by Insiders (Abuse 6)

Loans to the bank   Silver (1987, p. 10) cites the SEC Study's report on the Central-Illinois Securities Corporation. It was established just before the 1929 stock market crash. Fortunately, its funds were not yet invested, and its board of directors decided to avoid the stock market and purchase loans from the sponsoring bank and its security affiliate (ibid., p. 149). The SEC Study states that these were 'mainly of an unmarketable character' (ibid., p. 149). In response to the possible inference that these obligations were 'unloaded' by the sponsoring bank on the investment company, Clarke (who was not president of the company when the loans were purchased by it) declared (ibid., p. 150):

> I have always had the impression that that was all purposely done in order to give this investment trust everything that the Central-Illinois Company had in its portfolio that might possibly not qualify for an investment house, in other words, not be subject to distribution in the normal course of its business and, at the same time, give this company the largest amount of earning assets at the earliest possible time.

The questioner then states that these transfers 'might create in some [people's] mind . . . an inference of [an] unloading, isn't that so?' (ibid., p. 150, insertions and omissions in original). Clarke replied: 'I wouldn't want to go so far as to say that. I think it certainly demonstrates that the Central-Illinois Securities was, of the three affiliated companies, the one to which long-term investments were to be turned over' (ibid., p. 150). Thus, the record does not support

Silver's (1987, p. 10) characterisation of abusive 'fund loans to the bank'.

Loans to the Bank's Securities Affiliate One instance that the record Silver (1987) cites concerns the Central-Illinois Securities Corporation, which made a $1 million secured loan to the Central Trust Company's security affiliate, which the affiliate repaid. The corporation used the proceeds to buy the stock of a bank with which its sponsor bank was merging (SEC Study, pp. 157–8). There is no indication that the shareholders of the investment company incurred losses from these transactions.

The other instance that the record Silver (1987) cites concerns the Chatham Phenix Allied Corporation, which made loans to its sponsor-bank's security affiliate that the affiliate apparently completely repaid when due (ibid., p. 130). There is no indication in the SEC Study that the loans were not beneficial both to the bank's and the investment company's stockholders.

Loans to bank officers and directors Silver's (1987) charge concerns loans that the Liberty Share Corporation made to officers and directors of its sponsor and manager, the Liberty Bank of Buffalo (ibid., p. 2655). At its peak percentage in 1933, loans to insiders (including officers and employees of the investment company) were 45 per cent of the investment company's total assets. The SEC Study describes these and loans to customers (about 18 per cent of assets) as 'margin or brokerage accounts, the purpose of which was to enable the borrower to buy and sell stocks of the bank, the investment company and its affiliate . . . on margin' (ibid., p. 2659). The margin required appears to have been less than the percentage asked of other customers. In 1936 insiders connected to the bank or the investment company still owed the successor to the investment company $3.4 million (ibid., p. 2669). These transactions appear to have been to the detriment of those investment company stockholders who did not participate in the favored transactions. Insider loans to bank officers and directors, of course, are a continuing problem that governments have tried to control, often without success. That insiders used these loans for stock purchases tell us nothing about the wisdom of requiring the separation of commercial and investment banking.

Silver (1987) does not mention the only other case of this kind that the SEC Study discusses. It concerns the M&T Securities Corporation, which Manufacturers & Traders Trust Company of Buffalo sponsored. The corporation made loans to bank officers and employees amounting to $744,430 in 1931. (The SEC Study does not give the corporation's total assets.) The corporation also made a $2,600,000 loan to accommodate the bank; apparently it was repaid (ibid., p. 2672). In 1937, loans to officers and employees of $454,452 were charged off. The investment company also borrowed from the bank. The SEC Study (ibid., p. 2674) states: 'Excepting during the years 1929 and 1935, the bank loans of the company were always seriously under-secured' (ibid., p. 2674). The SEC study indicates that the company's stockholders do not appear to have been informed about these intra-bank and company practices. Whether or not those stockholders lost as a result of these transactions is not discussed in the Study.

Loans to companies controlled by insiders   Silver's (1987) citation is to the Chatham Phenix Allied Corporation. The investment company lost 70 per cent of the amount of loans made to companies associated with insiders (ibid., p. 133). Losses on these companies' securities were 61 per cent compared to losses of only 30 per cent on investments in unrelated companies (ibid., p. 135). But the sponsoring bank's securities affiliate and the bank appear to have played no role in these transactions – the SEC Study identifies all of the insiders as directors of the investment company.[1]

Fund Purchases of Securities from the Bank or its Securities Affiliate (Abuse 7)

In February 1939, the securities affiliate of Chatham Phenix National Bank transferred a collateralised note for $2.2 million from the syndicate constructing the Empire State Building to reduce the affiliate's indebtedness to the investment company. The record does not indicate whether the transfer was effected at other than an arm's-length price. In April 1931, the collateral agreement was modified to give the bank, to which the syndicate also was indebted, a senior position in the collateral. The bank eventually was paid in full, but the investment company took a loss of $380,063 (17 per cent) (ibid., p. 130). Thus, there is evidence that the bank improved its position

---

[1] As noted above, Silver (1987) gives an irrelevant citation to a Fox Theatres Corporation loan.

at the expense of the investment company it controlled, as Silver (1987) implies.

Funds Investments in Companies in Which Insiders Had an Interest (Abuse 8)

Silver's (1987) citation is to the Chatham Phenix loans discussed above under 'loans to companies controlled by insiders', and to the Fox Theatres Corporation loan, discussed in the first part of this section of this chapter. In the first instance, the insiders were directors of the investment company, not the bank. The Fox Theatres loan also did not involve a bank. Therefore, Silver's (1987) charge, whether or not correct, is irrelevant.

Fund Purchases of Securities Being Underwritten by the Bank's Securities Affiliate (Abuse 9)

Silver's (1987) citation is to a 5 per cent allotment of Film Securities Corporation two-year 6 per cent secured gold notes that the Chatham Phenix Bank's security affiliate received, which it later sold to the investment company it managed (ibid., p. 134). The security affiliate kept its participation bonus of 2,500 shares of common stock. There is no indication that the affiliate's sale to the investment company was at other than an arm's-length-market price. However, the SEC Study questions why the common stock was not included in the sale, presumably for free. The president of the investment company replied: 'I suppose they thought that was their commission probably for handling the transaction. If they had not sold them [the bonds] to us, they would have sold them to somebody else' (ibid., p. 135). Thus, the record does not support Silver's (1987) implication of wrongdoing.

Evidence from the SEC Study (1940) on Non-bank-sponsored Investment Companies

The chapters of the SEC Study (1940 and 1942) concerning abuses and mismanagement give as examples investment companies and trusts that investment houses and individuals sponsored, not organisations that banks sponsored. Bank-sponsored companies may not have been included because the study was begun in 1937, some five years after the Glass–Steagall Act separated investment and commercial banking. Much of the general narrative, examples, and statistical material, however, cover the years when banks operated investment companies: the years 1927 through 1936 in particular. The SEC staff also gathered material from the pre-Glass–Steagall period and included detailed analyses of the activities of three commercial-bank-sponsored investment companies; the Study also incorporates a supplemental report on bank-administered commingled trust funds (Securities and Exchange Commission, 1939b).

The SEC Study, Part 3 (1940 and 1942) includes three chapters (I, II, and VII) that describe 'abuses' by investment company sponsors. Chapter I provides a background emphasising the period 1927–9. Chapter II, entitled 'Detailed Histories of [Eleven] Various Investment Trusts and Investment Companies', covers 727 pages, exclusive of appendices. Two of the investment companies discussed were bank sponsored (65 pages) and nine were sponsored by individuals or investment houses (662 pages).

Chapter VII (339 pages), entitled 'Problems in Connection with Management of Assets of Investment Trusts and Investment Companies', includes four general kinds of abuses. As an indication of the kind of sponsors the chapter charged with the abuses analysed in detail, I follow the title of the abuse by the number and type of sponsor discussed (bank-or non-bank sponsored):

1 the benefits (to the sponsor) of sponsorship – 3 major investment houses;
2 purchase and sale of portfolio securities by sponsors – 15 non-bank, and 1 bank sponsor;
3 loans by investment trusts and investment companies to insiders and affiliates, with 8 sub-varieties:
   loans to insiders for speculative purposes – 2 bank sponsors;
   loans to brokers threatened with expulsion from exchanges – 2 non-bank sponsors;
   loans to sponsors to float security issues – 3 non-bank sponsors;
   loans to sponsors or their affiliates to operate trading accounts – 2 non-bank sponsors;
   transfer to investment companies of loans made to sponsor – 1 non-bank sponsor and 1 bank;
   loans to sponsors as a device for draining funds from an investment company – 3 non-bank sponsors;
   loans to support market of stock of companies affiliated with investment companies – 1 non-bank sponsor;
   loans for indirect purposes of sponsor – 8 non-bank sponsors;

4 pyramiding of investment in investment companies – 3 non-bank sponsors;
5 creation of fictitious asset values – 7 non-bank sponsors.

A simple count of the number of sponsors by variety reveals 3 bank sponsors and 48 non-bank sponsors of investment companies and trusts. Adding these numbers to the 11 examples of abuses discussed in the SEC Study Chapter II (1940), there are 5 bank-sponsor examples compared to 57 non-bank-sponsor examples.

Summary of Evidence from the SEC Studies

The Investment Company Institute's claim that there were 'widespread abuses in the operation of bank-sponsored funds' (Silver, 1987, p. 9) rests on the dubious activities of three banks and their affiliated investment companies. The 'abuses' (not all of which appear actually to be abuses) that the record supports (reference numbers given in parentheses) include fund purchase of loans from the bank (2), fund loans to accommodate bank customers (3), fund purchase of stock in other banks in anticipation of branching (part of 4), fund investment in the stock of the bank (5), and fund loans to bank officers and directors (part of 6). But the record does not indicate the extent, if any, to which most of these 'abuses' resulted in costs rather than benefits to the shareholders of the investment companies and trusts. In particular, the SEC Study does not show that banks transferred or sold the securities of their troubled borrowers to the investment companies they sponsored. There is no evidence that the investment companies took their sponsor-banks' illiquid (in the sense of worth less than face value) loans, made loans to bank customers at less than market rates, or purchased slow-moving or less-than-good (or, for that matter, any) securities from the bank or its securities affiliate, whether underwritten by them or not. The only exception concerns an intermingled bank and investment company management. Because in that case each organisation had different stockholders, the managers had a conflict of interest. From the one case cited, it is not clear which group benefited and which lost. Had the stockholders of the organisations not been different, the intermingling might have benefited and would not have damaged the stockholders.

The other and most important abuse revealed is insiders' and sponsors' use of investment companies to fund their stock transactions and business interests (including transactions in the stock of the sponsor). This abuse is not special to bank sponsorship and management of an investment company. Nor were commercial banks charged with imposing excessive or hidden fees on investors, as were operators of other companies. Indeed, the SEC study of abuses and management problems (Part 3) is devoted mostly to investment companies operated by investment bankers and individuals. Because I have not undertaken a detailed analysis of the data and documents underlying the report of the SEC study, I cannot conclude that these organisations' and persons' operations, which the Glass–Steagall Act does not inhibit from offering shares in and managing mutual funds and investment companies, were indeed characterised by 'widespread abuses'.

Furthermore, 8 per cent of the abuses that the SEC Study describes (by simple count, $5 \div 62$) involved commercial banks. In comparison to the three commercial banks criticised, thirty-five non-bank sponsers of investment companies and trusts are criticised. Therefore, the record it cites does not in general support the Investment Company Institute's assertion that there were 'widespread abuses in the operation of bank-sponsored funds'.

I cannot determine from this record how many or what proportion of commercial banks engaged in abusive practices, unless we can assume that the SEC Study is complete in its coverage. Considering that the Glass–Steagall Act was enacted only a few years before the SEC Study was undertaken, and that bank sponsored investment companies still existed, it seems unlikely that the researchers or their supervisors would be sympathetic to banks or mistakenly overlook their shortcomings. Instead, I suggest that banks had strong incentives to manage their sponsored investment companies carefully and correctly. Banks were regulated and examined by federal and state authorities. Their depositors' funds were not covered by deposit insurance. Consequently, their reputations for probity and prudence were important to them. These factors may explain the paucity of SEC criticism of bank-sponsored investment companies.

VII SUMMARY AND CONCLUSIONS

The record cited and available provides evidence on four overall sources of conflicts of interest and abuses by commercial banks related to their securities operations: (1) National City Bank and its affiliate, National City Company; (2) Chase National Bank and its affiliate, Chase Securities; (3) bank trust departments; and (4) bank-sponsored investment companies and trusts. The charges made against National City and Chase are based on the record of the Pecora Hearings (1933, 1934).

A detailed examination of this record reveals surprisingly little support for the charges of abuses by either organisation. Although some observers might consider the information provided by the National City to investors for some bond issues it sold as insufficient, the record does not support allegations that commercial banks' securities activities were abusive or otherwise contrary to investors' interests. Furthermore, a detailed examination of the charges against the chief executive officers of the banks, Charles Mitchell and Albert Wiggin (presented in the Appendix to this chapter), finds that their actions were not nearly as heinous as the major historians who have written about the period of claim or imply.

The record also provides almost no support for the Investment Company Institute's charge (Silver, 1987) that banks abused their fiduciary responsibilities to trusts. To the contrary, there is strong evidence that they were scrupulous (with one small exception) in insulating trust investments from the banks' securities activities. I find some support for Silver's (1987) contention that some banks sponsoring investment companies intermingled the banks' and the companies' activities. But the abuses reported in the record he cites, the SEC Study (1940, 1942), to a much greater degree concern non-bank sponsors of investment companies than bank-sponsored companies and trusts.

Thus, the record does not support the belief that the pre-Glass–Steagall period was one of abuses and conflicts of interest on the part of banks involved with securities transactions, either directly or through affiliates. Indeed, very little evidence exists of such abuses, and those abuses that the record does describe seem far more prevalent among non-banks. This finding is consistent with the observation that regulated depository institutions benefit from maintaining reputations for integrity and prudence.

APPENDIX: ALLEGATIONS NOT RELEVANT TO GLASS-STEAGALL

1 NATIONAL CITY BANK AND COMPANY AND MITCHELL

Personal Income Tax Avoidance by Mitchell (Charge 1)

Carosso (1970a, p. 334) declares:

> Even more shocking [than the revelation that National City Company executives made large salaries and participated individually in the company's flotations of securities] was the disclosure that these distinguished, respected pillars of the financial community had employed every legal trick to avoid, if not evade, paying any income taxes on their huge earnings.[1]

Actually, Carosso mentions only one 'legal trick'. Mitchell sold 18,300 shares of National City Bank stock to his wife, in 1929, to establish a capital loss of $2.8 million that could offset other income (which was permitted at that time). As he explained in his testimony (Pecora Hearings, 1933, p. 1811):

> MR MITCHELL   Well, I bought 28,300 shares [in 1929], which I had hoped to hold only temporarily. It was done in order to help the situation.
> MR PECORA   To sustain the market?
> MR MITCHELL   Yes. Of that, 10,000 shares were sold, leaving me at that time the holder of 53,300 shares of stock.

He repurchased the 18,300 shares (the balance of his 1929 purchase) from his wife in 1933 at the same price she paid for it, so that (he said) she would not take a loss. Mitchell explained: 'I sold this stock, frankly, for tax purposes'. This quotation appears in Carosso (p. 334), Seligman (p. 26), and Pecora (p. 194). Only Pecora provides the balance of the questioning on p. 1812:

---

[1] Pecora (1939, p. 194), Kennedy (1973, p. 125), and Seligman (1982, p. 26) do not make as strong a statement, but simply report that Mitchell testified that he sold the stock to his wife to avoid income tax. Peach does not mention Mitchell's taxes as an abuse.

SENATOR BROOKHART   That was to avoid income tax?

MR MITCHELL   Throwing my fortune into the breach as I did for the benefit of this institution, Senator Brookhart, in 1929 I had a definite loss in that stock which I was forced to take.

Mitchell bought the 28,300 shares from the National City Company to bail out the Company (and the bank's shareholders, including himself). During the October 1929 crash, the company had purchased the shares in the open market in an attempt to keep the price of the shares from declining below the level at which they were to be exchanged in a merger with the Corn Exchange Bank. As Huertas and Silverman (1986, p. 14) explain the situation, '[t]he City Company did not have the cash to pay for the stock and could not borrow from the bank for that purpose. To dump the stock back on the market would have driven the stock down further'. So Mitchell borrowed some $10.6 million from J. P. Morgan and purchased the shares from the company.

Mitchell was prosecuted for criminal tax evasion three and a half years later and was acquitted, but he was found guilty in a Tax Court proceeding and ordered to pay $700,000 in back taxes.[1] Interestingly, had he sold the stock in 1929 in the market rather than to his wife, he would have shown an undisputed tax loss for 1929. Had he then bought the stock back after expiration of the wash sale period and then sold the stock in 1933 in the market, he would have been able to deduct an additional tax loss for 1933. Indeed, had his wife sold the stock in the market in 1933 rather than to him, she would have had an undisputed 1933 tax loss.[2] It appears that Mitchell chose the method of writing down his loss in National City Bank stock via a sale to his wife because he wanted to be able to say publicly that he had still had faith in the bank, as evidenced by the 'fact' that he had not sold his shares. His statement to this effect was used against him at his trial. The Circuit Court stated: 'In January, 1932, at the annual stockholders' meeting of the National City Bank, Mitchell was asked by a stockholder whether he had disposed of any of his stock and replied: "Not a single share, sir. As a matter of fact I am buying all

---

[1] See Huertas and Silverman (1986) for a more complete analysis.

[2] Cleveland and Huertas (1985, p. 406) point out that 'Thomas S. Lamont, a Morgan partner, sold stock to his wife at a loss on December 30, 1930, lending her the money to buy it. On April 8, 1931, Lamont repurchased the stock from his wife and his wife repaid the loan. Pecora, *Wall Street under Oath*, pp. 196–197. Lamont was never prosecuted for tax evasion; Mitchell was'.

I can possibly get and that I can possibly pay for." [1] An alternative explanation, that Mitchell wanted to maintain control of the National City Bank, does not appear to be correct, since the 18,300 shares in question represent only about 2.5 per cent of the total shares outstanding at year end 1929.

In any event, Mitchell's stock sales certainly were neither a 'legal trick' nor related to National City Bank's operation of a securities affiliate. Nevertheless, the revelation of his not having paid taxes despite having earning a very large income was instrumental in his having to resign his position as chief executive officer of the National City Bank and National City Company, and in the passage of the Banking Act of 1933.

High Undisclosed Salaries and Bonuses Paid to Mitchell and Other Top Executives (Charge 2)

Carosso (1970a, p. 333) charges:

> Mitchell and other top National City executives saw themselves, he said, as 'the equivalent of partners in a private banking or investment firm'. They conducted the bank's and the affiliate's affairs in the same way, entirely oblivious of the fact that they were employees of a corporation and responsible to its stockholders. Besides drawing substantial salaries, they voted themselves huge annual bonuses, not reported in annual statements.

However, a review of the bonus system described by Mitchell at the hearings reveals a procedure that can benefit shareholders by reducing the common principal-agent problem, where employees (agents) tend not to maximise the wealth of owners (principals), but instead maximise their own well being at the expense of owners. [2]

This system may have been an important reason for the National City Company's success. Each officer received the same salary, $25,000 per year. The bonuses mentioned were determined as follows. The stockholders first received 8 per cent of stockholders' equity plus 80 per cent of the remaining net earnings. The company's board of directors distributed half of the 20 per cent balance to the officers and established each officer's share of that balance at the

---

[1] Mitchell v. Commissioner of Internal Revenue, F.Rep. 2d, 873, 875 (2d Cir., 1937).
[2] See Jensen and Meckling (1972)

beginning of the year. The board advised officers of their shares at that time. The other half was distributed twice a year according to three ballots. As Mitchell described the process (Pecora Hearings, 1933, p. 1787):

> The first ballot is an unsigned ballot lodged in a ballot box with the cashier of the bank, as to what portion of the management fund accumulated that I personally should receive.
>
> The second is a signed ballot as to how much of the management fund after the portion which I receive is deducted, should be distributed to each other eligible officer, each man voting eliminating himself. The third ballot is a signed ballot indicating what men other than the eligible officers should be considered in the distribution of the fund, what men have contributed most effectively during the period under review to the advancement of the interests of the institution.

This hardly describes the situation that Carosso depicts.[1]

Pecora and some senators viewed the bonus system as giving the National City Company officers incentives to oversell securities. Carosso (1970a, p. 334) quotes Senator Couzens's question to Mitchell: 'Does it not also inspire a lack of care in the handling and sale of securities to the public [because each individual officer has a split]?' Carosso (ibid., p. 334) reports that 'Mitchell replied affirmatively, saying that the practice may have had "some influence" on the fact that almost $1 billion, a fifth, of the securities issued by the National City Co. during the past ten years were in default'. But Mitchell actually said (Pecora Hearings, 1933, p. 1772):

> [MR MITCHELL] I can readily see, from your point of view that that would seem so, and I must grant that it must have some influence, Senator Couzens. At the same time, I do not recall seeing it operate in that way.
>
> [SENATOR COUZENS] You would not see it. Only the customers would see it after they had gotten the securities. May I ask you at that point . . . how many securities that you have sold are now in default?

---

[1] Kennedy (1973, p. 123–4) provides an accurate description of the bonus plan; she references pages in the hearings rather than only pages in Pecora and the Pecora Hearings, as does Carosso.

Mitchell answered that $1 billion of $20 billion were in default, which is 5, not 20 per cent.

In any event, neither the Glass–Steagall Act nor any other legislation forbids securities underwriters, dealers, or brokers from paying employees commissions or performance-based incentives rather than straight salaries. Nor is it unlawful for commercial bankers to reward employees with incentives based on the amount of deposits they generate or loans they close. Hence, whatever one's views on the merits or demerits of incentive employment rewards, the issue is not relevant except as an indication of kind of activity the Pecora Hearings (1933, 1934) and some senators and commentators identified as 'abusive'.

Special Lending Facilities for Officers of National City Bank (Charge 3)

Carosso (1970a, p. 334, footnote reference omitted to Pecora, 1939, pp. 127–8) states:

> When the stock market collapsed, and the speculators among National City's officers found themselves in trouble, the bank went to their rescue promptly by establishing a special 'moral loan fund,' from which they might borrow without interest or collateral. Nearly all the 'loans' made by this fund, amounting to some $2.4 million, never were repaid and, as in the case of many of its other transactions, the stockholders, whose money it was, were not told of their bank's solicitude for the morale of its executives.

Kennedy (1973, pp. 124–5) and Pecora (1939, pp. 128–9) also point out that the bank did not forgive instalment loans it made to ordinary employees for purchases of bank stock, despite the drop in the market value of the stock.

Pecora correctly reports the operation of the loan fund (titled officers, but not other employees, were not required to repay outstanding balances), with two exceptions. First, titled officers subscribed to two-thirds of the instalment stock purchase plan, which initially involved $12 million of indebtedness (Pecora Hearings, 1933, p. 1878). Second, no testimony appears indicating that the officers to whom loans were made were 'speculators'. The term was never mentioned; it only was stated that the loans were made principally because of the officers' prior purchases of National City Bank stock (ibid., p. 1875).

In any event, this issue is irrelevant to any actions that might support the separation of commercial and investment banking.

Loan by National City Bank to a Public Official (Charge 11)

Seligman (1982, p. 29) reports that:

> The nine days of hearings devoted to Mitchell and National City concluded with the revelation that the company had 'lent' $10,020 to John Ramsey, general manager of the Port Authority of New York, before receiving the right to sell $66 million worth of Port Authority bonds. The 'loan,' never repaid, was charged off as an expense of the bond issue.

Although this 'revelation' is irrelevant to the Glass–Steagall Act separation of commercial and investment banking, it does appear to indicate a lapse of ethical standards. The National City Bank made the loan, and apparently the bank assumed it to be an expense of the company. Hence, the bank's creditors were not disadvantaged. (The bank actually made the loan on 2 June 1931, while the underwriting, in which NCC participated, had occurred in March 1931).

2 WIGGIN OF CHASE NATIONAL BANK AND CHASE SECURITIES CORPORATION

Wiggin's Large Salary and Personal Fees from Bank Customers (Charges 4 and 11)

Pecora summarises his view of Wiggin's improprieties thus: 'Mr. Wiggin was able to make an income many times in excess of his salary, in large part by using his unique opportunities as the trusted and all-powerful head of a great bank, for his personal advantage' (Pecora, 1939, p. 147).

In particular, Pecora (ibid., 1939, p. 142) castigates Wiggin for receiving a salary from Chase National Bank 'of $175,000 in 1928, an equal amount in 1929, $218,750 in 1930, and $250,000 in 1931'. Pecora continues: 'As the reader will note, the deeper the depression, the higher Mr. Wiggin's salary. In 1932, Mr. Wiggin took a "cut" in salary, and received a mere $220,300.' In addition, Wiggin received bonuses of '$100,000 in 1928, $100,000 in 1929, and, even in 1930, $75,000', plus bonuses from Chase Securities Corporation, 'which in some years ran as high as $75,000' (ibid., p. 143). He also received thousands of dollars per year in directors' fees from some 59 directorships. Thus, the public might regard Wiggin's remuneration as obscenely high at a time when many people were out of work or getting barely enough to live on.[1]

The charge that Wiggin obtained substantial fees (possibly as a director, but not identified as such in the record) from corporations that were borrowing from Chase is potentially more serious. Pecora put into the record Wiggin's receipt of annual payments labelled 'salaries' of $40,000 from Amour and Co., $20,000 from the Brooklyn-Manhattan Transit Co., and that had an unidentified association with the International Power & Paper Co. Pecora then asked about these companies' borrowings from Chase. Wiggin replied that Amour & Co. became a large depositor but was not a large borrower. (Subsequent testimony brought out, however, that Amour had a $40,00,000 commercial paper loan, which it fully repaid; Pecora Hearings, 1934, p. 2916). Pecora established that the chairman of the board of the Brooklyn-Manhattan Transit Co. (Gerhard M. Dahl) had borrowed up to $4,758,000; some $2,500,000 was in default. Chase made substantial loans to the executive head of the International Power & Paper Co. (Mr. Graustein), of which some $3,339,000 had been charged off (ibid., 1934, pp. 2325–30). Wiggin responded that the loans had been adequately secured when Chase made them, but they went bad as a consequence of the depression. Subsequent testimony revealed an uncollateralised $502,083 loan to Continental Paper Bag Mills (ibid., 1934, p. 2918). I could find no other specific mention of loans to companies from which Wiggin received payments. Nor does the record report further information about the interest rates charged on the loans compared to loans from other borrowers.

Thus, without further explanation, one might interpret the amounts Wiggin received as bribes or as other evidence of self-dealing. These amounts did not give rise, however, to calls for legislation forbidding bankers from receiving directors' fees or other payments from companies that did business with their banks. Indeed,

---

[1] A similar charge appears in the SEP Report (1934), pp. 208–9, not on pp. 195–205, as Carosso reports (1970, p. 346).

the receipt of such fees for services rendered has been a common practice for a long time. This practice can benefit bank stockholders, because it provides the banks' officers with information about customers' affairs that allows the bank to serve these customers more effectively.

Wiggin's Income Tax Avoidance[1] (Charge 8)

The public and investors apparently did not know that Wiggin had established six personal corporations (three incorporated in the United States and three in Canada) through which he channelled securities and other transactions in which the Chase Securities Corporation also participated. Wiggin stated that he established these corporations in part to reduce income taxes, which, he maintained, was perfectly legal and proper. He presented a table showing that his three US corporations had net income of $2,798,787 from 1928 through 1932 and paid $924,814 in federal income taxes (33 per cent). Over this period, he personally received $5,802,200 in income and paid $1,365,235 in federal income taxes (24 per cent) (Pecora Hearings, 1934, pp. 2997–8). I could find no mention of the net profits from Wiggin's Canadian corporations. Whether or not the primary purpose of the corporations was to reduce taxes legally, they gave the impression of gross impropriety if not outright dishonesty even though tax avoidance is not illegal.

Personal Trading (Including Short Sales) by Wiggin in Chase Bank Stock (Charges 5 and 6)

According to Pecora, his questioning revealed that 'Mr Wiggin made [a profit] by trading in Chase National Bank stock, $4,008,538 to be exact . . . in the amazingly short period between September 19, 1929 and December 11, 1929, and in the very midst of the great Wall Street crash. . . . Mr Wiggin made all that money by selling Chase National Bank short' (Pecora, 1939, p. 153). Furthermore, Pecora

---

[1] This issue merited a chapter in the SEP Report (1934) – Chapter V, pp. 321–31. The report also discusses Wiggin's activities on pp. 325–8. Mitchell's 1929 sale of National City Bank stock to his wife to establish a tax-deductible loss and reporting of a bonus as an advance, both of which are generally considered instrumental in turning the public against the banks, receive no mention. However, the non-payment of income taxes in 1930 by the partners of J. P. Morgan & Co., which revelation helped bring about passage of the Banking Act of 1933 (Seligman, 1982, p. 38), leads off the chapter.

continues, 'the [Chase National] bank . . . loaned over $8,000,000 to one or another of Mr. Wiggin's family corporations, and it was this money that Mr. Wiggin used to buy the stock with which he covered his short sales, on December 11, 1929' (ibid., p. 155). Pecora (1939, p. 156) concludes, '[t]o make the story complete, Mr. Wiggin did not pay one cent of income tax on this $4,008,538 profit'.

We should consider three aspects of this charge. First, Pecora (and Carosso) imply that Wiggin's selling his bank's shares was particularly reprehensible, because the shares were sold short. In terms of the effect on his wealth or the wealth of other investors, it does not matter whether Wiggin owned the shares that were sold at the time of the sale (except for transactions costs). In any event, Wiggin claimed that he did not sell shares short, because he and his wife held more than enough to cover them. He used a complex means of selling the shares to delay income taxes on the gain.[1]

Second, perhaps Wiggin used inside information to profit at the expense of other shareholders, although this charge does not arise in the hearings or later in Pecora's book (1939). While this possibly explains the sale of 42,506 shares of stock (whether short or long), Wiggin and his family owned 194,000 shares in December 1932. (Pecora Hearings, 1934, p. 2851). They did not sell the shares over the period even when the price per share dropped from a high of about $280 to a low, in December 1929, of $40. Thus, if Wiggin had inside information, he did not use it.

Third, Pecora's statement that 'Mr Wiggin did not pay one cent of income tax on this $4,008,538 profit', is correct, but it misleadingly implies tax evasion. Wiggin declared the gain on the transaction in

---

[1] The following describes the sequence of transactions (Pecora Hearings, 1934, pp. 2949–68):

1) Shermar Corporation (which Wiggin and his family personally owned) sold 42,506 shares short.
2) Wiggin borrowed the shares from his family trust.
3) Wiggin placed the proceeds from Shermar's short sales with trusts (apparently to collateralise the borrowing) until the shares were returned.
4) Mr and Mrs Wiggin loaned their (other) shares to Shermar Corp, which returned those it borrowed from the trusts in exchange for the cash. (Wiggin could give no reason for not lending the shares directly to Shermar in the first instance; he stated that no tax advantage was achieved).
5) Murlyn Corp. (another Wiggin corporation) borrowed $6,588,430 from Chase National Bank to purchase 42,506 shares at $155 per share. Presumably, Murlyn repaid the money to Chase.
6) Shermar Corp. merged with the Murlyn Corporation in Feb 1931, and returned Mr and Mrs Wiggin's shares to them (which it received in the merger).

1931, but he paid no tax because of offsetting losses in that year. Furthermore, Pecora knew the reason that Wiggin did not pay taxes on the transaction.[1]

No other mention appears of Wiggin's trading in Chase National Bank stock, although a table (Pecora Hearings, 1934, pp. 2858–9), shows that the Shermar Corporation (which Wiggin owned) participated in two Chase National Bank stock units (see Table 4.1).

Insider's Profits and Intermingling of Wiggin's Private Business With the Bank's (Charges 3 and 12)

Pecora (1939, p. 148) charges:

When the Chase Securities Corporation, the bank's affiliate, was involved in what promised to be some especially profitable bit of financing, for example, it was considered more tactful and proper to 'cut in' the impersonal-sounding 'Shermar Corporation,' rather than crudely mention Mr. Wiggin by his everyday, noncorporate name.

This revelation, in addition to the amount of Wiggin's salary, bonuses, and fees and profits from short sales of Chase National Bank stock, was particularly damaging to Wiggin's reputation. Pecora (1939, p. 152) contrasts the profits made by Wiggin's corporations made with those made by Metpotan Corp., the Chase affiliate established to deal in the bank's stock:

Whereas Metpotan, as we have seen, in pool transactions aggregating over $860,000,000, made only a miserable $159,000 profit for the whole period of 1928–1932, Mr. Wiggin and his corporations, during substantially the same period, from trades in the same stock, actually realised a cash profit of over $10,425,000 – sixty-five times as much! [additional emphasis in original omitted].

---

[1] After testimony brought out that the lending of stock enabled Wiggin to delay reporting a profit, the following dialogue indicates that Pecora understood what happened (Pecora Hearings, 1934, p. 2966):

MR PECORA   Well, it seems quite clear. The fact of the matter is that in 1931 the Shermar Corporation was able to offset the entire amount of profit that accrued to it that year from the covering of these short sales made in 1929 by the losses that the Shermar Corporation was able to show for the taxable year 1931?

MR WIGGIN   Yes, sir.

In the hearings (Pecora Hearings, 1934, p. 2854), Pecora asked Wiggin about the difference in performance from 'trading in the same stock. How can you account for it, if you can account for it at all?' Wiggin replied: 'I do not know that I can add to that [my previous] answer. The two accounts were two entirely different kinds of accounts. The Wiggin family corporations were long-time accounts and these other [Metpotan] accounts were in and out'.

Wiggin's answer was incomplete, in two respects. First, a table printed later in the hearings shows a combined net profit from the three Wiggin corporations of only $2,798,787 for the five years 1928–32, not the $10,425,000 Pecora claims. Pecora might have confused this figure with the *gross* sales amount of the Chase National Bank stock Wiggin sold short (although this amount was $10,596,968). Second, the Wiggin corporations dealt in securities other than that of Chase. Thus, it appears that Wiggin possibly could have accounted for much of the difference.

Pecora's (1939) book gives no specific examples of stock transaction other than the short sale just described and transactions in Sinclair stock (discussed earlier under 'stock pools and market manipulations'). But the hearing reports do include a table showing 'trading accounts in which Chase Securities Corporation participated other than trading accounts operating in connection with security offerings' (Pecora Hearings, 1934, pp. 2858–9). It shows that Wiggin's personal corporations (through which he did all his securities transactions) participated in 7 of the 34 trading accounts, and possibly in 8 more (where the participants appear only as 'Chase Securities Corporation and others'). The Wiggin corporations' (Shermar and Murlyn) participants are less than Chase Securities's participations in 4 of the 8 where percentages or numbers of shares appear and the participants are equal in the other 4. The hearings provide no data about Wiggin's participation in underwritings. Wiggin testified that his corporations suffered a net loss of $5,139,698 from sales and market-price depreciation from securities 'taken down from syndicates' in which Chase Securities participated (Pecora Hearings, 1934, p. 2894). Most of this loss was realised; it appears principally to reflect price depreciation, although no details appear in the record. Wiggin also testified that his corporations almost always purchased securities from Chase Securities at more than the price that Chase paid for them (ibid., 1934, p. 2897). The record gives no indication that the price Wiggin paid was less than the price at which he could have bought the shares on his own. Nor is there evidence about the price that Chase Securities would have had to pay had it not been for Wiggin's personal contacts. Hence, the record provides no evidence that Wiggin's participation in Chase Securities activities were at the expense of Chase's other shareholders.

Wiggin's corporations also borrowed from Chase Bank. The loans totalled $11,820,000. Wiggin pointed out that '[t]hose loans were all subsequently repaid in full, and they were always secured by collateral by an ample margin' (ibid., 1934, p. 2907). While Wiggin testified that the loans were 'specially authorised by the board in all cases' (ibid.), Pecora implied that Chase's other officers and directors did not question Wiggin's personal transactions (and perhaps loans from the bank) because '[h]e stopped their mouths, and killed any possible disposition to cavil, by intermingling his private business with the bank's; by making his interest their interests too; by being generous and considerate to them, just as the bank was to him' (Pecora, 1939, p. 158). No information appears about the rates charged or whether the terms of these loans were commensurate with those charged in similar, though clearly arm's length, transactions.

An extended colloquy illustrates well the difference in understanding between Wiggin and Pecora as to the propriety and effectiveness of rewarding bank officers (including Wiggin) with participations in the business. After listing loans made by Wiggin corporations to several Chase officers and directors, Pecora (1939, pp. 159–60, Pecora Hearings, 1934, pp. 2937–8) quotes testimony from the hearings. The portions that Pecora omits appear here in italics.

[MR PECORA] Well, has there developed through the years a system whereby those executive officers of the Chase Securities Corporation, in the exercise of their judgement, gave your family corporations a subparticipation in interests, such as Chase Securities Corporation Syndicate accounts, and you and your family corporations gave to those individual officers subparticipations in some of your syndicate interests?

[MR WIGGIN] Occasionally.

[MR PECORA] What was that? A sort of log-rolling scheme?

[MR WIGGIN] No. It was that they wanted to reduce the risk, *the amount of underwriting of the Chase Securities Corporation.* And I also had the theory that those key men should have, that it should have, that it was wise for them to have something besides their salaries. *It did not work out that way in the long run, but that was my theory. I thought where they originated business the*

> *best test of that business was their own belief in it, and if they were willing to take a risk in it, it was good business for the Chase Securities Corporation to go along with it.*
>
> [MR PECORA]   *Did they originate any of this business?*
>
> [MR WIGGIN]   *They originated business frequently.*
>
> [MR PECORA]   *Do you think it is a good thing for executive officers of financial institutions, who receive adequate salaries for their work, to also be engrossed in extensive private matters at the same time?*
>
> [MR WIGGIN]   *Well, I can only say –*
>
> [MR PECORA]   *(interposing)   Do you think it makes for greater effectiveness on their part as officers of financial institutions?*
>
> [MR WIGGIN]   You will understand that this is not a case of heads I win and tails you lose. They took the risk. *It was not a case of waiting for the profit and then taking a piece of it.*
>
> [MR PECORA]   *Do you think it was a good thing to put them into enterprises where they took financial risks?*
>
> [MR WIGGIN]   *Yes, sir.*
>
> [MR PECORA]   *Do you think that improved their efficiency of their effectiveness as officers of the bank or of the security company?*
>
> [MR WIGGIN]   That is my theory, that their self-interest made them better judges of the matter than otherwise.

This quotation shows both Pecora's belief that *any* trading in securities by officers associated with a bank is evidence of inappropriate, if not illegal, actions, and Wiggin's belief that giving responsible employees a stake in their decisions was beneficial to shareholders. While one can make arguments for both positions, there appears to be little justification for these arrangements to be kept secret from the shareholders. I could obtain no direct evidence about whether the arrangements were, indeed, unknown to shareholders. The revelation of these arrangements, though, did result in Wiggin's having to resign his pension and in his being denounced by his successor, Winthrop Aldrich.

In sum, the record shows that, while Wiggin did not separate his personal transactions from those of Chase Securities or Chase Bank, Chase stockholders appeared not to have suffered and might have benefited as a consequence of Wiggin's actions. Wiggin never took a greater participation than Chase, and when his corporations did participate, they were one among several other participants. One finds no mention of profitable transactions that Wiggin made that excluded Chase Securities. Nor is there evidence of especially risky transactions in which Wiggin put Chase Securities, possibly as a means of reducing the risk that he and his friends may have faced. Indeed, one could argue that Chase's stockholders benefited from Wiggin's contacts with pool operators and from his having had a personal monetary interest in the success of securities transactions in which the stockholders also risked their investments. (Whether joint trading accounts serve in the public interest is irrelevant for determining the cost to Chase National Bank's stockholders or depositors of Wiggin's personal sharing in the profits from the accounts). While Wiggin may not have been subject to down-side risk (although this limitation receives no mention in the testimony), Chase stockholders would have benefited from his participation in upside gains only, if the board of directors and stockholders were aware of the arrangement. One might interpret protection from down-side risk as an alternative to salary while participation in upside gains is a form of risk sharing.

3 CONCLUSIONS

The charges reviewed here are primarily against actions of National City Bank and Company, rather than those of Mitchell. His principal personal 'crime' was in attempting to *avoid* personal income taxes, which was then and remains now legal. He did not try to *evade* these liabilities, which would have been illegal. The charges against the bank and company also are weak. Indeed, today National City Company's wage and bonus arrangements appear eminently sensible. The lending arrangements did benefit officers as compared to other employees, but they were not as Pecora and others describe them. The 'loan' made to a public official associated with an underwriting in which the National City Company participated, however, does not appear to have been proper.

The charges against Wiggin and Chase relate mostly to Wiggin's intermingling of his personal affairs with those of the bank and company. His tax avoidance does not appear to be reprehensible in the light of analysis. Nor was his receipt of fees (probably as a director) from corporations that were customers of the Chase National Bank contrary to ordinary banking practice then or now. His personal participation in underwritings and securities trans-actions in which Chase Securities Corporation also participated, and his having borrowed from Chase National Bank, would not now be considered proper, although they were not illegal at the time. It is not clear whether Chase's shareholders accepted these practices or whether they were other than beneficial to the shareholders and the bank's depositors. In any event, in common with the other situations that this appendix analyses, the charges delineated relate to events the Glass–Steagall Act does not address.

5 Securities Services: Improper Banking

I SENATOR BULKLEY'S CONCEPTION OF THE PROPER ROLE OF COMMERCIAL BANKING

It is possible that the press, public, and perhaps the Congress were so outraged by what they perceived to be serious abuses by commercial banks and bankers, that legislation forbidding commercial banks from offering most kinds of securities services was enacted. One reason that the Pecora Hearings may have had such a strong impact was the prior belief, shared by several important senators and some writers, that mixing commercial and investment banking inevitably results in abuses. Senator Glass in particular was convinced that bank lending, and to a lesser extent securities underwriting and sales, had fuelled rampant speculation that had perverted and endangered the banking system and the Federal Reserve.

A speech by Senator Bulkley (*Congressional Record*, 1932, pp. 1931–2), a member of the Committee on Banking and Currency, presents the clearest, most well developed exposition of the beliefs and concerns of proponents of the Glass–Steagall Act. Its rhetorical quality has led to its citation by commentators (particularly proponents of the Act, such as the Securities Industry Association) and by the Supreme Court in *Investment Company Institute v. Camp* (401 US 617, (1971)). Both Senator Bulkley and those who cite his speech view his words as a conclusory recital of findings of congressional inquiries, anecdotes, and allegations of actual occurrences. Therefore, I quote in full the key portions of his 1932 remarks to the United States Senate.[1]

Bulkley begins his speech by tracing the history of commercial bank involvement in securities activities. He observes (*Congressional Record*. 1932, p. 9911; italicised portions quoted by Securities Industry Association, 1985, p. 18): '*When the national banks, through their affiliates, followed into the investment-banking business* after the State

---

[1] The quotations are from the *Congressional Record* (1932) pp. 9910–12. It is tempting to reproduce the entire speech, as it is so well done.

123

banks had established their bond departments and subsequently their own affiliates, *the idea of increased profits more and more obsessed our bankers. . . . Did not professional pride become diverted from the pride of safe and honest banking service to that of profits, greed, expansion, power, and domination?*[1] He then gives the basis for his belief that abuses will result from commercial banks having bond-sales departments or affiliates (ibid., p. 9911; quoted in full by Securities Industry Association, 1985, p. 19):

> Can any banker, imbued with the consciousness that his bond-sales department is, because of lack of securities for sale, losing money and at the same time losing its morale, be a fair and impartial judge as to the necessity and soundness for a new security issue which he knows he can readily distribute through channels which have been expensive to develop but which presently stand ready to absorb the proposed security issue and yield a handsome profit on the transaction?

Bulkley continues with what apparently he believed were factual historical descriptions that speak to the safety and soundness issue. In particular, consider his observation that '[i]t is easy to see why the security business was overdeveloped and why the bankers' clients and country bank correspondents were overloaded with a mass of investments many of which have proved most unfortunate' (ibid.). In retrospect we know that this observation is incorrect, as chapter 3, section III shows. Bulkley then expresses the basic assumption underlying macroeconomic concerns about commercial bank involvement with securities (ibid., pp. 9911–12; italicised portions quoted by Securities Industry Association, 1985, p. 19):

> While the banks competed with each other in the business of finding and distributing issues of investment securities, yet they had at all times one great common interest – none of these profits could be made unless the condition of the securities market was

---

[1] In his appraisal of the Banking Act of 1933, H. Parker Willis (Senator Glass's adviser) evaluated the benefit of the Glass–Steagall provisions thus: 'Under this heading [safeguarding the general stability and responsibility of member banks] we may enumerate the abolition of the security affiliates and the separation of directorates so as, if possible, to recreate the older type of bank board when at its best – a group of non-partisan, disinterested men who have an eye singly to the welfare of the community' (Willis, 1934, pp. 108–9).

such as to assure the absorption of securities. Most of the banks, certainly all the great ones, were interested, therefore, in a good market for capital securities. Can there be any doubt that under such pressure of competition there was an overproduction of capital securities? Can there be any doubt that in order to maintain the market conditions which would absorb the great production of capital securities and produce the big profits for the affiliates and bond departments commercial banks went astray by encouraging an overdevelopment of collateral-security loans? Is it not fair to attribute the vast development of loans on collateral security at least in part to the necessity for keeping up a market condition capable of absorbing capital issues? It does not matter whether this motive was deliberate or subconscious; the fact remains that the banks generally were involved in it, and that if they are permitted to continue in the investment-security business the same motive will be provided for a repetition of the same performance. If, on the other hand, *the business of originating and underwriting investment securities is confined to houses not engaged in deposit banking, then the extent and the desirability of new issues will be subjected to an independent and impartial check.* This should tend to restore public confidence.

Many, if not all economists do not accept Bulkley's claim that bank-loan-fuelled speculation 'pumped up securities prices' or led to or exacerbated the depression.[1] In any event the Glass–Steagall Act does not prevent banks from lending to securities brokers or purchasers. On the other hand, the passage of the Glass–Steagall Act did not restore public confidence in the securities market and in the economy. Economic activity remained depressed until 1941 or 1942, and securities underwriting and trades did not reach pre-depression levels until the 1950s. Indeed, concern for the paucity of new securities issues (particularly those of heavy industry) was such that Senator Glass supported a proposal (not adopted) in 1935 that would have permitted commercial banks to underwrite some investment securities. His last-expressed expectation, that commercial banks might independently and impartially check on new new stock issues if they could not make them, is illogical and inconsistent with the evidence

---

[1] See, for example, Presidential Task Force on Market Mechanisms (1988), study VIII, and Staff of the Board of Governors of the Federal Reserve System (1984), chapter V.

presented later in this chapter. Competition between commercial banks and other underwriters provides the check Bulkley wants; mandated specialisation is more likely to lead to a 'live-and-let-live' division of the market for firms' deposit and underwriting business.

The rest of Senator Bulkley's speech includes exhortations about the proper role of commercial banks and assumptions about abuses. He expresses his philosophy with respect to individuals and households thus (ibid., p. 9912; quoted in full by Securities Industry Association, 1985, p. 19):

> The banker ought to be regarded as the financial confidant and mentor of his depositor. . . . Obviously, the banker who has nothing to sell to his depositors is much better qualified to advise disinterestedly and to regard diligently the safety of depositors than the banker who uses the list of depositors in his savings department to distribute circulars concerning the advantages of this, that, or the other investment on which the bank is to receive an originating profit or a trading profit or any combination of such profits. . . . If we want banking service to be strictly banking service, without the expectation of additional profits in selling something to customers, we must keep the banks out of the investment security business.

Again, the evidence does not support Bulkley's assumption about how bank affiliates operated and the consequences of their securities operations. The only evidence available, the Pecora Hearings (1933, pp. 2018–20), reveals that National City Bank did not solicit its depositors (who were restricted by state-imposed bank branching laws to the New York City area) to do business with the National City Company (which had offices throughout the country). More important, though, is the empirical evidence presented below in this chapter that incorporated commercial bank underwritings performed as well as securities underwritten by private investment and commercial banks and somewhat better than specialised investment banks.

Bulkley then turned to corporate customers (ibid., p. 9912):

> A corporation, having carried its account with a bank, having borrowed from that bank for its ordinary commercial requirements, is confronted with the question of raising long-time funds by the issuance of securities. If it is to have the advice of its banker untainted by the prospect of obtaining an originating or

underwriting profit we must keep the banks out of the investment security business. If we are to relieve the banker of the temptation to put pressure upon his commercial borrower to put out a security issue on which the banker will make either an originating or an underwriting profit we must keep the banks out of the security business.

Senator Bulkley's solution to a possible conflict-of-interest in advice-giving is ill-conceived, for two reasons. First, apparently he assumes that advice given by banks that do not engage in underwriting and other securities services, as a result of their not engaging in such activity, would not be 'tainted' by the banks' concerns for profits that they might be earned indirectly from the advice. A bank that was inclined toward obtaining such profits, however, still could urge its customers to take bank loans rather than issue securities, or it could suggest that its clients use the services of other bank customers, such as investment bankers, who then would compensate the bank with non-interest-bearing deposit balances and recommendations to their customers to use those banks' services. Second, Bulkley does not consider that bank customers have incentives to evaluate advice according to the self-interest of the advice giver. One can more readily perceive the extent of this self-interest when a bank can provide underwriting services directly. Furthermore, if the law prevents banks from engaging in securities underwriting, their customers cannot benefit from economies of scope and from the banks' expertise in underwriting; hence banks' advice would not be worth as much as it would have been had they been active participants in the market. In addition, customers are disadvantaged by having fewer securities sellers and underwriters vying for their business.

There follows Senator Bulkley's recitation of 'abuses' concluding with a rhetorically effective refrain (ibid., p. 9912):

If the public is to be protected against the possibility of bad bank loans being set up into bond issues to be sold to savings depositors of the same banks without the exacting scrutiny of an independent underwriter interested primarily in the soundness of the securities he is about to sell we must prohibit the banks from engaging in the security business. If we are to keep banks from being tempted to make security loans in order to help make a market or to finance the purchase of securities on which the lending bank is making an originating or underwriting commission we must keep banks out of the investment security business. And if we are to save banks from the embarrassment of having to appraise, as collateral security offered by prospective borrowers, the very securities which their own affiliates have sold to those customers we must keep the banks out of the investment-security business.

The evidence from the Glass Subcommittee Hearings (1931 and 1932), the Pecora Hearings (1933 and 1934), and the SEC Report (1940) of investment trusts and companies reviewed in Chapter 4 does not offer proof of 'the abuses here intimated' (as Bulkley put it in the sentence following the last quotation). Nor does the evidence reviewed in section II of this chapter on the performance of commercial-bank-sponsored and other firms' securities underwritings and investments offer proof of deleterious effects of such 'abuses'.

II   THE PERFORMANCE OF SECURITIES UNDERWRITTEN BY BANK AFFILIATES

Had events borne out Senator Bulkley's expectations and if commercial bank customers were not aware that their banks gave them poor advice, then, *ceteris paribus*, the returns on bank-underwritten securities should have been significantly less than the returns on investments presumably disinterested firms underwrote. Here I report on some studies that speak to this comparison of returns. But the reader should keep in mind some caveats about these studies.

The measurement of returns is very difficult. One problem is that *ex ante* expected returns may differ from *ex post* realised returns and yet not indicate good or bad performance. An investor or his or her adviser optimally might choose wisely, but because all risky investments involve an expected distribution of returns, the actual and expected results may differ significantly. Therefore, one cannot learn from *ex post* data whether the initial decision was optimal unless one is willing to assume that the sample is such that extraneous events average out and that the realised average returns equal the returns expected.

One should take into account the risk associated with a security (particularly a bond) that a given issuer brings to market. If investors are risk-neutral or risk-averse, then higher risk securities should offer higher yields, *ex ante*. (*Ex post*, higher risk securities would show higher yields only if investors were risk-averse). Therefore, the investor should take into account the kinds of securities that the different kinds of organisations originate. The size of the organisations also might be an important determinant of the kind of securities handled and of their performance. Fortunately, the two available studies reviewed next have different strengths and weaknesses with respect to these qualifications. Together, these studies offer a reasonably good indication of the performance of securities that commercial bank affiliates and other securities underwriters originate.

Security Originations by Large Banking Houses

Terris Moore (1934) studied the stock market performance of securities originated by the eight largest securities affiliates of commercial banks and by the eight largest private investment banking houses over the years 1925 through 1932. Regardless of their origination year, he evaluated all securities as of 1 March 1933, so his analysis includes most of the Great Depression experience. The study includes 2,526 issues, about one-half of the total dollar volume and one-tenth of the total number of issues sold during the eight-year period. In terms of numbers, 88.7 per cent were bonds, 9.5 per cent were preferred stocks, and 1.8 per cent common stocks. Because there were a much larger number of private investment banks than bank affiliates, Moore's choice of the eight largest from each group results in an underrepresentation of smaller houses. Because Moore and Edwards (whose study I review next) find that smaller organisations tend to originate lower quality securities, the results are biased towards finding that the performance of the private investment banking industry is better than that of the commercial banking industry. Furthermore, J. P. Morgan was a bank, although Moore includes it as one of the eight investment houses. (Indeed, after the passage of the Glass–Steagall Act, Morgan opted to continue operations as a commercial bank rather than as an investment banker.) Kuhn Loeb also accepted deposits. These two firms ranked first and fourth best in the investment banking group with which they are included.

Moore measures bond performance in terms of the percentages of issues (measured in terms of dollars and numbers) rising in price, called, falling in price by various percentages, or defaulted. He measures preferred stock performance by whether the stock is paying dividends, called, passed dividends, or in receivership or bankrupt. The small amount of common stock data precluded its analysis. Moore presents the data for each bank and for aggregates of the commercial bank affiliates and private investment banks. In comparing each group, Moore concludes (ibid., p. 483):

> [T]here is very little, if any, significant difference between the success of the originations of the two groups. The percentage columns for bonds show a slight indication in favor of the security affiliates of commercial banks. . . . The preferred stock history . . . indicates that there is little significant difference in the success achieved by the two groups. Calculated by dollar volume, the private investment bankers show a slightly more successful records; calculated the other way, by number of issues, the security affiliates show a slightly better record.

There is some diversity among the individual originators. The best private investment bank (which also accepted deposits), J. P. Morgan & Co., does better than any security affiliate. But 'the poorest investment banking houses of the eight have a poorer record than the worst of the eight security affiliates' (ibid., p. 482). If Moore had included Morgan and Kuhn Loeb with the commercial bank affiliates as combination commercial-investment banking organisations, this group's underwritings would be seen as outperforming the underwritings of pure investment banking houses.

Moore also divides the data into three periods, 1921–4, 1925–9, and 1930–2, to test the hypothesis that security originators' critical faculties deteriorated during the boom years. He reports that '[t]he originations brought out by these sixteen houses during the 1925–9 period are seen to be only slightly poorer in quality than those brought out in the other two periods' (ibid., pp. 483–4).

Domestic Corporate Bond Flotations Disaggregated by Kind of Company and Originator

Edwards (1942) compares the performance of bonds that affiliate banks (incorporated commercial banks and their affiliates), non-affiliate banks (investment banks that performed no commercial banking operations), and private banks (unincorporated banks that conducted both deposit and security banking) floated. The data include 2,633 bonds with a par value of $20 billion that were outstanding at year-end 1936 and that were issued before the effective data of the Glass–Steagall Act. He classifies the originators by large and small size, large being 'the major investment houses in the period before the passage of the Banking Act of 1933, as listed by the *Wall Street Journal*' (ibid., p. 226). He also identifies the kinds of bonds floated by industry and size of issuer, and finds significant differences among them. Edwards measures performance according to the coverage of the bonds (earnings over a ten year period available to meet fixed charges), price stability between 1930 and 1936, whether or not defaulted, net original return (the higher the return, the riskier the bond, *ex ante*), and a measure of change in value.

After presenting and discussing his various measures, Edwards (ibid., p. 232) concludes:

[T]his study shows that there is no statistical foundation for the belief that specialised banking was superior to integrated banking. There was practically no difference in the investment results of the bonds of non-affiliate and affiliate banks. In fact, the bonds of the private banks performing both commercial and investment operations were superior to those of the non-affiliate and affiliate banks. It would seem therefore that the Banking Act of 1933 separating commercial from investment banking did not rest on factual foundation.

III   SECURITIES UNDERWRITTEN BY THE NATIONAL CITY COMPANY

The securities affiliate of the National City Bank, the National City Company was the largest and most prominent commercial-bank-related securities underwriter.[1] From 1921 through 1933 the company originated or participated in offering securities that other banking houses originated with a total value of $14.4 billion. Of this total, it sold $5.3 billion during 1928 through 1933, representing 33 stock issues valued at $0.4 billion and 538 bond issues valued at $4.9 billion. Independent ratings of the bonds (US and foreign) show that 90 per cent were rated 'investment grade' – Baa or better. Over 85 per cent of the US corporate bond issues offered were of investment grade. In comparison, 75 per cent of all new US corporate

---

[1] I draw the statistics and other descriptions from a Citicorp application to the Federal Reserve Board to engage in some aspects of underwriting and dealing in investment securities (Citicorp, 1985).

straight bonds issued during those years were of investment grade.[1]

Citicorp (1985, p. 6) states that NCC 'provided extensive information regarding securities available for sale. Prospectuses were prepared for new issues, and information was provided at regular intervals regarding issues trading in the secondary market.' Also, as I note in chapter 4 section V, it was contrary to National City Bank's policy for its trust affiliate, the Farmers Trust, to purchase securities from the Bank or Company.

These data and observations are inconsistent with some of the concerns that Senator Bulkley expressed.

IV THE PERFORMANCE OF COMMERCIAL-BANK-SPONSORED INVESTMENT TRUSTS, COMPANIES, AND FUNDS

We can glean some data on the performance of commercial-bank-sponsored investment trusts, companies, and funds and those managed independently or by other firms from the SEC Investment Trusts and Companies study (1940). Only one figure appears there for performance according to the kind of fund and sponsor. This is investors' return over the years 1928–35 calculated as net gain or loss (in parentheses) as a percentage of investors' capital investment at year end. These returns for all investment trusts or companies over the years 1927–35 are (SEC Study, Part 2, 1940, p. 517):

242 management investment companies[2]	(32.3)%
44 semifixed investment trusts	(0.3)
580 unclassified management investment firms	(33.9)
16 common trusts funds[3]	(0.4)

Approximately 15.4 per cent of the 242 management investment companies were bank or bank affiliate sponsored and managed. None of the 44 semifixed investment trust or 580 unclassified manage-

---

[1] Citicorp (1985, footnote 7) points out that the NCC underwritings include convertible debentures, income bonds, and equipment trust certificates in addition to straight debt; hence the comparisons are not precise.

[2] With the companies in the Atlas and Equity groups (which did particularly badly) excluded, the remaining 196 companies returned on average (20.0) per cent.

[3] Source: SEC Study (1939) p. 21.

ment investment firms appears to be commercial bank related. Banks managed all of the 16 common trust funds. Thus, these data indicate that commercial-bank-managed investment companies and trusts did no worse, on average, than non-bank-managed companies and trusts. Unfortunately, the available data do not permit a more precise conclusion.

V CONCLUSIONS

Senator Bulkley's evaluation of the risks to the financial system and to consumers of banking services clearly is based on a moralistic and inoperative concept of how banking ought to operate, and is not at all supported by evidence. Indeed, the evidence is consistently contrary to his and Senator Glass's expectations. Commercial banks offering securities services did not endanger the financial system or abuse the public. To the contrary, the evidence indicates that these banks had lower failure rates and tended to serve the public at least as well as did the underwriters who did not also offer commercial banking services.

6 Restraints on Competition and Political Necessity as Explanations

There is reason to believe that an important reason for the legal separation of commercial and investment banking was a political demand or at least a willingness by both investment and commercial bankers to eliminate competition for a shrinking market and to secure other benefits and avoid more restrictive legislation. In particular, investment bankers not affiliated with commercial banks had incentives to bar their rivals from the investment banking business; many commercial bankers were no longer interested in securities operations; and by this ploy bankers could relatively inexpensively assuage demands by the public, legislators, and the Roosevelt administration for reform.

Prior to the 1930s depression, commercial banks had made great inroads into the business of underwriting and distributing securities. Indeed, the share of private bankers (compared to the share of commercial bankers, directly and through affiliates) in originating bond issues (exclusive of refundings) shrank from 78.0 per cent in 1927 to 54.5 per cent in 1929 and 55.4 per cent in 1930. Private bankers' participations in bond issues similarly declined from 63.2 per cent in 1927 to 48.9 per cent in 1929 and 38.8 per cent in 1930.[1] From 1921 through 1930 the volume of new securities issues was $66 billion, of which $10 billion were issued in 1929. (Peach, 1941, p. 37). Thus, commercial banks were getting an increasing share of an increasing market before the onset of the 1930s depression.[2]

We may attribute their success in the securities market to several

---

[1] Source: Peach (1941), tables III and IV, pp. 109 and 110. Houses issuing less than $20 million per annum are not included. The participation figures reveal only whether a commercial or private bank participated in an issue, not in the amount of its participation. Thus the percentages may overstate the commercial banks' participation. The relative percentages, however, provide a meaningful indication of the growth of commercial bank participation over the period.

[2] However, these numbers understate the market served by organizations that were affected by the Glass–Steagall Act. J. P. Morgan and several other important private bankers also took deposits.

factors. One factor is the banks' apparent positive reputations among their customers, which provided them with goodwill that they could transfer to securities products. Prior to 1933 (when the Federal Deposit Insurance Corporation was established), banks attracted and held depositors by emphasising financial strength and responsibility. By the time individuals were beginning to invest in securities, the banks that offered these services had successfully come through several depressions and recessions.

A second factor is economies of scope and scale in production and distribution that could be realised by joining commercial and investment banking. Although commercial banks' deposit operations were limited to state boundaries, they could (and several did) establish affiliated securities corporations that were permitted to operate nation-wide.[1] Indeed, some of the decline in the pure investment houses' share of the market reflects mergers of these houses with commercial banks (see, for example, Harris, Forbes's merger with Chase Securities and Blair's merger with Bank of America NY).

It is reasonable, therefore, to expect that pure investment bankers would have wanted to use the law to eliminate superior commercial bank competition.[2] Macey (1964) suggests this motive for the passage of the Act. He uses interest-group theory to argue 'that the actual motive behind the passage of the [Glass–Steagall] Act can only have been that of protecting one group – investment bankers – at the expense of another – commercial bankers' (ibid, p. 2). Macey points out that 'any notion that Glass–Steagall can be justified on grounds that commercial banks are somehow made safer by the Act's prohibitions is clearly misguided, since the law, if anything, accomplishes precisely the opposite result' (ibid., p. 13). The Act prevents banks from optimally diversifying their portfolios and from earning higher net profits. Both prohibitions increase the probability of failure. Nor, Macey argues, did the Congress act to increase public confidence in commercial banks or reduce conflicts of interest. 'By removing the

---

[1] See Peach (1941), chapter II for a description of the 'Factors Contributing to the Entrance of National Banks into the Investment Securities Business' and chapter III for a discussion of the 'Legal Aspects of Securities Affiliates'.
[2] Perkins (1971) reviews the hearings that Senator Glass held in 1932 and points out that, while several commercial bankers testified against divorcing investment from commercial banking, '[n]o one from J. P. Morgan & Co, or Kuhn Loeb & Co. had made the trip to Washington. The older investment banking houses who had been losing the competitive battle with the more aggressive commercial banks now thought they saw an opportunity to reestablish their former dominant position in the underwriting field' (ibid., p. 516).

banks' ability to profit from the sale of securities, Congress was not ensuring that banks would provide better advice than investment banks. Congress was ensuring that commercial banks would provide no advice at all' (ibid., 1984, p. 15). We cannot conclude the Glass–Steagall Act to be public interest legislation, he declares, because it reduces public welfare. Hence, he concludes, 'public-spirited justifications for the Act are best achieved by not enforcing the statute rather than by enforcing it' (ibid., 1984, p. 19). Nor, he states, can one describe the Act as 'public sentiment' legislation, because '[i]ncreasing taxes [on banks] would have been a more effective punishment' (ibid.). Consequently, Macey concludes 'that Glass–Steagall clearly represents an agreement between a special interest group and the legislature' (ibid., p. 20).[1]

A review of the key features of legislation related to financial institutions and markets passed in 1933 supports Macey's interest-group explanation.[2] In addition to separating investment and commercial banking (which benefited pure investment banks at the expense of larger commercial banks), the Banking Act of 1933 made illegal the payment of interest on demand deposits (which benefited generally larger, correspondent commercial banks at the expense of depositors, including smaller country respondent banks)[3] and established federal deposit insurance (which benefited small country banks at the expense of large banks). The Act did not permit state, region, or nationwide branching for national banks, which was a change strongly opposed by predominantly small unit banks that wanted federal deposit insurance. The Securities Act of 1933, which the Roosevelt Administration wanted (the President, however, was against deposit insurance), benefited large investment banks at the expense of their smaller rivals, because it imposed requirements that were costly to those rivals but not to the larger investment banks, because those banks' practices were similar to the requirements.

---

[1] Macey also concludes that a judiciary that is subservient to the will of Congress would enforce the bargain struck in 1933 among special interest groups and the legislature. However, he says, the 'judiciary was not a party to the original deal struck in Congress and thus were not privy to the true motives informing the Act' (ibid., p. 34). Furthermore, the 'courts . . . [should] be given some basis in logic to enforce it [special interest legislation]. No such logical underpinnings accompanied Glass–Steagall, and the Act [in recent years] has been eviscerated' (ibid.).

[2] See Benston (1982) for a more complete discussion.

[3] Tom Huertas pointed out to me that National City Bank did not support this provision of the Banking Act of 1933. Apparently, the bank preferred to compete for deposits rather than join with its rivals in a government-sponsored and enforced cartel arrangement.

The stock registration and disclosure requirement, though, exempted commercial banks on the grounds that they already were regulated.

Other special interest motives also probably shaped the legislation. One important consideration was the sharp reduction in new securities flotations before the Act was passed. From 1931 to 1934, the *total* volume of new issues was only $6.4 billion (Peach, 1941, p. 37). By 1933 the number of banks engaged in the securities business had shrunk from 591 in 1929 (459 directly and 132 through affiliates) to 379 (271 directly and 108 through affiliates) (ibid., 1941, table 1, p. 83). Relatively few banks, therefore, had much to lose from the Act. Indeed, considering the low levels of the investment business they were doing, they were able to obtain savings by firing the staff of the affiliates while continuing to maintain the image of banking as secure, though possibly low paid, employment.[1]

Second, considering the public opprobrium that was being heaped on commercial bankers as a result of massive bank failures, losses on securities investments that the bankers had sold, and damaging charges of dishonesty against bankers, it seems likely that most bankers would consider the forced separation of commercial and investment banking a cheap price to pay to forestall more onerous legislation. In particular, as Kennedy (1973, pp. 212–13) points out,

> The sensational manner of these [the Pecora] hearings, as well as their timing, on the eve of the national moratorium [bank holiday], inflamed public resentment. Outrage centered upon the security affiliates. . . . Separated banking encountered no opposition after March 1933. After the testimony of Charles E. Mitchell before the Banking and Currency Committee [the Pecora hearings], few defended the affiliate. Bankers who had rejected the idea now saw the virtue of the divorce and climbed aboard Glass's bandwagon.

Third, Senator Glass acquired an important ally in Winthrop W. Aldrich, the new chairman of the Chase National Bank. In March 1933, he publicly reversed the bank's opposition to the legal separation of investment and commercial banking voiced by the former chairman, Albert Wiggin, attempting to distance himself and the Rockefeller interests (who controlled Chase) from the previous administration of the bank. Chase had announced it was separating

---

[1] Perkins (1971, pp. 523–4, citing the *NY Times*) reports that '[b]y the end of 1933, over one thousand employees of the Chase Securities Company had been released'.

from its securities affiliate. It made this announcement during the March Bank Holiday when Chase (and other banks) had to secure a licence from the Treasury Department to reopen for business. Aldrich not only supported the divorcement of investment and commercial banking for all banks, but also proposed additional measures that would remove private investment bankers (J. P. Morgan, in particular) from competing with commercial bankers by making private bankers also subject to the provisions of the Glass–Steagall Act.[1] The Act included these restrictions.

Thus, a legislative bargain may have been struck. Investment bankers and commercial bankers were able to divide a dwindling market. Smaller unit bankers did not have to contend with greatly expanded branch banking and with depositors' switching to larger, apparently safer banks, and larger correspondent bankers got a government-enforced cartel that reduced to zero explicit interest payments on demand deposits. Congress protected the small depositor from loss and appeared to be doing something about the banking crisis. The administration reformed the securities markets that appeared to contemporaries to have been the root cause of the 1930s Great Depression. And bankers made the best of a bad situation. The organised interest groups appear generally to have benefited, at that time, although consumers of investment services lost out in this now less competitive environment, as they were left with fewer options.

---

[1] Aldrich proposed that: 'First, no corporation or partnership should be permitted to accept deposits without being subject to the same regulations as commercial banks; second, no corporation dealing in securities should be permitted to take any deposits at all' (Bacon, 1933, p. 3955).

7 Commercial Banks' Federal 'Safety Net'

Those who do not want the Glass–Steagall Act rescinded argue that the federal government provides commercial banks with a 'safety net', which it should not extend to cover securities activities. As the Securities Industry Association (SIA) (1987, p. 2) testifies: 'The federal government and the taxpayer support the banking system so that banks will perform their role of objective lender to the rest of society, not to support dealing in the capital markets or investment in real estate'. The SIA entitled section II of its statement, 'The Federal Safety Net, Taxpayer Risk and Unfair Advantage'. Unfortunately, I cannot find a precise definition of the federal 'safety net' either in this document or elsewhere. I believe, nevertheless, that those who argue against the federal government's allowing banks to engage in securities activities have four, somewhat interrelated, aspects of the federal 'safety net' in mind: (i) federal deposit insurance; (ii) loans from the Federal Reserve banks' discount windows; (iii) government intervention to prevent bank runs and a loss of depositor confidence in the banking system; and (iv) government intervention to prevent disruption that the failure of financial service firms might cause.

Our concern about the four aspects of the 'safety net' takes two forms. One is the cost to the federal agencies and to taxpayers of maintaining the 'safety net'. The second is the cost to the economy should the government have to use the 'safety net', and the suboptimal allocative effects that its presence engenders. Both concerns are based on an assumption that banks' involvement with securities would increase the costs of the system and the probability that it might fail. Chapter 8 explores the competitive advantages that banks might obtain from the federal 'safety net'.

I FEDERAL DEPOSIT INSURANCE

Federal-agency deposit insurance for up to $100,000 per account at each institution protects depositors in almost all chartered depository institutions (commercial and savings banks, savings and loan associations, and credit unions). For commercial and most savings banks, the Federal Deposit Insurance Corporation (FDIC) administers two funds, the Bank Insurance Fund, which covers the deposits insured by the FDIC, and the Savings Association Insurance Fund, which covers deposits formerly insured by the Federal Savings and Loan Insurance Corporation (FSLIC).[1] The National Credit Union Insurance Fund (NCUIF) insures credit union deposits.

The federal insurance agencies impose direct and indirect insurance premiums and fees on their member institutions. The direct premiums are a flat percentage of domestic deposits, unadjusted for the risks the institutions take. The indirect 'premiums' assume the form of examinations, supervision, and regulations that impose costs on the institutions in rough proportion to the risks they impose on the agencies. For example, federal (and state) examiners spend more time at and demand more material and employee time from banks that appear to be operated in an unusual or unsafe and unsound manner. Such banks also get supervisory criticisms, which require managers' and directors' time to resolve, and cease and desist orders, which subject the banks to legal and other costs. Regulations and laws impose reporting and capital requirements on banks, and prevent them from supplying some services, such as securities underwriting and trading.

In addition, depository institutions pay fees that offset some of the examination and supervisory costs that federal and state agencies incur. The Comptroller of the Currency and many states impose per diem fees on banks they examine and supervise, and all Federal Reserve member banks and other chartered institutions offering transactions (demand deposit) accounts must keep non-interest-bearing accounts at Federal Reserve banks. Furthermore, the imposition of a risk-based capital requirement (imperfect though it be), which is scheduled to go into effect by 1992, will tend to equate the costs and benefits of deposit insurance.[2] Thus, it is not clear whether the deposit insurance aspect of the federal safety net is a net benefit to commercial banks in the aggregate.[3] It is likely, however, that the

---

[1] The Financial Institutions Reform, Recovery, and Enforcement Act (FIRREA) (enacted 9 August 1989) dissolved the FSLIC and the Federal Home Loan Bank Board (which chartered and supervised savings and loan associations), transferring their functions the FDIC and the Office of Thrift Supervision, a newly created burea of the US Treasury Department.

[2] The requirement follows the capital standard adopted by the Basle Committee on Banking Regulations and Supervisory Practices (the Cooke committee) sponsored by the Bank for International Settlements.

[3] See Kane (1985) for a contrary view.

cost of deposit insurance is less than the benefit derived for some, if not all, banks.[1]

One might think that all insured banks find FDIC membership worth the cost, because all but a few hundred US chartered banks are members. Federal Reserve member banks (which includes all national banks), however, are legally required to be members of the FDIC. Most states also require the banks they charter to be members of the FDIC. Hence, one cannot tell how many banks might opt for privately provided or no deposit insurance if they had the opportunity to do so.

To date, the cost of commercial banks' federal deposit insurance has not been imposed explicitly on the general taxpayer. The FDIC's operating costs and insurance payouts and the operating expenses of the other bank regulation agencies have been met entirely with assessments and fees imposed on banks, and from earnings on reserve deposits banks must keep at Federal Reserve banks. The only cost imposed on the taxpayers has been the contingent opportunity value of possible transfers from the US Treasury should the FDIC be declared bankrupt.[2] This could occur as the solvency of the FDIC is endangered by losses to some banks on loans to depressed industries, such as farming and petroleum exploration and development, and to foreign countries. (Interest-rate losses and real-estate-loan losses at savings and loan associations have bankrupted the FSLIC.) As a consequence, the taxpayers' resources may be called upon, although for commercial banks, at least, it is much more likely that banks and their customers will pay the cost.

Federal deposit insurance nevertheless involves a potentially important moral hazard problem that could result in costs being imposed on the economy.[3] To the extent that these agencies do not directly or indirectly charge depository institutions an actuarially correct rate for insurance, institutions have incentives to incur more risks. Effective control of the moral-hazard problem requires answers to two ordered questions. The first is, to what extent is there a

---

[1] Marcus and Shaked (1984) estimate the value of federal deposit insurance for 40 bank holding companies in 1979 and 1980, using an option pricing model and stock market data. They find that deposit insurance is 'overpriced' on average, although some banks are charged considerably more or less than its estimated value. Ronn and Verma (1986) conduct a similar analysis of 43 bank holding companies for 1983. They report that the average value of deposit insurance is almost exactly the same as the amount charged, with the value to some banks being considerably more or less than the amount charged.

[2] Deposit insurance and bank regulation also may have resulted in a non-Pareto-optimal level of risk taking, resulting in welfare losses to society.

[3] See Kane (1985) and Benston *et al.* (1986, chapter 3) for elaboration.

true moral hazard problem, which determines the extent to which opportunistic bankers must be constrained? The second is, how effective are alternative methods of dealing with risk-taking? I defer a discussion of these methods of control until I consider the federal 'safety net' aspects of Federal Reserve loans and prevention of banking crises, because the control procedures also relate to them.

II FEDERAL RESERVE BANK DISCOUNT WINDOW LOANS

The Federal Reserve banks may make secured loans to banks (including savings and loan associations) that keep reserves with them. (Because the Federal Reserve banks originally made these loans by discounting member banks' loans presented to them, they are called 'discount window' loans.) Ordinarily, discount window loans are a very small percentage of most banks' borrowing and are made at rates close to market rates. Hence, there is usually not much of a subsidy present. But when a bank faces a liquidity crisis, generally as a result of an unexpected run off of deposits, and the market is unsure of its solvency, the bank can turn to the Fed as 'the lender of last resort'. In this event the loan usually is at less than the market rate, because if this were not the case, banks presumably would borrow in the market. But banks also must hold reserves at Federal Reserve banks on which no interest is paid. The subsidy on discount window loans, therefore, is more than offset by the tax paid by banks in the form of foregone interest on their non-interest-bearing required reserves.

Whether or not borrowings from the Federal Reserve include much of a subsidy, the possibility that these loans might be made provides little in the way of a 'safety net' that benefits banks, because the loans are almost always fully secured.[1] Hence, if the loans are not repaid, the borrowing bank's stockholders and other creditors absorb the loss. Furthermore, as I discuss next, the Federal Reserve can maintain the stability of the banking system without serving as a lender of last resort. Therefore, this aspect of the 'safety net' is not relevant to the issue of the separation of commercial and investment banking.

---

[1] The existence of a borrowing facility that banks *might* use necessarily confers a benefit.

III FEDERAL RESERVE INTERVENTION TO PREVENT A BANKING SYSTEM CRISIS OR FAILURE

The Federal Reserve can prevent (or cause) a financial-system crisis by its control of the money supply. The Fed most efficiently exercises this control with open market operations, wherein it buys and sells US Treasury obligations, thereby increasing and decreasing bank reserves and the nation's money supply. The other, less efficient and less used methods of affecting banks' reserves include controls over discount window loans and changes in required reserve ratios. None of these methods depends on regulation of the activities that banks conduct or limitations on the assets in which they invest.

Some hold out loss of depositor confidence in individual banks as an important concern for the stability of the banking system. Before federal depositor insurance was established, bank runs were an occasional problem, although the importance of runs as a cause rather than an effect of economic distress has been questioned.[1] Whatever the past record, this concern is presently not relevant. Now only depositors with balances of more than $100,000 need be concerned with their banks' solvency (assuming that the federal deposit agencies do not default on their obligations). But virtually no depositors have incurred losses. In all but a few instances other banks (often with FDIC assistance) assumed all liabilities of failed banks, depositors with account balances over the insurance limit could withdraw their funds before the authorities closed the bank, or depositors could offset their deposit balances with their loan liabilities at the same bank. In any event, US banks have not experienced economically significant (contagious) runs since the FDIC's establishment.[2]

But even were depositors to lose confidence in a particular bank or group of banks, there need not be a systemic problem. The consequence would be either a redistribution of banking resources

---

[1] See Kaufman (1988) for a review of the record of bank runs and an analysis of their impact and means of resolving them. Also see Tallman (1988) for an analysis of bank panics during the National Banking era (1863–1914). Both papers question the generally held belief that bank runs and panics were primarily responsible for major economic downturns.

[2] Depositors with uninsured balances appeared to have withdrawn funds in the period immediately prior to the failure of Franklin National, Continental Illinois, and First Republic (Texas). However, these banks were insolvent. Swary (1986), however, found no evidence of runs on other banks (contagion) as a result of the problems and failure of the Continental Illinois bank.

to other, more respected banks, which would not change total bank reserves and little affect total bank lending; or there could be a run to currency, which the Federal Reserve could facilitate with open market operations so as to maintain the money supply. For example, consider what might happen if even a very large bank's depositors thought it was insolvent. Depositors with accounts under $100,000 would not be concerned. Other depositors might remove their funds. But they would be unlikely to keep the funds in currency, as they then would be subject to the risk of theft and be unable to write cheques and deposit new funds received. Hence, they would either transfer their accounts to banks they believed to be sound or they would buy safe securities, such as US Treasury obligations. The sellers of the securities would be most unlikely to keep the funds in currency, because they would have traded safe interest-bearing obligations for unsafe, non-interest-bearing cash. Instead they would deposit the funds received in a bank. In either event, therefore, large depositors would transfer funds among banks rather than from banks to currency. Although these transfers of deposit accounts would affect individual banks, there would be little effect on the banking system.[1] Even if some depositors were so fearful of the entire banking system's (but not the government's) solvency that they converted their deposits to currency, the Federal Reserve could replace the lost reserves by open market purchases of US Treasury obligations or of other assets. Hence, depositor confidence in individual banks is not necessary for maintaining a stable money supply or for banking system stability.

IV GOVERNMENT INTERVENTION TO PREVENT DISRUPTIONS DUE TO THE FAILURE OF FINANCIAL SERVICE FIRMS GENERALLY

A final concern is that the government might take actions to prevent the failure of non-bank firms or the non-bank affiliates of banks because of fear that such failures will disrupt the economy. These actions can have two outcomes that some many consider undesirable. One such outcome is the transfer of resources by the government

---

[1] *Ex post* the economy would suffer transactions costs. But *ex ante*, the costs of the economy are likely to be smaller or negative as banks conduct their operations to avoid runs and less dramatic transfers. See Kaufman (1988) for a further explication.

to a particular group, for example stockholders, customers, and employees of the firms that would have failed absent government intervention. The second such outcome is the welfare cost of suboptimal resource allocation because of additional risk-taking by the protected firms' managers. More failures might occur because the market prices of securities often are more variable than the prices of assets in which banks presently can invest. Thus, opponents of repeal of the Glass–Steagall Act warn that banks that deal in and underwrite securities or that hold equity securities (either as long-term direct investments or as a consequence of being securities dealers and underwriters) are more likely to fail and would have to be 'bailed out' by the Federal Reserve, the FDIC, or some other government agency.

One counter argument to the possible extension of the federal 'safety net' to banks were they permitted to deal in securities is that the government already has extended protection to the securities markets. The Federal Reserve intervened in the market in 1970 by increasing the money supply when it feared that the commercial paper market would be disrupted should the Penn Central Railroad default on its debts. The Fed also intervened after the October 1987 market crash, to increase the liquidity available to securities firms. A second counter-argument is that the government effectively can restrain banks' excessive risk-taking. A third is that securities operations and holdings are not likely to cause bank failures, directly or indirectly. The following sections review evidence about the last two counter-arguments.

V THE ADDITIONAL RISK OR RISK REDUCTION OF BANKS' SECURITIES ACTIVITIES

In sum then, only two of the four federal 'safety net' aspects might be affected by activities (such as securities operations) undertaken by banks: deposit insurance and extension of the safety net to securities markets. Both are of real concern because the extension might give banks and securities firms incentives to take excessive risks. This concern, however, requires that securities activities provide banks with an opportunity they presently do not have to take such risks.

Before I review the evidence on the riskiness of securities activities, I must point out that there is little reason to believe that banks' involvement with securities would increase their propensity or ability to take risks. First consider risk-taking propensity, which is a function of the returns expected from risk-taking and the decision maker's preference for or aversion to risk. Such preferences are matters of taste. Banks *per se* are not people – banks have no taste for risk – and bank owners can express their preferences by constructing portfolios of securities and other asset holdings that provide their desired combinations of risk and return. Bank owners and managers whose wealth is concentrated in a specific bank, though, may operate their banks to fulfill their preferences concerning risk. Most economists assume that people's tendencies in these instances are towards risk aversion, on the assumption of decreasing marginal utility of wealth.[1] Bank owners and managers with diversified portfolios of wealth are more likely to be risk-neutral. Thus, there is little reason to expect risk-preferring behaviour, *ceteris paribus*. And, in any event there is no reason for bankers' involvement with securities compared to other kinds of activities to affect their attitudes towards risk, unless it can be shown that securities offer them opportunities to take or avoid risk that the range of activities in which they presently can engage cannot meet.

The return from risk-taking depends on the distribution of expected outcomes and the probabilities that each outcome might occur.[2] Deposit insurance affects those outcomes only if it is not correctly priced. If the premium does not reflect the risk of loss that the FDIC might bear, bankers could benefit by taking more risks. In effect, they could play the game, 'heads I win, tails the FDIC loses'.[3] A riskier project, then, would have a higher expected return than a safer project, all other things equal. The higher the capital required, though, the lower the return from risk-taking, because the

---

[1] Decreasing marginal utility assumes that a given additional amount of wealth is valued less than the same amount of wealth already in hand, or losing wealth reduces one's welfare more than gaining the same amount of wealth. Consequently, people will not take risks unless they are compensated more than proportionately to the expected gain. (The fun or thrill of gambling is part of the compensation.)

[2] For example, an investment might yield -100, $+130$ or $+150$ with probabilities .30, .50 and .20. The expected return, then, is calculated thus:

Outcome	×	Probability	=	Expected Return
-100	×	.30	=	-30
$+130$	×	.50	=	$+65$
$+150$	×	.20	=	$+\underline{30}$
		total return	=	$+\underline{\underline{65}}$

[3] In the example given, if the FDIC absorbs the -100 outcome, the expected return is $65+30=95$.

capital holders would have to absorb a greater proportion of the loss.[1] The activities in which banks lawfully can engage do not affect the returns, though, unless a particular activity allows them to take more risks than they otherwise could have taken *and* they want to take more risk.

It seems clear that, except for conducting presently prohibited securities-related activities, banks now are permitted to take as high a level of risk as they demand. Banks can make loans to such risky borrowers as oil and gas explorers, developers and producers, real estate developers, single-crop farmers, underdeveloped and Communist countries, and capital goods manufacturers. They can invest in fixed-interest long-maturity obligations, purchase and sell interest rate options and futures contracts, and they can take positions in foreign exchange. They can expand and contract branch networks (where state law permits), develop new services that may not succeed (such as home computer banking), and construct buildings much larger than their operations required. All of these permitted activities have resulted in banks incurring losses, some sufficient to cause insolvency. It is difficult to understand how securities activities could increase the amount of risk that a bank is now legally permitted to take, with the exception that some bankers may be so inexperienced that they would not realise the extent to which securities activities expose them to risk.

Proponents of allowing banks to deal in and hold all types of securities suggest that the result could be a decrease in bank risk. The decrease could come from two sources. The first source is increased profits from higher returns and, hence, higher capital. Litan (1987, pp. 65–6), for example (in a discussion of benefits to competition of unrestricted bank entry into investment banking), provides these statistics:

> between 1975 and 1984, securities underwriters as a group earned 16.2 per cent on equity after taxes. This return on equity is the highest profit level recorded by any of the financial services listed. However, profits were even higher at the ten largest investment banks, which . . . dominate corporate securities writing in the United States. . . . These institutions earned an average of 21.5 per cent on equity after taxes between 1975 and 1984, or more

---

[1] In the example, if the capital holders absorb half of the loss, the expected return is 15+65+30 =80.

than nine percentage points more than commercial banks. Even if the variability (or riskiness) of profits that these institutions recorded is considered, their profits still outdistance those of other financial services. . . .

The high profits among securities underwriters conceal the high salaries and profit-sharing draws that investment banks pay their personnel, a fact consistent with the tendency of firms in imperfectly competitive markets to incur excessive costs.

Similarly, Morgan (1984, table 4, p. 20) reports annual after-tax returns on equity from 1970 through 1983 for large investment companies ranging between 19 per cent and 30 per cent compared to a range of 13 per cent to 16 per cent for the ten largest bank holding companies.

I should point out several important shortcomings of the numbers indicating higher profits for securities firms than for banks. First, the returns to investment banking during the period include a large proportion of fee income from services that banks can legally offer (for example, advice on leveraged buyouts). The higher reported returns to investment banking, therefore, may represent the comparative advantages that investment bankers enjoy.[1] Second, the higher returns may reflect the higher variance of earnings that investment bankers experience. Third, if banks were to engage in investment banking by buying existing securities firms, they would most likely pay a premium that captures any higher-than-normal returns. Hence, the banks' after-acquisition returns would not be a simple weighted sum of pre-merger returns. Similarly, banks' *de novo* entry into investment banking would entail significant start-up costs. But banks could achieve higher net profits if they experienced economies of scope when they produce and market securities products together with their other financial services.

The second source of potentially lower risk is a less than perfect correlation of returns or cash flows from securities activities and banks' other activities that is sufficient to offset any higher standard deviation (a generally employed measure of risk) from securities activities. Total standard deviation is the square root of a weighted sum of the variances of each individual activity and the covariances

---

[1] These advantages, however, may be enhanced by the investment bankers' legal ability to underwrite and distribute securities, a service that commercial banks are not permitted to offer.

of the activities. Thus, although a new investment alone may present a greater standard deviation than existing ones, if its returns or cash flows are negatively correlated with those of existing investments, the total (portfolio) standard deviation could be lower than each of the individual standard deviations.[1] If the returns from commercial and investment banking are positively but less than perfectly correlated, the two activities combined offer less risk than the sum of each risk.

The appropriate measure of risk, however, is not total standard deviation, but the probability that a bank will become insolvent and impose costs on the FDIC, other banks, and the economy. Total standard deviation does not measure this risk, because the statistic treats the up-side and down-side occurrences equally. For example, consider a bank that experiences a return on equity that varies between 7 and 9 per cent per year and an investment company that experiences a return of between 10 and 30 per cent, with zero covariance between their returns. If the bank purchases the investment company for the amount of its equity, the resulting firm's variance of returns will be higher than that of the old bank, all other things being equal. But its risk of insolvency will be lower, because both its new lowest expected return and expected average return are higher than those for the bank alone. A correct analysis would compare the amount of the combined institutions' expected loss and their economic capital with the same measure for the bank alone.[2]

VI EVIDENCE ON THE RISK OF COMBINING COMMERCIAL AND INVESTMENT BANKING

Researchers have taken four approaches to studying the effect on total risk and return of combining investment and commercial banks, should the Glass–Steagall Act be repealed: (i) failure rates of banks in the pre-Glass–Steagall period that engaged in securities transactions or held securities compared to similar banks that did not; (ii) analyses and simulations based on the measured returns to commer-

---

[1] Standard deviation is the square root of variance. The formula for total (portfolio) variance is $w^2 var_i + (1-w)^2 var_k + 2w(1-w) covar_{i,k}$, where w = the weight of asset i or k in the portfolio, var = the variance of each asset, and $covar$ = their covariance. Covariance is related to correlation ($corr$) as follows: $covar_{i,k} = corr_{i,k}\ sd_i sd_k$, where sd = standard deviation.

[2] See Santomero and Vinso (1977) for a formal analysis.

cial and investment banking and the distribution of those returns; (iii) correlations of cash flows from commercial and investment banking; and (iv) distribution of gains and losses from common stock underwriting.

Failures of Banks Related to Their Securities Activities or Holdings

As reviewed in Chapter 3, Section V, White (1986) studied the survival experience during the Great Depression of national banks that did compared to those that did not actively deal in securities. He reports that only 7.2 per cent (15 in number) of the banks with securities operations failed. In comparison, 26.3 per cent of all national banks failed. All but one of the banks with securities operations were relatively small; the largest had total assets of $180 million, and its security affiliate's assets were 10.7 per cent of its total assets. The next largest had total assets of $37.1 million, and the third largest had $7.8 million in total assets. Thus, almost all of the 15 failed national banks with securities operations were relatively small. Furthermore, considering factors other than securities activities, White (1986) found a lower probability of failure for banks that engaged in securities activities. Data analysed in Chapter 3 Section VI on the relationship between banks' holdings of securities (other than domestic governmental obligations) and their failure rates during the 1930s depression also indicate that losses on securities played a very minor role in the over 11,000 failures and mergers experienced at that time.

Since 1933, the law has allowed US commercial banks to conduct securities operations only at overseas branches or affiliates. Only one of these banks failed, Continental Illinois National Bank. But loan defaults, especially oil and gas loans purchased through the Penn Square Bank, account for its failure, not its overseas securities operations. Thus, the only available evidence does not support the hypothesis that banks' securities activities or holdings increase the only relevant measure of risk, the failure of banks that imposes costs on depositors or on other banks and the economy.

Returns and Their Distribution

The second method of estimating the effect of combining commercial and investment banking examines the returns and their distribution from commercial and investment banking. Returns are measured with both accounting and securities market data. The researchers then combine these data and conduct statistical tests to see how the combined return and the standard deviation of the returns (the measure of risk) might change. The numerous extant studies have been cited as supporting the repeal or continuation of the Glass–Steagall Act. These studies, unfortunately, suffer from five basic shortcomings, which I delineate next. These limitations should be kept in mind when reading the brief reviews of the studies that follow this subsection.

Important Shortcomings

One shortcoming, discussed earlier in section V, is the inappropriate use of total (portfolio) standard deviation as a measure of risk. This measure provides information only if it is lower as a result of combining commercial and investment banking. If this measure is higher, then without considering the amount of economic capital available to absorb expected losses, one cannot discern whether the consequence might or might not be a greater probability of insolvency.

A second shortcoming is that returns are measured with accounting data. These data often provide poor measures of economic values and changes in these values over time. In particular, the data are not adjusted for price level changes. Hence, *ceteris paribus*, rates of return will appear to be higher for longer-lived organisations during periods of inflation. Assets and liabilities (particularly those of banks) generally are not stated at economic market values. Hence, banks' net income will be misstated and appear to be less variable than the net income that investment banks report. Banks can smooth earnings by choosing the amounts of credit losses to recognise and by selling assets (particularly bonds) to record already experienced losses and gains. Expected returns to equity capital are not included as expenses. Hence, *ceteris paribus*, more heavily capitalised firms will appear to have higher returns. Investment banks tend to record returns on their human capital as salary expenses. Hence, *ceteris paribus*, investment banks' net profits appear lower than those of commercial banks.

Third, many studies use past data only from existing firms, thereby excluding failed firms. This sample truncation imparts to the data a selection bias that tends to understate the probability of failure.

Fourth, the use of variance as a measure of risk assumes that the probability of failure follows a normal distribution with independently distributed annual outcomes. An additional assumption is that . the period from which the data are drawn includes all possible negative outcomes. Experience indicates otherwise. Banks that fail, for example, often have stable income for years that they derive from undiversified portfolios. Then some unfortunate event occurs, such as a sharp reduction in oil prices or a drought; the banks suffer massive defaults, and the losses cause insolvency. Thus, the distribution of past failures and losses may not be normally distributed, and the sample from which the standard deviation of returns is derived may not include disasters (such as a major drought or depression). As a result, a sample of past measured experience may provide a poor measure of the probability of future failure.

Fifth, studies using data from the post Glass–Steagall period necessarily cannot measure the actual effect of combining commercial and investment banking. Economies of scope and scale from the combination cannot be measured. Nor are the costs to banks of acquiring or establishing investment operations included. In actual practice bankers should try to combine only activities that would tend to optimise their desired risk-return combination. Researchers cannot know enough about the data they use to simulate these combinations. Hence, their results need not predict what would happen were banks permitted to engage in securities activities.

Review of Empirical Findings

White (1986) is the only researcher who used data from banks that actually conducted a full range of securities activities. Other factors accounted for, he found that these banks had higher returns and similar variances of returns compared to banks that did not engage in securities activities. As I note above, banks with securities operations also experienced lower rates of failure, *ceteris paribus*. (See Chapter 3 Section V for a more extensive discussion of White's study.)

Heggestad (1975) correlated the annual profitability (net profits/ assets) of commercial banks with the profitability of investment companies over the period of 1953–67. He found a correlation coefficient of −.12, which indicates that combining the activities would reduce the variance of total returns. Litan (1987, p. 86) conducted a similar study for the period 1962–82. He found a statistically insignificant correlation coefficient of −.11 for this period, and a correlation coefficient of .06 for the subperiod 1973–82. Stover (1982), however, found a relatively large, positive correlation between the earnings of commercial and investment banks. This finding suggests that the variance of commercial banks' returns would be higher were the two activities combined, assuming that the variance of investment banks' returns is greater than the variance of commercial banks' returns.

Several other papers calculate efficient combinations of various financial activities. Meinster and Johnson (1974) used profitability data for the period 1954–69. Litan (1987, pp. 89–95) conducted a similar study for the period of 1961–82. Eisemann (1976) did the same, using average monthly rates of return between December 1961 and December 1968 on the shares of corporations principally engaged in commercial or investment banking (as well as on other activities). All three studies found significant improvements of returns relative to risks when commercial and investment banking (and other congeneric activities) were combined. Stover (1982) similarly found that an optimal portfolio of activities from the point of view of higher total market value would include both commercial and investment banking.

Brewer, Fortier, and Pavel (1988) used stock market returns to measure risk.[1] They found that the standard deviation of daily returns, measured over three years (1980, 1982, and 1986), was considerably greater for securities brokers and dealers (3.07) compared to bank holding companies (0.47). The correlation between the returns, however, was relatively low (.30). Brewer, Fortier, and Pavel calculated the standard deviation of returns from a hypothetical combination of a bank holding company and a securities broker-dealer. With securities at 5 per cent of the total, the standard deviation (s.d.) is .51; with securities at 10 per cent of the total the s.d. is .65; with securities at 25 per cent of the total, the s.d. is .94. They do not provide data that would allow an interpretation of the magnitude of these numbers, other than the obvious ordinal conclusion that combining securities with banking increases the standard deviation of returns. If no other gains were forthcoming, such as economies of scope and higher returns, this study indicates that combining commercial and investment banking would increase risk somewhat.

Boyd and Graham (1988) use both accounting and stock market

---

[1] They also provide a useful table summarising the findings of 18 earlier studies.

data for samples of 146 bank holding companies and eleven securities firms measured over 1971–84. Unfortunately, they misclassify 6 of the 11 securities firms because these engage primarily in other activities.[1] The other 5 firms are large securities companies or diversified financial service companies with large broker-dealer subsidiaries.[2] Their sample does not include large, privately held securities firms, such as Goldman Sachs or Drexel Burnham Lambert, or firms such as Bear Stearns or Morgan Stanley that went public after 1984. Nor is Shearson-Lehman-Hutton, perhaps the largest securities firm in the United States included, because it is owned by American Express. Hence, the comparison Boyd and Graham report between banks and securities firms is of doubtful usefulness for the present issue.

Boyd and Graham report a median accounting return on equity (and standard deviation on the return) of 13.12 per cent (0.03) for the bank holding companies and 16.52 per cent (0.09) for the 'securities' firms. These groups' stock market returns (and associated standard deviations) are 15.62 per cent (0.27) and 28.65 per cent (0.52) respectively. Thus, although the 'securities' firms experienced higher risk than bank holdings companies, the 'security' firms' returns were significantly greater. If these data were normally distributed, they would indicate a very small (much less than 1 per cent) probability of negative income for either type of company. Boyd and Graham calculated the effect on return and standard deviation of random combinations of a bank holding company and 'securities' firm. Because the bank holding companies are larger, their median share of the combined total assets is 79 per cent. The resulting median annual accounting return on equity (and standard deviation) is 14.06 (0.05) per cent, compared to 13.02 (0.03) per cent for bank holding companies alone. In terms of market values, the median return (and standard deviation) is 21.56 (0.36) per cent, compared to 15.62 (0.27) per cent for bank holding companies alone. They present a measure

---

[1] The 6 firms include Diversified Industries (whose principal activity is metal trading and reclaiming metals), Dryfus Corporation (primarily an investment adviser and manager of mutual funds), Fidata Corporation (a provider of computerised record keeping and trust services), Integrated Resources (which deals in limited partnership investment programmes and insurance underwriting), Inter-Regional Financial Group (a diversified financial services holding company with broker-dealer and real-estate syndication subsidiaries), and A. G. Edwards (a holding company with a mid-sized broker-dealer subsidiary). I am indebted to Brian Gendreau for identifying this misclassification.

[2] These five are First Boston, E. F. Hutton Group, Merrill Lynch & Co., Paine Webber, and Philbro Saloman.

of possible bankruptcy, calculated as the probability that a loss for a year would exceed average net profits plus equity. The probability is greater for the combination of 'securities' and banking than for banking alone, but (assuming normality) it is trivially small in either case.[1]

Eisenbeis and Wall (1984) took a somewhat different and theoretically more defensible approach. They reasoned that the prices of a bank's fixed-income securities (bonds) would decline if 'the market' viewed the merger of the bank with a securities or other firm to be risk-increasing, because bond-holders cannot obtain the gains that the merged firm might achieve, but they would absorb the losses. Eisenbeis and Wall examine four kinds of mergers: banks acquiring discount brokers; financial firms acquiring other financial firms; financial firms acquiring non-bank banks; and non-financial firms acquiring financial firms. They find no significant bond market reaction to any of these combinations.

Finally, several studies examine the effect on risk of actual combinations of banking and other financial activities in subsidiaries of holding companies. Although these studies do not include investment banking (as this combination is not legal), they do provide some interesting insights. Wall's (1987) paper is perhaps the most comprehensive of the group (which includes several of the papers just discussed). He investigates separately, in combination, and as actually consolidated the returns on equity, standard deviations, and probability of failure of 267 bank holding companies' (BHCs) banking and non-banking subsidiaries (the universe for which data were available), over the period 1976–84. He finds that 'diversification into non-bank activities may lower risk . . . [but] the differences in prob-

---

[1] Wall and Eisenbeis (1984) use industry data over the period 1970–80 and report a higher coefficient of variation for investment banking than for commercial banking, but a negative correlation between the returns. I do not review their work here because the authors inform me that they found some errors in the data. Nor do I review a working paper by Kwast (1988) because of some important measurement problems. Kwast calculated the returns, etc. to the securities and non-securities operations of banks by quarter over the years 1976–85. Unfortunately, he could only measure returns before operating expenses, which tends to bias securities returns positively. Securities returns are based on mark-to-market data, while non-securities returns are based on historical accounting data, which imparts a positive bias to the standard deviation of securities returns. Furthermore, the securities activities he analyses are only those permissible under Glass–Steagall: essentially government obligations and (to a much smaller extent) bankers' acceptances. He finds much higher returns and standard deviation of returns for securities compared to non-securities operations and small opportunities for costless diversification.

abilities are statistically insignificant' (pp. 321–2). Wall's paper is particularly notable, because he also explored the risk posed by the non-bank subsidiaries of holding companies that had the most and least risky bank subsidiaries. He reports that '[o]verall, these results suggest that non-bank subsidiaries may reduce the riskiness of the most risky BHCs'. Brewer's (1988) work, which used the daily stock market returns of 40 BHCs over the period of 1979–85 to study the relationship of risk (measured as the standard deviation of returns) and the percentage of assets invested in non-bank activities (and other variables) compliments Wall's findings. Brewer (1988, p. 6) reports that '[t]he sign of the coefficient on non-bank activity indicates that increases in non-bank activity tend to lower BHC total risk'.

All of these studies indicate that there would be benefits in terms of higher returns from combining commercial and investment banking. They also report higher standard deviations of returns from investment banking than from commercial banking. Some find that total risk, measured by the total standard deviation of returns, from combining the two activities would not increase significantly or might decline, while some find higher total standard deviations than banks alone experienced. Several studies find that an efficient portfolio of activities (measured by assets) would include from five to ten per cent in securities operations. But all the studies reviewed suffer from the important shortcomings discussed earlier. Hence, we cannot view them as anything more than suggestive. Perhaps the only conclusion we should draw is that total risk, measured in terms of the standard deviation of returns, is unlikely to decline if commercial and investment banking were combined, while total return might increase.

Studies of actual (rather than simulated) combinations of banking and other activities, however, provide some additional, and I believe, more useful insights. These studies, particularly White's (1986), covering the pre-Glass–Steagall period, indicate that the activities that banks undertake affect total risk very little. This finding is consistent with bankers having a preference towards risk bearing that they can exercise in a variety of ways, regardless of the activities in which the law permits them to engage.

Cash Flows from Commercial and Investment Banking

The third research method examines cash flows from commercial and investment banking. This approach is superior to the accounting-data-based returns and their distribution studies just reviewed because cash flows measure the resources that the organisations can use immediately and provides some information on economies of scope from combining investment and commercial banking.

Saunders (1985a) compares quarterly changes in commercial and industrial loans with similar changes in new publicly offered nonconvertible debt issues plus their sum over the 1973–83 period. His graph of the two sets of data shows that they move in generally opposite directions. The sum of the loans and debt issues is between the individual series in 26 of 41 quarters (63 per cent). This visual conclusion is confirmed by a −.5 partial correlation coefficient between the two series. Thus, these data indicate that risk, as measured by net cash flows, would decline and economies of scope might be achieved were commercial banks permitted to offer nonconvertible debt underwriting.

Risk and Returns from Common Stock Underwriting

The fourth method of estimating risk and return, net profits or losses from underwriting common stock, provides a direct and relevant measure. Giddy (1985) studied 2,540 common stock issues (all SEC-registered common stock issues of $5 million or more) offered over the period 1976 through 1983. He measured the net profit of underwriters (spread less holding loss), assuming they had held the issue one, five or ten days after issue, and that the subsequent market price was lower than the net price to the underwriter. Because underwriters ordinarily sell an offering almost immediately, these assumptions are unrealistic and result in an understatement of the underwriters' net profit. The mean net profit per issue, standard deviation (in parentheses), and range in millions of dollars, and the percentage of the total number of issues that result in losses are thus (Giddy, 1985, table 6.4):

Period	Net profit	*Millions of dollars* Standard deviation	Range	*Percentage of issues that yield losses*
First day after issue	1.3	(1.8)	−10.4 to 25.6	3.4
Fifth day after issue	1.1	(2.0)	−18.7 to 25.6	11.1
Tenth day after issue	1.1	(2.1)	−13.8 to 25.6	12.2

These numbers indicate that very few underwritings result in losses, even if the underwriter very uncharacteristically holds the issue for as long as ten days. Profits are slightly lower than if the issue were held ten rather than one day ($1.1 million instead of $1.3 million); only 12 per cent of the issues yielded losses. Thus securities underwriting does not appear to be a very risky business, particularly when we recall that underwriters typically do not hold an issue even for one day.

Morgan (1984, table 2) presents what appear to be the same data as does Giddy (1985), but in annual aggregates. Over the eight years 1976–83, the average reduction of the underwriters' net profits from a decline in market price of an issue following its offering would have fallen by 15 per cent had the underwriters held the issues for one day, by 31 per cent had they held the issues for five days, and by 41 per cent had they held them ten days. In the worst year, 1980, the holding losses would have reduced underwriting profits by 21 per cent (one day), 41 per cent (5 days), or 58 per cent (ten days). Furthermore, Morgan (ibid., p. 17) shows that 'for the entire period, the number of transactions in which such [price] declines occurred on the first day after the offering date is only 4.4 per cent of the total number of issues'. These numbers overstate the risk, because the underwriters could have sold and almost surely did sell out the entire issue before the price declined, or they could have hedged against losses.[1]

Giddy (1985, pp. 163–5) also finds that corporate bond offerings offer more risk of loss than common stock issues. Over the period 1979–83 he calculated the mean of net profit, its distribution, and the percentage of issues showing a loss, as he did for common stock issues, with these results:

Period	Net profit	Millions of dollars Standard deviation	Range	Percentage of issues that yield loss
Same week of issue	0.14	0.82	−20.8 to 8.5	28.6
Second week after issue	−0.01	2.09	−20.8 to 5.7	28.6
Third week after issue	−0.06	2.45	−28.8 to 7.4	28.4

---

[1] Were bankers to hold inventories of securities as investments, they could experience either gains or losses as a result of changing market prices. As I note earlier, this was not a significant cause of the failures of the 1930s. Nor is there reason to believe that market declines in securities prices, including the October 1987 market crash, have been greater than declines in the values of such loans as those made by commercial banks to many South American and African countries, to oil and gas producers, and to farmers.

Unfortunately, the statistics are not completely comparable, because the common stock returns refer to 1976–83 while the bond returns refer to 1979–83. Assuming that the difference in time period does not bias the results toward greater returns to common stock issues, these data show considerably lower mean profits, greater variance, and a higher proportion of losses for bond compared to stock underwriting. Nevertheless, commercial banks lawfully can underwrite many kinds of bonds, but not equities. Within the United States, commercial banks may underwrite municipal obligation bonds and some varieties of municipal revenue bonds, and they may underwrite corporate bonds abroad. (Overseas subsidiaries of US bank holding companies may underwrite equities, subject to a cap of $2 million per issuer.) Thus, commercial banks at present can undertake an apparently riskier securities activity than that from which the Glass–Steagall Act bars them. If the primary purpose of the Act is still to prevent banks from taking securities-related risk, it is ironic that they may not underwrite equities, which the data indicate pose less risk than bonds, which they may underwrite.

VII   METHODS OF CONSTRAINING EXCESSIVE RISK-TAKING BY BANKS

Because the evidence on the relationship between risk and banks' securities activities is not (and probably cannot be) conclusive, we should review the methods available to the banking authorities for keeping banks from taking advantage of deposit insurance, as it presently is administered, by assuming excessive risks. This brief review indicates that the present system is not the best alternative, even if repeal of the Glass–Steagall Act provisions results in banks taking more risks. Excessive risk-taking by banks can be controlled by using three, not necessarily mutually exclusive or equally effective, means: (i) specific regulation, such as the prohibition or restriction of activities believed to increase risk inordinately; (ii) the general risk-sharing constraint of capital requirements; and (iii) a timely bank reorganisation policy.

Specific regulation seeks to control risk-taking by limiting or prohibiting banks from engaging in particular activities, such as securities underwriting. Knowledge about the riskiness of an individual activity or investment alone is not sufficient, however, for this purpose. The regulator should estimate how the activity affects the probability that a bank will become insolvent, given its other activities and investments. As I discussed earlier, a risky activity conducted in combination with other activities may reduce total risk.

Capital requirements constrain risk by imposing risk-sharing on banks, because the shareholders bear the cost of risks that turn out badly before the cost is imposed on the FDIC. The capital requirements could be adjusted for the risks undertaken by individual banks (as has been proposed by the Federal Reserve), but this would require the same sort of knowledge as is required for control of individual activities. However, if a general capital requirement were imposed, the supervisory authorities would only have to be assured that the capital was sufficiently great to absorb the losses a bank might incur before its capital had declined to the point where the bank had to be reorganised or closed.

Timely bank reorganisation is an important method of control. If the authorities could intervene and prevent a bank from taking additional risks while it still has economic capital, the FDIC and other banks would experience no losses. For this method (or any capital standard) to be effective, capital is best measured in terms of economic market value, not accounting value.[1] Because the only relevant concern is protection of the deposit insurance fund, capital can include subordinated debentures as well as equity.[2] The reorganisation rules would specify that a deposit-insured institution shall maintain capital amounting to, say, ten per cent of its assets. If the institution allowed the percentage to decline below ten per cent, it would be subject to more intensive supervision and might be required to suspend dividend payments, at the discretion of the supervisory agency. When a bank's capital percentage declined below, say, seven per cent of assets, it would be required to suspend dividends and interest payments on subordinated debt that is counted as capital. At this point, the debt holders might move to reorganise the bank. A bank with less than three per cent of capital to assets would have to submit to reorganisation by the authorities.[3]

---

[1] See Benston and Kaufman (1988, pp. 47–53) for a description of how this measurement could be made and monitored.

[2] Other advantages of allowing subordinated debentures to count as capital include the tax deductibility of interest, the ability of small banks to increase their capital without losing equity control, the availability of capital funds when bank stock is not traded, and revelation of market measures of risk as banks go to the market to sell and renew debentures. See Benston and Kaufman (1988).

[3] See Benston and Kaufman (1988, Chapter IV) for a complete discussion and explanation of the capital requirement and timely reorganisation proposal. Implementing

If timely reorganisation rules were established and followed, the federal 'safety net' would not be called into play as a result of banks' engaging in securities activities, regardless of the riskiness of these activities, unless it appears that losses attributable to securities might use up a banks' capital before the authorities could act. *Ex ante* imposition of risk-adjusted deposit insurance premiums would preclude concern for the riskiness of these activities, except as they affected the calculation of the premium rate. If specific regulation or risk-based capital requirements were imposed, however, the effect on total risk of securities activities and holdings would have to be calculated and taken into account, instead of the risk of securities activities and holdings alone.

VIII SUMMARY AND CONCLUSIONS

We can distinguish four aspects of the federal 'safety net': deposit insurance, Federal Reserve loans, government intervention to prevent runs, and government intervention to avert financial crises. Of these, only deposit insurance and, to a lesser extent, intervention to avert financial crises, are affected by activities that banks undertake, including securities operations. The deposit insurance safety net would not be extended to cover additional risk-taking by banks if the insurance premium charged were adjusted for risk, banks' capital were required to be sufficient to absorb losses, or the authorities followed an expeditious policy of reorganising banks before their capital went below zero. In any event, the federal 'safety net' has already been extended to cover disruptions to securities markets.

Furthermore, there is reason to believe that the repeal of the Glass–Steagall Act would have no detrimental effect on risks undertaken by banks. Bankers already have sufficient opportunities to increase risk to the point their managers find optimal. The availability of securities activities and holdings would not increase either bankers' proclivities or opportunities for risk taking. Evidence from the pre-Glass–Steagall period indicates that banks conducting securities operations had lower rates of failure than did other banks, *ceteris paribus*. Studies using data from recent years are of limited

---

the proposal might require legislative action permitting the authorities to take actions against a bank even though its legal capital was positive or a regulatory redefinition of legal capital.

value because of serious shortcomings. Nevertheless, they show that banks would obtain higher returns but not much in the way of reduced risk through diversification if they lawfully could acquire securities firms. More direct and relevant evidence shows reduced liquidity risk, because cash flows from corporate bond underwriting and loans are somewhat negatively correlated. Most importantly, underwriting is almost uniformly profitable.

In short, there is no reason to believe that banks would be more likely to become insolvent or in any other way would put additional strains on the federal 'safety net' were the Glass–Steagall Act repealed. Whether the banking industry would become much more profitable, and hence safer, also is doubtful. Banks and their customers probably would make some gains from economies of scope as banking and securities operations were conducted together. Consumers also would gain from increased entry and competition. But the securities industry is much smaller than the banking industry, and many banks do not have the skills or enjoy a demand for securities services. Hence, repeal of the Act is a benefit, but not a panacea, for the banking industry.

8 Concern for Unfair Competition

Those, such as the Securities Industry Association, who oppose giving commercial banks the right to deal directly in securities argue that '[b]anks are inherently unfair competitors outside of banking, if, as is now the case, they can use their federally-derived banking relationships, credit sources and credit tools to promote their non-banking business' (Securities Industry Association, 1987, p. 12). Mehle (1975), who presented probably the best and most influential statement of concern about unfair competition, enumerates the specifics of the unfair advantages banks are said to possess. In analysing the arguments on bank underwriting of municipal revenue bonds, Mehle finds that 'neither the default nor the market risk argument militates against bank underwriting of revenue bonds' (ibid., p. 1132, footnote excluded).[1] He finds unpersuasive the evidence for and against predictions that bank entry into revenue bond underwriting would lower costs to municipalities. Nonetheless, he concludes that banks should not be allowed to engage directly in underwriting, because they 'enjoy significant competitive advantages over non-bank underwriters – lower cost of capital, tax deductibility of carrying costs, and captive markets – making underwriting competition between the two groups unfair'[2] (ibid., p. 1155).

The Glass–Steagall Act allowed banks to underwrite some government obligations, Mehle argues, only 'because of the exceptional

---

[1] In the excluded footnote, Mehle observes: 'If this discredited "risk" argument were the sole rationale for restricting banks from underwriting, then logic would dictate that certain high quality corporate debt securities should be eligible for bank underwriting also'.

[2] Mehle dismisses concerns about 'conflicts of interest' in a footnote (98), in which he states that 'opponents [of a change in Glass–Steagall] have more effectively [than commercial bankers] advocated the conflict of interest argument . . . but have been hard pressed to exemplify such conflicts'. After quoting some testimony by Federal Reserve Governor Balderston in response to a question by Representative St Germain to the effect that he knows of no evidence of 'abuse by the underwriting banks underwriting GO's [general obligation bonds], and selling to their correspondent banks', Mehle reports: 'To date, no witness has appeared before Congress in the sole capacity of bank depositor, borrower, trust account beneficiary or correspondent to claim that bank revenue bond underwriting is detrimental to his interest.'

need perceived in the early thirties for bank participation in the federal government and general obligation bond markets' (ibid., p. 1146). They should be permitted to underwrite other obligations, he suggests, 'only through creation of security affiliates, capitalised and regulated like non-bank dealers, and insulated as completely as is practicable from the fortuitous advantages bank affiliation would otherwise provide' (ibid., pp. 1155–6).[1] The US Department of the Treasury adopted Mehle's proposal (he served as Assistant Secretary of the Treasury for Domestic Finance from January 1981 through May 1983), and in 1988, the US Senate passed a bill sponsored by Senator Proxmire that would permit commercial bank holding companies to engage in securities activities only in a separate affiliate that would be completely insulated from the banking organisation.[2] (The US House of Representatives did not consider similar legislation.)

We can delineate four concerns by securities industry underwriters about unfair competition by commercial banks: (i) banks enjoy a lower cost of capital than do securities firms, because banks have federally provided advantages; (ii) banks enjoy lower funding costs because they have special tax advantages related to the underwriting of municipal bonds; (iii) banks benefit from captive markets; and (iv) banks' correspondent banking networks give them an unfair advantage over securities firms. I consider each of these arguments in turn.

---

[1] The securities industry organisations appear to agree with Mehle's suggestion, with three possible exceptions. First, they do not agree that the Glass–Steagall Act's restrictions should be weakened. However, if the provisions were changed, they agree with Mehle, but are more specific about the restrictions that would be imposed on banks and powers that should be granted to securities firms. The Securities Industry Association (SIA) (1985, appendix C) would completely separate a bank from its affiliate to the extent that the two would really be separately managed corporations with common ownership. The SIA also would have securities firms given the same banking powers as commercial banks enjoy. The Investment Company Institute specifically emphasises the necessity of 'permitting securities firms to engage in all banking activities and to do so throughout the nation' (Silver, 1988, p. 22). I discuss this proposal in section IV of this chapter.

[2] The bill would permit some securities activities – such as swaps – to remain in the bank.

I LOWER COST OF FUNDS (INCLUDING UNDERPRICED DEPOSIT INSURANCE AND THE PROTECTION OF THE FEDERAL 'SAFETY NET')

Mehle (1975, p. 1139) believes that commercial banks have lower cost of funds than do non-bank underwriters, because '[a] large percentage of any bank's liabilities is low-interest or interest-free deposit liabilities, as contrasted with those of its underwriting competitors which must themselves borrow from banks to finance their operations' (footnotes omitted). He concludes that '[t]he privilege of accepting deposits thus creates a competitive advantage' (ibid., p. 1140). He could have added possibly underpriced federal deposit insurance and Federal Reserve discount window borrowing as advantages granted only to banks. Assuming that banks finance their securities activities with deposit funds (actually, they now generally raise funds from the same sources as non-bank securities firms, mainly through repurchase agreements), Mehle's conclusion relies on his defining the cost of funds solely in terms of explicit interest payments, which is an incomplete measure of the cost of funds. The actual economic cost of money is its opportunity cost, the amount that a bank gives up when it uses the money for one purpose and not for the next best alternative purpose.

One way to measure the cost of deposits is in terms of what a bank must give up to get the use of the funds, because one alternative is to forego this source and borrow money in the open market (which many banks do). Depositors also have alternative uses of funds and must be paid for the use of their money. Interest is only one means of payment. A more prevalent means, particularly for demand deposits for which the Banking Act of 1933 made illegal the explicit payment of interest, is 'free' services, such as cheque and deposit clearing. These services are costly to the bank, for to obtain demand deposits it must make investments in such assets as buildings, equipment, computer programs, employee training, and customer goodwill, and incur such operating expenses as salaries, supplies, and utilities. These amounts should be added to explicit interest paid on savings and time deposits and NOW and money market accounts to calculate the full cost of deposits.

Another measure of the opportunity cost of funds is the net revenue that a bank would forego by allocating the funds to underwriting and investments rather than to alternative uses. Because banks can lend to non-banks (as Mehle notes), if a bank used the funds internally, it would give up the amount that non-banks would have paid it for the use of the funds. Thus the cost of funds to a bank can be no less than the cost of funds to a non-bank underwriter, with one exception. By using deposit funds directly, a bank would not have to estimate default risk, and it also might save some transactions cost. But these amounts are likely to be relatively small, because the bank must assess the risk of its direct investment, and it must maintain records for internal as well as external transactions. Thus, banks have no advantages over non-banks, except those that result from lower transactions and information costs.

Nor does underpriced deposit insurance or Federal Reserve borrowing opportunities (the federal 'safety net'), which can reduce banks' cost of funds, give banks a competitive advantage over non-banks with respect to underwriting. It is true that, as long as depositors believe that the federal deposit insurance agencies will not default on their obligations (either because they are sufficiently well funded or will be protected by US Treasury loans and Congressional appropriations), chartered depository institutions can obtain funds (under $100,000 per account) at close to a risk-free rate. The federal agencies charge for deposit insurance directly and indirectly in the form of examinations and supervision. Because the direct charge is a flat percentage of the total dollars of domestic deposits, it is likely that the charge is not actuarially correct for all banks. But there is some question as to whether federal deposit insurance is underpriced for all or even for most banks. For present purposes, I assume that underpricing prevails. Although banks would benefit from this (or any other) subsidy, unless they prefer to give resources to investors and companies rather than to their shareholders, there is no reason to believe that they will offer their services as underwriters at a lower price than would non-bankers, *ceteris paribus*.

One could maintain, however, that banks should not be permitted to use a subsidy to finance competition with non-subsidised competitors. Were this position accepted as public policy, banks should not be permitted to make commercial and consumer loans, because insurance companies, manufacturers, consumer finance companies, department stores, and other firms also offer these products. Nor should banks be permitted to invest in US government securities, because many unsubsidised companies and individual investors also hold these obligations. Nor, perhaps, should banks be allowed to distribute the subsidy to their stockholders, because these people would then enjoy a similar competitive advantage over other consumers or suppliers with whom the stockholders compete.

The relevant issue, though, is not that banks get a federal subsidy (assuming that it exists), but whether the subsidy is greater if banks lawfully could underwrite and deal in securities. Chapter 7 examined this issue. As that chapter reports, the subsidy is a positive function of the risks banks impose on other banks, the deposit insurance agencies, and the economy in general. Banks have incentives to increase these risks to some optimal point, given the expected gains from the federal subsidy, compared with the loss they might incur should the gamble turn out badly. The range of permitted risk-taking possibilities (for example long-term, fixed interest US treasuries and loans to underdeveloped countries) is now sufficiently great to allow bankers to take almost any level of risk they desire. It is very likely that banks now tend to get the maximum subsidy amount. Therefore, there is no reason to believe that their undertaking securities operations would increase the amount of risk that they would take. Regardless, the authorities could ameliorate this situation (if it exists) by charging banks risk-related deposit insurance premiums or subjecting them to risk sharing by means of higher and more effectively administered capital requirements.

II TAX DEDUCTIBILITY OF CARRYING COSTS

Mehle (1975) points out that non-banks may not deduct against taxable income the interest expense of carrying bonds paying tax-free interest. Before this benefit was phased out, beginning in 1982, banks alone could deduct interest carrying costs from taxable income, regardless of the extent of their tax-free income from state and municipal securities. But banks no longer have this advantage for obligations acquired after 7 August 1986. However, they still may deduct the non-interest cost of deposits from taxable income. These costs, which include salaries and other expenses incurred to process deposit accounts and serve customers, represent interest-in-kind, and are substitutes for interest-in-funds. All taxpayers, including banks and securities firms, may deduct interest and other carrying costs from taxable income.

But, while the tax law did, and to a far lesser extent, still does permit banks to pay lower taxes than most other corporations pay, this tax subsidy does not give them a competitive advantage over non-banks with respect to securities underwriting. Banks can get the subsidy simply by holding tax-free obligations; they need not underwrite them. Furthermore, they already can underwrite general obligation state and municipal bonds. Their underwriting of municipal revenue bonds would add nothing to their present tax advantages. Nor would their underwriting of corporate bonds or equities provide any comparative advantage, because income from these securities is taxable to all holders.

III   CAPTIVE MARKETS

Mehle (1975) asserts that banks have an unfair advantage in being able to sell underwritten bonds to 'captive markets'. One market he identifies is the bank itself, in its capacity as an investor. Mehle sees the underwriter/investor bank as being 'able to bid more aggressively and consistently than a non-bank competitor who has no such fallback'. (pp. 1143–4, footnote omitted). He also suggests that a bank might abuse its legal responsibilities as a trustee: 'At the bank's suggestion, such purchases [by or for a trust] may be made in aid of a slow-moving underwriting account' (ibid., pp. 1144–5, footnotes omitted). Or, correspondent banks may agree to purchase securities from a bank underwriter in return for services such as cheque clearing and loan participations that the bank provides. I consider each of these possibilities.

The Bank as Investor

Mehle's argument that a bank enjoys an unfair advantage from being an investor is illogical. If a bank bids aggressively for a securities underwriting, such that it incurs losses, it bears them whether or not it keeps or sells the bonds. Furthermore, because securities held in a trading account are marked to their market prices, the loss incurred will be recorded whether or not the bonds are sold. While a bank that holds bonds it underwrites might benefit from transaction and search cost economies, this saving of resources would not usually be called an 'unfair' advantage. Indeed, in a competitive market the bank will pass these savings along to buyers.

Bank-Administered Trusts

Mehle's concern that a bank underwriter might 'sell' slow-moving securities to the trusts it administers would be valid only if the bank were willing to violate its legal and ethical obligations. Chapter 3 section V reviews evidence about this possibility gathered from the pre-Glass–Steagall period. There is no support for the charge that the feared conflict of interest actually happened. More recently, Herman (1980) very thoroughly studied conflicts of interest generally in commercial bank trust departments. He states that for a trust department housed within a profit-oriented entity (the bank), '[t]he potential for serious conflict would seem on its face to be considerable' (ibid., p. 120). His investigation (ibid.) found

> scattered but convincing evidence of bank abuses in past years in accommodation loans and dispositions of estate property, holdings of trust cash in excess or at less than competitive rates, discriminatory treatment of customers of different status and power, and improprieties in the allocation of trust-generated brokerage. But these abuses do not appear ever to have reached massive proportions. . . . Conflict abuses have always been constrained by the legal rules applicable to fiduciaries and the fear of surcharge and adverse publicity.

Thus, even in situations less easily monitored than securities purchases, there is little evidence of breaches of banks' fiduciary responsibilities towards trusts.

Potential conflicts of interest might arise if commercial banks could underwrite and deal in securities. Chapter 4 Section VI reports some evidence of misdealings with respect to bank-sponsored and managed investment companies. Non-bank-sponsored investment companies, though, turn out to be subject even more to conflict-of-interest abuses. Indeed, investment firms that manage mutual funds today have at least as great an opportunity and incentive as do banks that administer trusts to shift slow-selling securities to those funds. Both kinds of firms, however, are constrained by the common law, the Investment Company Act of 1940, and by the forces of competition, which give firms incentives to deal fairly with customers and to expose competitors who do not.

Correspondent Banks

Correspondent banks are hardly a captive market for banks that might underwrite or deal in securities. As Mehle (1975) correctly describes the situation, the smaller banks might purchase bonds from their correspondent as a means of paying for services. But in this event the bank underwriter does not obtain a net benefit, as it could charge for services directly. Indeed, the Banking Act of 1933's prohibition of interest payments on demand deposits (including bankers' balances), if it were binding, might cause banks to underprice bonds they underwrite as a means of paying for correspondent balances. With respect to securities sales, then, the bankers' advantage over non-bank underwriters would arise from the terms of another section of the Glass–Steagall Act and not from their having a 'captive market'. It is highly likely, though, that banks now compete for correspondent balances by giving their correspondents other 'free' services.

Senator Glass and his supporters make similar claims before passage of the Glass–Steagall Act. As Chapter 3 Section VI shows, these claims enjoy no empirical support. Nor, to my knowledge, does evidence, direct or indirect, from a later period support such claims of abusive market power.

IV   UNEQUAL POWERS – COMMERCIAL VERSUS INVESTMENT BANKING

The Investment Company Institute's president raises an additional aspect of 'unfair competition'. Silver (1987, p. 5) states that 'piecemeal repeal of Glass–Steagall is likely to result in a competitive situation slanted sharply in favor of large bank holding companies'. Not only should the law allow investment firms to offer a full range of banking services, he argues, but Congress also should repeal the geographical limitations of the McFadden Act and the Douglas Amendment. Otherwise, Silver fears that banks will have a competitive advantage, because 'they can be expected to utilise the correspondent banking system to distribute securities through their well-established relationships with local banks' (ibid., p. 5).

Silver's argument is faulty in the same manner as is Mehle's: neither considers the banks' competitive situation. Again, nothing would prevent respondent banks from purchasing securities from and distributing securities for investment companies as well as commercial banks, if Congress repeals the Glass–Steagall Act's securities provisions. Nor could correspondent banks have any economic power over their respondents. Such a situation appears very unlikely, considering that, according to a 1970 survey, the average small bank (deposits in 1970 of less than $5 million) maintains balances with five correspondents, while banks with $50 to $100 million in deposits have an average of thirteen correspondents (Knight, 1970, p. 9). With so many alternatives, respondent banks hardly can be dictated to by one of their correspondents.

A later survey finds a wide variety of levels and kinds of charges for correspondent services, which evidence is inconsistent with collusion among correspondent banks (Knight, 1976). But even if the present commercial banks had some degree of economic power over their respondents, the larger banks already would have already exploited their advantage. They would get no additional advantage from underwriting and marketing all kinds of securities and from forcing their correspondents to take these securities rather than those that investment bankers offered when the respondent banks' products are inferior. Because the respondent banks already should have extracted the maximum amount they could garner from their economic power, they, and not their respondents, would bear the cost imposed on correspondents from asking them to take a presumably inferior product.

The evidence reviewed in Chapter 3 Section VI also does not support the assertions made before passage of the Glass–Steagall Act that larger banks 'forced' securities on smaller banks and caused their failures. Neither then nor now is there reason to believe that respondent banks fail to operate in their own self interest.

Silver's (1987) argument, that investment firms should have the opportunity of using their own, at present geographically unconstrained, branch system, has merit. A law allowing these firms full banking powers should not also force them to restructure their organisations to conform to the branching constraints of commercial banks. Indeed, the public would be better served and the banking system would be less prone to failures if Congress removed the present geographical constraints from all providers of financial services. Interestingly, Senator Glass originally proposed permitting national banks to establish branches state wide and within areas of trade to the extent of fifty miles into adjacent states, regardless of state law. But Senator Long's ten-day filibuster killed that proposal (see Kennedy, 1973, pp. 207–8). Thus, if Congress adopted Silver's suggestions for complete repeal, the public and the banking system would benefit. Had Congress removed the geographic restraints in the 1920s, it is very doubtful that the massive failures of the 1930s would have occurred; branches, rather than whole banks, would have been closed as was the situation in Canada, which enjoyed nationwide banking (see White (1983) for an excellent analysis).

9 Concentration of Power and Performance

I PRE-GLASS-STEAGALL ACT

Some proponents of the Glass–Steagall Act are concerned that commercial banks might dominate corporate finance if Congress gave them the right to underwrite and deal freely in securities. Fear of centralised financial power has long been an issue in US politics. Congress only twice accepted federally chartered banks that could operate across state lines, in the form of the First and Second Banks of the United States. In both cases Congress failed to renew their twenty-year charters as a result of political opposition from state-chartered banks. In 1864, when federal chartering was established, national banks could not branch. Only in 1927, with the passage of the McFadden Act, did they receive the right of limited intra-state branching. Because of strong opposition, Congress removed the provision in the first drafts of the Banking Act of 1933 which would have allowed national banks to branch intra-state and within economic regions.

Therefore, concerns about centralised power never entered the early 1930s debate over the separation of commercial and investment banking. And the separation never found support as a desirable means to keep commercial banks from dominating the securities market. On the contrary, concern centered around the notion that excessive competition among bankers – commercial and investment – had resulted in an inflation of security prices and, as Senator Bulkley put it, 'an overproduction of capital securities' (*Congressional Record*, 1932, p. 9911).

II CURRENT CONCERNS ABOUT SECURITIES UNDERWRITING

Commercial bankers have raised the issue of concentration in the securities industry as an argument in support of repealing the Glass–Steagall Act. J. P. Morgan & Co. (1984, p. 30) claims:

'Research shows that corporate underwriting markets are concentrated and that legal barriers to competition in these markets result in high costs and other adverse conditions for issuers of securities, as well as unusually high profits for the securities industry'. It points to 1983 data which show that the top four firms managed 60 per cent of the total dollar volume of US corporate debt obligations underwritten by the largest (top twenty) securities firms. (For 1987, the number is 56 per cent.)[1] The top four firms also earned 28 per cent of the industry's revenue in 1980 (the latest year then available) (ibid., tables 4 and 2). In comparison, the top four firms in the Euromarket, in which commercial banks (including US banks) can offer underwriting services, managed 35 per cent of the obligations. (The number is 31 per cent for 1987.) In the United States commercial banks also can underwrite municipal bond general obligations but not revenue bonds. In 1983, the top four firms managed 18 per cent of the general obligation offerings (30 per cent in 1987), and 27 per cent of the revenue bond offerings (37 per cent in 1987).[2] Morgan (ibid., p. 36) concludes: 'Major investment banking firms earn very large profits, which may result from lack of competition in many segments of their business, including corporate underwriting and dealing. Their returns on capital typically are disproportionately greater than those of companies in other industries, and very high earnings are concentrated in the most prominent firms'.

The Securities Industry Association (SIA) (1985, p. 24) counters these arguments by saying that '[t]he securities industry is among the easiest of businesses to enter. Other than banks, no category of enterprise is prohibited from engaging in the securities business'. It questions the concentration data, stating that since 1974 'the number of over-the-counter market-makers and the average number of market-makers per security have increased' (ibid., p. 28). The SIA continues: 'the composition of the top ten corporate underwriting firms also has undergone a significant shift in recent years' (ibid., p. 29). It concludes: 'Since the securities industry already is open to all manner of competition, there is no evidence that the entry of commercial banks . . . would increase long-run competition in the securities industry' (ibid., p. 29).

Pugel and White (1985) very thoroughly and competently reviewed

---

[1] Source: IDD Information Services. The total amount of an issue is credited to the firm serving as lead manager.
[2] 1987 percentages per IDD Information Services.

an extensive body of evidence on the concentration and performance issue. They generally agree with the data that both Morgan and the SIA present, but they also point out that the national data are irrelevant for many issuers, because 'the effective market for underwriting services may be a local one, with the choice restricted to a handful of broker-dealers. Although published evidence is not available, the effective concentration ratios in these local markets are likely to be quite high' (ibid., p. 108).

Pugel and White also conducted an empirical study of underwriting spreads on 216 initial public offerings (IPOs) during the first six months of 1981. This analysis finds that cost factors (size of issuer and issue, complications about the issue, and variety of underwriting) are significant determinants of the spread. Competition was also significant; when the lead underwriter was a large, nationally oriented firm the spread was 10.3 per cent lower, on average, than when the lead underwriter was a local firm (ibid., pp. 120–1). They offer two explanations for this difference (ibid., pp. 11–22):

> If an IPO issuer has been able to attract the attention of a leading underwriter, he has (in essence) probably been able to create a more competitive environment for the underwriting of his issue; he is not limited to the (usually small number of) local, smaller broker-dealers who would otherwise be interested in the underwriting. . . . An alternative explanation is that the leading underwriters are selecting (are attracted to) particular IPO issuers who are, in some way that is not measured by our other variables, less risky or have other lower-cost attributes than the remaining IPO issuers in our sample.

Pugel and White also point to the evidence revealed in a number of studies finding that new issues are underpriced by considerable margins. Citing a study by Ritter (1984), they report that 'for the period January 1960 through December 1982, the average underpricing for all new issues was 18.8%' (ibid., p. 123). They conclude (ibid., pp. 130–1): 'The entry of commercial bank affiliates into the underwriting of corporate securities would provide valuable new competition in this area. Lower spreads and improved services, including better pricing of issues – in sum, lower costs of and superior opportunities for raising capital for issuers – would be the likely result, with benefits spreading throughout the U.S. economy'.

The reason for IPOs being 'underpriced' is not entirely clear. The issuers may benefit from lower costs of future issues as a result of a successful sale (that is, complete acceptance) and an immediate and sustained increase in the market price of the securities presently issued. Underpricing also might reflect one way that firms address investors' concerns that the issuers have incompletely disclosed private information. Or, the management of the issuers may benefit personally from having obtained shares and options at less-than-market prices. Limited competition among investment bankers may permit them to underprice issues so that they can benefit from lower selling costs and a lower probability that an underwritten issue might not sell for the amount guaranteed. It also is possible that investment bankers persistently underestimate the market value of new issues.[1] While the entry of commercial banks is likely to have little effect on the first two explanations (demands by issuers and managements), adding to the number of suppliers of underwriting services must increase competition and reduce error.

Neither the commercial nor investment bankers have presented any evidence on economies of scale or scope showing that commercial banks would dominate securities underwriting if they legally could offer this service. On the other hand, A relatively few investment bankers presently dominate the top portion of the market.[2] If these few investment bankers obtained this position by offering the superior abilities and reputations of their partners, commercial banks would find entry into the market very difficult. The investment banks' higher returns, moreover, would reflect rents on their partners' personal and collective assets, not monopoly pricing. However, as Hayes, Spence, and Marks (1983, p. 24) point out, 'the Glass–Steagall Act, by barring commercial banks from participating in most aspects of underwriting, created barriers to entry that effectively excluded the best-positioned potential entrants'. Considering that there is no evidence supporting allegations of unfair competition or abuses, there would seem to be no reason not to remove the Glass–Steagall barrier and let the chips fall where they may.

---

[1] See Beneviste and Spindt (1988) for a review of and references to the literature on the subject, and an analysis supporting the view that underpricing 'is a cost to the firm that reflects the value of private information' (ibid., p. 27).

[2] Hayes, Spence and Marks (1983, p. 58) conclude: 'The analysis of this chapter has confirmed that a relatively small group of investment banks . . . occupied a dominant position at the beginning of the 1970s and, by and large, sustained that position through 1978, the end of our sample period'.

III CURRENT CONCERNS ABOUT COMMERCIAL BANK TRUSTS AND CORPORATE EQUITIES

The Investment Company Institute (ICI) (undated) points to the possibility of commercial bank control of companies and industries through a combination of equity holdings in trusts they hold and manage and of mutual funds and insurance companies they might acquire were the Glass–Steagall Act's prohibitions repealed. The ICI presents statistics showing that, at year-end 1982, '[t]he stock holdings of bank trust departments account for 44.2 percent of the total stock holdings of all financial institutions', and that '[t]he ten largest groups of bank collective trust funds have 44 percent of the total assets of such funds' (ibid., p. 11). Seven companies and five industries are listed with data showing that if the top twenty bank trust departments were combined with the top twenty mutual funds advisory organisations and insurance companies, the percentage of equities held (in some manner) would approximately double. These data, the ICI claims, together with 'an array of activities' in which banks engage, show that 'multiple activities may bind customers to their banks and also create a significant potential for conflicts of interest' (ibid., p. 12). The ICI then cites several papers that speculate about possible conflicts of interest and abuses that might occur, but it presents neither anecdotes, studies, or other types of evidence to support this claim.

Farrar (1981) much more rigorously studied the question of institutional management of equities.[1] He found companies with stock held in a bank's trust accounts and whose employee retirement plans were managed by a bank had significantly more financial service relationships (contacts) with that bank than with other institutional holders (property-liability companies, life insurance companies, and investment advisers). Furthermore, banks charged these companies significantly lower management fees than did the other institutions. Farrar (ibid., p. 31) concludes that the banks' relatively high management of equities probably reflects their charging lower fees, and the difference between banks' and other institutions' fees 'owes its existence to the prohibition on payment of interest on demand deposits contained in the 1933 and 1935 Banking Acts and would be eliminated by their repeal'. This result, he says, is the 'legacy of Glass–Steagall', referring to the sections of the Banking Act of 1933

---

[1] A similar version of his paper is cited by ICI (undated), footnote 16.

prohibiting interest payments on demand deposits, rather than those sections mandating separation of commercial and investment banking.

Aside from the relationship that Farrar (1981) describes, the ICI's concerns appear to be ill-founded. With the exception of common trust funds, trust owners rather than bank managers control or can control trust assets. Furthermore, there is no evidence that banks ever have colluded in voting the shares in trusts they manage. In addition, the ICI offers misleading indicators of the extent to which commercial bank trust departments or mutual funds might dominate other corporations. The numbers presented give percentages of financial assets held or managed only by financial institutions, rather than the more relevant total amount of financial assets outstanding. Hence, the percentage of equities held in bank trust departments or the percentage managed by the twenty largest bank trust departments can tell us little about the extent to which banks may have power over corporations, and how repeal of the Glass–Steagall Act might affect this power, if it exists.

IV   CONCLUSIONS

While concerns for concentration of power by commercial banks over other corporations did not arise before the passage of the Glass–Steagall Act, both supporters and opponents of the Act subsequently have raised them. But there is little meaningful evidence showing that bank trust departments either have power over corporations whose shares they hold or manage or could control these companies were they lawfully able to underwrite and sell mutual funds. Some evidence indicates that the market for securities underwriting is concentrated. Whether or not this market is now competitive (and there is reason to believe that it is), it seems clear that competition would increase if banks legally could offer their services to issuers of securities.

10 Universal Banking

Universal banks offer the entire range of financial services, including securities underwriting and transactions. Non-banks can own them. They can also vote the shares of companies they own and that are deposited with them (if they are delegated as proxies for the owners), and they can elect their employees as members of the boards of directors (supervisory boards) of those companies. West Germany today and Germany before the Second World War offer the best examples of universal banking.

I IMPUTED ADVANTAGES AND DISADVANTAGES OF UNIVERSAL COMPARED TO SPECIALISED BANKING

Because universal banking is the antithesis of specialised banking, we can best consider the comparative advantages and disadvantages of each kind of market structure from a single viewpoint. I frame the issue in terms of arguments in favour (pro) and against (con) specialised banking, because that is the system now mandated in the United States. Within each set of arguments, I describe the disadvantages or advantages of universal banking as fully as possible, without regard to my own position. After presenting both sides, I draw my conclusions as to which argument is superior and when the outcome is inconclusive.

Specialised banking is said to offer eight, not mutually exclusive, advantages:

1 desirable for the maintenance of financial stability, avoidance of financial crises, and beneficial risk taking;
2 greater government ability to direct resources;
3 greater efficiencies through economies of scale;
4 promotion of entrepreneurship through the development of an active market for securities;
5 less concentration of power;
6 enhanced competition – greater consumer choice;
7 avoidance of abusive practices, such as tie-in sales and favouritism; and

8   fewer conflict-of-interest situations.

The disadvantages, which often follow from a view that interprets the claimed advantages as detrimental, include:

1   specialised banking reduces financial stability and is not necessary for conducting monetary policy;
2   inefficient and inequitable allocation of resources result from government's inability to direct resources to their most productive ends, and because politically effective groups can get resources transferred to themselves from others;
3   loss of efficiencies from foregone economies of scope;
4   reduced economic development and entrepreneurship, because banks' monitoring skills cannot be fully used;
5   concentration of power in groups whose specialised interests coalesce;
6   reduced competition as firms are kept from offering some services and products;
7   tie-in sales are not abusive and favouritism is not feasible; and
8   more conflict-of-interest situations are likely.

1   Financial Stability, Financial Crises, and Risk Taking

Pro: Specialised Banking Promotes Financial Stability While Allowing Desirable Risk-Taking

The larger the banks, the greater the effects of their failure on the system. Were universal banks to dominate financial markets, a failure could bring the entire system down or at least cause substantial distress. The government would be forced to step in to save the bank, even though the bank failed because of its managers' incompetence, lack of judgement, or dishonesty. Alternatively, government would tend to regulate banking too closely and directly out of fear that it could not leave universal banks to their own devices.

Universal banks are particularly vulnerable, because as Franke and Hudson (1984, p. 50) put it, 'it is the banks who bear a significant share of business risks'. The banks own shares in their customers' companies and have representatives on the companies' boards of directors. The failure of those customers can cause the banks to fail. Universal banking thus tends to subject the economy to the risk of 'putting all one's eggs into one basket'. In addition, Franke and

Hudson (ibid., p. 7) point out that universal banks often lend to businesses in anticipation of their customers' repaying loans with the proceeds of stock issues that the banks underwrite. This procedure, they say, 'did appear to make the recovery of their liquidity by the banks highly vulnerable to changes in the prevailing sentiment on the stock market and hence to the reception it would give to a flotation. This was even more the case if the bank retained substantial shareholding in the firm even after it has been successfully floated'.

Government can allow specialised institutions, by contrast, because their individual failures are less important. Government supervisory agencies also can more efficiently monitor specialised institutions, because their functions are limited. Consequently, government can allow these institutions to take more risks than it can allow universal banks to take, which is an advantage in two principal regards. First, desirable experimentation can take place without endangering the entire financial system. Second, specialisation permits a clearer aggregation and homogenisation of planned risks. Commercial banks, for example, should have a very low probability of failure, because they are the providers of the payments system and the conduits through which the government carries out monetary policy (Corregan, 1987). In addition, if commercial banks fail, the government will face political pressure to bail out depositors, whether or not their funds are covered by deposit insurance. Stock brokers, on the other hand, are known to deal in risky assets. The government should allow them to take risks and fail. Because consumers know stock brokers to be risk-takers, the government would not find it politically necessary to compensate investors for their losses.

Con: Specialised Banking Is Detrimental to Financial Stability and Not Necessary for the Conduct of Monetary Policy

Specialised firms are subject to substantial risks of failure, because their assets, liabilities, and operations are not well diversified. For example, farmers who suffer a severe drought or, in the light of subsequent conditions, have over expanded productive capacity, would have to draw down their deposits and might default on their loans. As a result, banks that specialise in this industry would be weakened and some would fail, thereby exacerbating an already bad situation. Similarly, intense foreign competition or foreign protective legislation that restricts imports can lead to the failure of both domestic exporters and export banks. Another example is the severe decline in oil prices, which resulted in the failure of US banks that were heavily involved in lending to oil and gas producers.

Maldistribution of maturities is the cause of the failure of hundreds of specialised thrift institutions in the United States. In the period 1981–6, over 230 savings and loan associations (SLAs) officially failed, 6 per cent of the number operating at the beginning of the decade. The authorities arranged mergers of over 300 more to avoid failures, and an additional 500 or more SLAs were economically insolvent in early 1986, although the authorities did not chose to close them down. These institutions, which specialised in fixed-interest long-term mortgage loans funded largely with short-term savings deposits, suffered massive capital losses when interest rates increased sharply, from 6 per cent in September 1977 to 15.5 per cent in August 1981 (US Treasury three-month bills). Although many SLAs became economically insolvent, the Federal Home Loan Bank Board (FHLBB) did not recognise their financial position, because they were not required to mark their assets and liabilities to market values.[1] These associations then had incentives to take risks, which substantially increased the industry's losses.[2] It is estimated that the federal deposit insurance agency, the Federal Savings and Loan Insurance Corporation (FSLIC), is contingently liable for losses of at least $100 billion on a present value basis. Thus, a specialised banking system can present considerable risks, and eventually, great costs to the economy and taxpayers.

In any event, the failure of several universal financial firms, even very large ones, need not cause a failure of the financial system, Chapter 7 argues. The central bank can both cause and prevent a systemic failure. If the bank maintains the money supply, there is no reason for the financial system to collapse, even though some banks or other financial firms fail. Nor does the structure of the financial system have much of an effect on monetary policy. The general conduct of monetary policy requires central bank control over the money supply or interest rates. The bank controls the money supply by means of its control over high powered money (bank reserves and currency outside of banks). Although the Federal Reserve can exercise control with open market operations, reserve

---

[1] Indeed, the federal regulator, the Federal Home Loan Bank Board, adopted regulatory accounting rules that served to hide the losses.

[2] See Benston (1985) for a complete analysis on which this brief narrative is based.

requirements and banks' borrowing from the federal reserve banks, open market operations are sufficient for this purpose. The central bank can influence interest rates with purchases and sales of securities (open market operations).[1] Hence, the central banks can conduct either aspect of monetary policy – control of the money supply or of interest rates – without regard to the organisation of the market for financial services.

However, if the government wants to conduct economic policy through control of bank loans, such control is likely to be more effective if relatively fewer firms made the loans. For this purpose, specialised banking would present the government with more of a problem than would universal banking.

Both US and German history (and the history of most other countries, as Schwartz (1988) and others document) bear out this explanation of financial crises. As Chapter 4 reports, banks' securities activities during the pre-Glass–Steagall Act era mitigated the failure of US banks. With respect to Germany, Franke and Hudson (1984) examined the relationship of universal banking to the three major financial crises that affected that country. The post-First World War (1923–4) inflation was the first crisis. Their analysis and references to scholarly work lead them to conclude: 'it is difficult to believe that the particular nature of that intermediation was in any meaningful sense responsible for the enormous difficulties experienced by the German financial system in the postwar inflation' (ibid., p. 9). But the inflation both weakened the banking system and resulted in increased concentration (ibid., p. 10). The central bank's inability to conduct open market operations to offset an outflow of foreign funds caused the depression crisis of 1931–2. In addition, forced lending by savings banks to the local authorities who controlled them put these banks into 'an almost totally illiquid position' (ibid., p. 11). The third crisis was the collapse of the currency following Germany's defeat of the Second World War, which, Franke and Hudson state (ibid., p. 14), one can hardly attribute to the banking system. Although Franke and Hudson mention that, compared to US and UK banks, the German universal banks were subject to the risk of stock market reverses, they do not cite any instance in which

---

[1] The press characterises the discount rate on borrowings from the Federal Reserve as the way the Fed changes interest rates. This is not true for the United States. A very small portion of bank reserves are borrowed; hence, a change in the discount rate has a very small effect on the cost of banks' funds. Furthermore, changes in the discount rate tend to follow rather than lead changes in market interest rates.

a bank failed or was seriously weakened as a result. Futhermore, the risk of payments system collapse is less under a universal banking system because these well-diversified banks are less likely to fail.[1]

Conclusions – Financial Stability, Financial Crises, and Risk Taking

The banking structure has little effect on the conduct of monetary policy. Central bank control of the money supply control and its actions to change interest rates can be as effective under a regime of universal or specialised banking or some hybrid thereof. Nor is a financial crisis or the collapse of the payments system more likely under either banking system, as long as the central bank takes appropriate action.

Individual universal banks are less likely to fail, because they can establish and maintain well-diversified portfolios of assets, liabilities, and collateral activities. Indeed, inadequate diversification (both in terms of products and location) is the major cause of US bank failures both in the past and present.[2] Therefore, if the government's primary concern is to lower or eliminate the failure of financial service firms, universal banking is preferable to specialised banking.

The failure of a large universal bank, though, is of greater concern to the authorities, who could permit specialised banks more latitude to experiment with activities that might result in failure. The government could reduce the risk of failures for all kinds of firms if it established sufficiently high capital requirements and followed a policy that forced reorganisation of banks before their economic (rather than book) capital fell below zero.[3] Such a policy would also reduce the required level of government monitoring of banks and eliminate its constraints on other banking activities.

2 Allocation of Resources

Pro: Greater Government Ability to Direct Resources

The 'specialisation' of banks usually results from government attempts to channel resources to particular industries and groups of people. For example, Congress limited US savings and loan associations to making home mortgages, to help the home building industry

---

[1] See Flannery (1988) for a thorough analysis.
[2] See Benston (1973) and White (1983).
[3] See Benston and Kaufman (1988) for a discussion and explication of this proposal.

and home buyers and owners. It established farm credit banks to aid farmers. It funded small industry banks because existing banks appeared to ignore smaller producers. And it created export credit and development banks to support the government's policy of encouraging exports and new industries.

Some specialised lenders found their origins as exceptions to usury laws. In the United States, consumer finance companies could lend limited amounts at rates that exceeded the usury ceilings when it became understood that established banks would not provide small loans at the ceiling rates and allegedly abusive illegal lenders ('loan sharks') were serving consumers.

Several justifications support specialised lending. One is that the universal banks are not serving particular markets.[1] This pattern might occur if these lenders were unfamiliar with or unskilled in lending to some industries or people. Creation of a specialised lender, then, might reflect the belief that the cost of getting universal bankers to learn to serve these borrowers would be greater than the costs that a specialised lender would incur.

A collateral argument holds that specialised financial institutions can overcome legal barriers to entry that prevent universal banks from serving a particular market.[2] These barriers often include restrictions on branching and other forms of entry, ceilings on loans and deposits that make provision of these services uneconomic, and outright prohibitions against the otherwise universal banks providing the services.

Another justification is the government's desire to subsidise a particular industry or group. While universal banks could provide the subsidy, the government could conceal the subsidy better by allocating funds and other resources to a specialised lender at less-than-market rates. Furthermore, because funds are fungible, a universal bank might take the subsidy but not pass it on to the preferred recipients.[3]

---

[1] This result could also occur in a specialised banking system; indeed, it would be more likely because specialisation yields voluntary or forced narrowness of interest.

[2] These barriers must be legal. Cost barriers (which are better described as constraints) are those just discussed (lack of skill or ignorance) or reflect economies of scale or scope, which I discuss later.

[3] The economy would be served better if cash payments rather than lower-priced loans were made to favoured persons or groups, because both the direct and indirect cost (which includes distortion of the capital market) would be lower. But such payments might be too obvious, and hence be opposed by non-recipients.

Con: Inefficient and Inequitable Allocation of Resources

To the extent that the funds borrowed from specialised lenders are fungible, the government never can be sure that borrowers will use loans as the government wants. For example, home-buyers who receive mortgages at subsidised rates could make smaller downpayments and use the funds saved to buy securities or expensive automobiles. Exporters can substitute loans for funds that they otherwise would have used to finance exports and then use those funds to speculate on real estate. Hence, a policy of directing resources towards specific ends is not likely to be successful, except perhaps in the short run, before borrowers learn how to avoid the rules.[1]

The allocation of resources through specialised lenders also is likely to be inequitable and not a reflection of the citizens' policy preferences to the extent that hidden subsidies are involved. Hidden subsidies make it difficult or impossible for citizens to participate in the decision to subsidise. The result is likely to be inequitable, because non-preferred borrowers and other users of financial services have incentives to obtain the subsidised funds and services intended for others. Government attempts to constrain the efforts of 'undeserving' people to get the subsidy inevitably result in increasingly complex rules and regulations. As a result, those who can work through and around those rules and regulations are better able to get the subsidy than those with lesser abilities of this kind. Consequently, the groups government wants to help need not be the same ones as those who will obtain the subsidy, particularly if it is not clearly identified. As an example, consider loans to farmers. How can the government be sure that the money borrowed is used for farming and not for speculation in real estate (including farm land)? The more complex the regulations designed to prevent abuse, the more costly it will be for unsophisticated farmers, who presumably are those who could not obtain funds from other lenders, to use the specialised facilities.

Furthermore, national priorities change as previously disadvantaged industries and groups become financially strong and as conditions change. But the previously established specialised institutions have had the means and incentives to develop a supporting political constituency, making it difficult for a government with different priorities from closing them down or substantially reducing their funding. Public officials, then, usually have only the option of estab-

---

[1] See review articles by Meltzer, Mayer and Jaffe, in Brunner (1975).

lishing new specialised institutions. The consequence is a proliferation of special purpose agencies and banks, some of which no longer serve the purposes for which government created them.

Conclusions – Allocation of Resources

Specialised banking is preferable to universal banking for governments that want to direct resources to particular purposes or people. But the evidence about these attempts indicates that these allocations are not successful in the long run, as those who are politically skilled subvert the government's professed intent. Furthermore, although government priorities change, it usually is politically difficult to close established special purpose institutions. Specialised banking (whether subsidised or not) also is not incompatible with universal banking. But if one kind of banking were economically superior to other varieties, it would become the dominant kind in the absence of subsidies to economically inferior institutions.

3 Efficiency – Economies of Scale and Scope

Pro: Specialisation Brings Greater Efficiencies Through Economies of Scale

Specialised firms can achieve economies from specialisation. They can afford to hire and train experts and use special purpose forms and equipment. They can reduce consumer search costs by informing potential consumers of their services. While evidence on economies of scale is incomplete and mixed, specialised financial institutions have survived in markets where they have not received subsidies and where alternative suppliers are not constrained. Examples in the United States include mortgage bankers who specialise in making and servicing mortgages (which they sell to investors), sales finance companies (such as General Motors Acceptance Corporation), and factors (such as Walter G. Heller & Co.). It may be that if specialised providers of financial services do not receive protection during their formative years, they cannot develop and grow to the point where they can achieve economies of scale.

Con: Specialised Firms Lose Economies of Scope

As noted, the evidence on economies of scale is mixed. With respect to the cost of operations, the most current studies find slight economies of scale for commercial banks with deposits below about $50 million, and neither economies nor diseconomies thereafter when the interest cost of money is included (Benston, Hanweck, and Humphrey, 1982; Hunter and Timme, 1986). Small loan companies obtain considerable economies of scale per office: costs increase by only 0.86 for each 1.00 in output (Benston, 1977). But these companies tend not to increase the size of their offices for fear of losing control and risking exposure to large losses. Furthermore, departments offering individual financial services can grow large within larger organisations.

Financial institutions may obtain economies when they produce or purchase different goods together (economies of scope). They achieve these economies through pooled central facilities and expertise, information they can use for several purposes, joint delivery of services, savings to consumers of search and other transaction costs, and reduced cost of risk as a result of more effective diversification. For example, a bank can use a computer to process deposits, loans, securities transactions, and so forth. Information about a customer's business can help the banker discern for that customer the optimal mix of funds transfer services, loans, equity securities, and financial advice. Consumers can save time and the cost of information by meeting all their financial requirements from a single organisation. Bank income from lending and from some other activities, moreover, may be imperfectly or (better yet) negatively correlated.

There is little formal empirical evidence on the extent to which banks have achieved economies of scope. But we can draw some inferences from the expectation that diseconomies of scope would tend to give specialised firms a comparative advantage over banks with respect to those services affected. In this event banks offering multiple services would not be able to compete with specialised banks, and they would not be in those markets. Almost all US banks offer all the services which they may lawfully offer, from which one can infer that economies of scope overwhelm diseconomies of scope. But one can measure economies of scope only if the firms studied produce different kinds of output of sufficient variety to produce measurable differences in costs.[1] Because most banks today offer

---

[1] One can study economies of scale because US banks are legally constrained to produce deposit services within states, and in many states, from only a single office or from offices in a geographically restricted area. Lending is similarly constrained because of consumer-borne costs and because of apparent economies of scope between business lending and deposits. Hence, some banks produce more than others because

almost the same kinds and proportions of services, it is difficult if not impossible to conduct meaningful empirical studies of economies of scope.

We can infer from the West German banking situation, however, that economies of scope may not totally overwhelm diseconomies of scale. Although all German financial institutions may offer all kinds of financial services, the universal banks do not dominate the market. In terms of total booked and unbooked assets (business volume) at year-end 1984, universal banks had 76 per cent of the market.[2] Included in this total is the volume of the three largest commercial banks (8 per cent of the market), all other commercial banks (regional banks, private bankers, and branches of foreign banks – 14 per cent of the market), and public savings banks and co-operative banking institutions (54 per cent of the market).[3] Thus, economies of scope are unlikely to be overwhelming, or may be overcome by other factors, including economies of scale from specialisation and customer preferences for trading with particular institutions.

There is little or no evidence on the extent to which specialised firms could achieve economies of scale if they were government protected during their early years. Casual evidence indicates that protection would not be helpful. If it were helpful, specialised firms eventually would dominate banking. But this has not occurred. Nor, for that matter, have limited service and universal banks in most countries put specialised institutions out of business, even when there have been no legal constraints against change. The West German banking situation is perhaps the best example. In the United States, large commercial banks in states (such as California and New York) that do not limit within-state branching have not displaced specialised institutions and small commercial banks. But, if allowed nationwide, universal banks would become relatively more important. For example, before the 1933 Glass–Steagall Act prohibited commercial banks from offering securities underwriting and dealing, commercial banks had increased their share of the bond underwriting market from 22 per cent in 1927 to 45 per cent in 1930, and their participations in

---

of the size of their market areas rather than because they enjoy comparative cost advantages.

[2] Business volume is defined as balance sheet total plus endorsement liabilities (Kempf, 1985, chapter 2, note 1).

[3] Kempf (1985), exhibit 2.8. Not included are building societies, which, Franke and Hudson (1984, p. 54) state, are of considerable importance in the Federal Republic [West Germany] in the financing of housing construction'.

underwritings from 37 per cent in 1927 to 61 per cent in 1930 (Peach, 1941, pp. 109–10).

Conclusions – Efficiency

The evidence does not support the expectation that government-mandated specialisation would promote economies of scale. But banks would lose economies of scope if they could not offer services and conduct some activities. Hence, if efficiency is a goal, Congress and the states should allow universal banking. They should also allow specialised banking, however, and the evidence indicates that such organisations can prosper despite the superior economies of scope that universal banks might achieve. In short, the appropriate configuration of product-line decisions is best left to private choice.

4   Economic and Market Development

Pro: Specialised Banking Encourages Entrepreneurship and Securities Markets

Large organisations can become bureaucratic and inflexible. Rules and hierarchies tend to dominate, and new ideas and risk taking may be discouraged. Universal banks necessarily are large, as they offer many varieties of financial and other services. They have an advantage in getting and keeping customers over smaller, specialised institutions because they enjoy economies of scope (including reduced costs to consumers of doing all transactions with the same organisation), and because consumers believe they are 'failure proof' as a result of adequate diversification or government policy.

Universal banks can practice limit pricing, whereby they lower prices to the point where potential new entrants cannot expect to offset the costs of entry with sufficient revenue. If a new entrant should become established, universal banks might engage in predatory pricing, reducing prices to below their competitor's marginal costs. Hence, even though entrepreneurs might have excellent ideas that they would apply to the operations of small banks, they cannot bring these to the market. This situation, though, requires the existence of significant economies of scale or scope.

Large banks also tend to work with large, established customers. Hence, supporters of specialised banking fear that, if universal banks dominated the market, smaller and newly formed businesses would not be as well served as would large firms. When universal banks trade and hold equity securities, furthermore, they discourage the development of an active stock exchange and independent stock brokers and dealers. As a result, the cost to new firms of raising equity funds might be greater.

Con: Economic Development is Retarded if Banks May Not Offer a Full Range of Securities Services and Hold Equity Securities

Universal banks may encourage economic development, because they can offer several important benefits to new enterprises that would not otherwise be available. One benefit is that universal banks can take more risk than outside investors would accept, because such banks have a comparative advantage in monitoring firms and the projects they undertake. Bond holders and outside investors often find it costly to review the operations of firms on a continuing basis. Banks, though, get continuous information from deposit customers and already engage in explicit monitoring when they make and renew loans.[1] The bankers' continuously updated knowledge of their customers thus enables them to evaluate and monitor those customers' equity positions and activities more efficiently than can many other investors. This advantage is particularly great for newly formed and small enterprises, for which the cost to outside investors of monitoring are likely to exceed the benefits they might expect to gain therefrom.

A related benefit of banks' providing securities services and holding equity securities is more efficient monitoring that can overcome agency problems. Pozdena (1987, p. 2) points out that universal banks, 'by simultaneously lending to and owning the equity of a corporation, can help control inefficiency arising from so-called "agency" problems in corporations'. These problems arise when the interests of the stockholders, bondholders, and managers of corporations are partly incongruent. Consequently, equity holders fear that managers will run the corporation in ways that do not benefit them, such as continuing negative net present value 'pet' projects that should not have been undertaken and protecting their jobs by not taking on risky projects that might yield high returns to equity holders. Debt holders fear that equity holders may reduce the value of their claims, as when riskier projects are undertaken than the debt holders expected when they loaned their funds at

---

[1] James (1987) finds that increases in bank loans are associated with increases in the market value of a company's stock.

interest rates that reflected lower risk (see Jensen and Meckling, 1976).

Agency problems can be reduced by several devices. Audits by independent accountants serve to assure equity and debt holders that the managers are operating the firms approximately as expected. Restrictive covenants written into debt agreements can restrain equity holders from changing the terms of debt agreements. Stock options and holdings can encourage corporate managers to act in the interests of equity holders. Fear of take-overs can encourage managers to operate the firm to keep the value of company's shares from declining.

Pozdena (1987, p. 2), however, argues that a bank operating as both debtor and creditor is a desirable alternative to take-overs and other means of reducing agency cost:

> If, instead [of being restricted to loans], a bank were to own the full range of classes of both the firm's debt and equity, the bank could gain the control necessary to effect re-organisation much more economically. The covenants of the loans and other liabilities can be designed to give the bank progressively greater authority to intercede in the management of the firm as dividend and interest payment performance deteriorates. Moreover, because the debt-holder is also the equityholder, there are no conflicts between holders of debt and equity securities to impede a needed re-organisation. The result would be fewer agency problems, lower costs in 'work-outs' of financial problems, and a resultant increase in organizational efficiency.

Thus, direct monitoring by banks is an efficient alternative to the capital formation and monitoring advantages of an active capital market, particularly for newer and smaller corporations. Universal banks, then, can offer entrepreneurs a full range of financing, from short-term loans to long-term bonds to equity at less cost than the entrepreneurs would have to pay for alternatives.

Furthermore, universal banks can offer entrepreneurs advice and counselling. In countries such as West Germany, bank representatives hold seats on corporate boards of directors. Some scholars (particularly Gerschenkron, 1962) have argued that the universal banking system, which provided the required capital funds in the absence of public willingness to accept the risk involved, considerably enhanced Germany's rapid economic development in the 1800s.

Although this view is not universally accepted (as Franke and Hudson, 1984, pp. 3–5, document), it seems reasonable that universal banks can play a valuable role as intermediaries in situations where individual investors do not have the skills to do their own analyses or are not disposed to trust securities brokers' and dealers' recommendations.

Cable (1985) provides some contemporary evidence on the capital formation role of universal banks in West Germany. He examines the variables related to the after-tax profits to total assets averaged over 1968–72 of 48 of the largest 100 corporations (all for which he could obtain data). Average profitability (net profit/assets) is higher for the 31 corporations with representatives of the universal banks on their boards of directors – 3.17 per cent compared to 2.83 per cent.[1] A regression analysis shows a statistically significantly higher profitability for corporations with universal bank representatives and with higher percentages of bank loans to overall debt, with firm and industry effects accounted for.[2] Thus universal bank involvement with companies is associated with higher profitability, *ceteris paribus*.

Conclusions – Economic and Market Development

Both theory and evidence support the belief that universal banking is beneficial to economic development and to the profitability of established firms. There is some concern, though, that universal banks might be biased towards large companies, although I am not aware of any evidence on this question.

Casual comparisons of the United States and West Germany only support the belief that stock markets do not develop under universal banking. I do not know of any studies that control for the effects of other variables, such as taxation, transactions costs, regulatory costs and benefits, and national propensities towards risk taking. In the absence of evidence, there is no way to determine whether the apparently less active West German stock market is the result of the universal banking system or of other factors. Because people in West Germany could own and trade securities directly if they wished, and because the market for financial services in West Germany is very

---

[1] Table 2, p. 123. Cable reports no tests of statistical significance.
[2] The firm effects include size, rate of growth, internal organisation structure, diversification, dispersion of private holdings, degree of private shareholdings, and industry of the firm. Cable (ibid., p. 137) reports that '[v]ery similar results were obtained using . . . before tax profits and returns to equity'.

competitive (as is discussed later), it seems reasonable to conclude that the organisation of West German stock markets primarily reflects factors other than universal banking, such as investors' preferences.

5   Concentration of Power

Pro: Specialised Banking Results in Less Concentration of Power

We should distinguish two kinds of concentration: concentration in the market for financial services, and the dominance of universal banks over non-bank companies. Those who support specialised banking fear both kinds, and they point to pre-Second World War Germany as an example of what occurs when universal banking is permitted. They charge universal banking with fostering cartels and enhancing the power of large non-banking firms. In particular, they claim that before the First World War large German universal banks were biased towards heavy industry (Neuberger and Stokes, 1974). But the basic German industrial firms had become so large by the turn of the century that they dominated the banks (Franke and Hudson, 1984, pp. 5–6). Furthermore, as Franke and Hudson (ibid., p. 6) point out, before the First World War 'a range of other financial intermediaries, especially the local savings banks and the credit cooperatives assembled and distributed funds on a scale that was considerably in excess of the joint-stock and private banks'. Thus, the German universal banks, while important, were hardly the dominant force.[1]

Some also fear that universal banks could dominate non-banks generally. The banks' influence comes from three sources: direct stock ownership, exercise of proxy rights of shares deposited with them, and membership on boards of directors (supervisory boards). Two official groups in West Germany studied the extent of universal bank involvement with non-banks: the Monopoly Commission (1976, 1978), and the Commission on Banking Structure (also called the Gessler Commission) (1979). The Monopoly Commission used 1974 data from the 100 largest corporations; the Gessler Commission's investigation lasted four years and concentrated on the 74 officially-quoted large corporations and on the stock holdings of 343 banking

---

[1] Franke and Hudson (1984) do not discuss the role of the German universal banks in the period leading up to and during Nazi rule. I have not undertaken research on this question.

institutions at year-end 1975. An article written by Wolfram Eckstein (1980), Secretary General of the Monopoly Commission reports the findings of both investigations. Hans-Jacob Krümmel (1980), a member of the Gessler Commissiion, reviews its findings.

With respect to stock ownership, the Gessler Commission found that 'universal banks' total holdings in non-banks measured by nominal values are small relative to the total equity of non-banks. But these holdings are concentrated in a few branches of industry [brewing and malting and construction], in particular, two branches whose nominal capital is a rather small fraction [2.8 per cent] of total non-bank capital' (Krümmel, 1980, p. 48). While the three large nationwide banks had the largest proportion of ownership of shares (41 per cent measured with nominal values), the balance was widely distributed among many banking organisations (Eckstein, 1980, p. 467). Thus, universal banks do not appear to dominate German industry through stock ownership alone.

A study of proxy votes in 1975 by the Monopoly Commission (1978) revealed that in 50 of the 100 largest corporations, 'credit institutions voted more than 10 per cent of the shares, and in 29 cases more than 25 per cent. . . . This investigation also found that the large banks exercised a predominant role: in 15 cases they voted more than 25 per cent of the votes as proxy holders, in 3 cases even more than 50 per cent' (Eckstein, 1980, p. 468). The Gessler Commission agreed with respect to the big banks. But its study of actual voting in 'officially quoted large-scale companies . . . found that the banks exercising proxy rights did not hold the majority of votes in the general meeting of any of these companies. Even having a bank represent voting rights of between 25 and 50 per cent [blocking minorities that can veto charter amendments by the general meeting] does not often occur' (Krümmel, 1980, p. 49). Therefore, the Gessler Commission concluded 'that the banks' influential power from voting shares . . . is not very great compared with non-banks on the whole' (ibid.). But it also found that the 'proxy rights of the big three [banks] together constituted a majority in 5 companies and the blocking minority or voting majority in 22 companies (out of 74)' (ibid., p. 50). Hence, the Gessler Commission concluded 'that, in the case of big industrial and trade companies [which have widely dispersed shares], the question of influential power by proxy rights is not irrelevant' (ibid.).

The Monopoly Commission (1978) found that '[a]t the end of 1974, credit institutions had at least one representative on the supervisory boards of 75 of the largest corporations. . . . In 31 cases, the chairman of the supervisory board was supplied by a credit institution. An executive of a large bank was chairman of 21 boards, a member of the Deutsche Bank A G alone of 18' (Eckstein, 1980, pp. 469–70). But the Gessler Commission's study of the 74 officially quoted corporations revealed that 'the proportion of seats held by banks exceeded one third in only one company' (Krümmel, 1980, p. 50). It also disclosed that the seats held were 'considerably concentrated in a few banks', which is consistent with the Monopoly Commission's study.

Taking the three means of influencing non-banks together, both studies find that the banks, particularly the big three and the regional banks, possess considerable influence, particularly in a few companies. This conclusion, rather than a finding of actual use of power, led the Monopoly Commission (1976) to recommend limiting stock ownership by banking institutions to 5 per cent of the total amount outstanding. The Gessler Commission recommended a limitation of 25 per cent plus one share (the present practice). No other substantive changes were suggested by either commission, other than disclosure of corporations' board of directors members' affiliations.

Con: Concentration of Power is Not an Important Issue, and in Any Event, Specialised Banking Leads to Concentration of Power in Groups Whose Specialised Interests Coalesce

Concern about universal banks' dominance over other financial service firms must reflect assumptions about either economies of scale and scope or political power. In the absence of political interference in the market, universal banks could not dominate specialised institutions if those institutions were more efficient than universal banks. Thus, if universal bank dominance is of concern, we must assume that they enjoy economies of scale or scope (including lower consumer-borne costs). Hence, were concentration of power in the financial services industry a fear and mandated specialised banking the response, we would reduce the feared consequences of universal banking at a cost of efficiency and consumer satisfaction.

Relatively inefficient universal banks could dominate the financial markets if they had sufficient political power to get laws passed or administered that constrained entry into their markets. For example, potential entrants might have to obtain state charters for which there would be requirements that they rarely could meet or that would keep new entrants from getting customers. Such requirements might include having to convince a government official that existing institutions were not meeting consumers' demands. Restrictions on the number and location of branches that could be opened, ceilings on interest rates that could be offered to depositors, and limitations on advertising and business promotion would favour existing institutions over new ones. (A high capital requirement, however, does not restrain entry as long as it is imposed equally on all suppliers). The response to unmet consumer demand, however, should not be to ban universal banks, but a relaxation of legal restraints on entry, except for requirements of adequate capital and general supervision.

Indeed, in West Germany the universal banks neither totally dominate the market nor are a few institutions dominant. As just noted, universal banks were responsible for 76 per cent of total business volume in December 1984. At that time, 3,250 financial institutions, including 6 national banks, 96 regional banks, 72 private bankers, 62 foreign banks, 591 savings banks, and 2,239 cooperative banks served West Germany (Kempf, 1985, exhibit 2.8).

With respect to domination over the economy, Eckstein (1980, p. 477) reports that '[o]ne general conclusion of the Commission on Banking Structure [the Gessler Commission] was that some frequently-described possibilities for banks to exert influence via their ownership of non-banks either do not exist or are sufficiently restrained by existing restrictions'. In particular, Krümmel (1980, p. 51) states that '[t]he Commission could not subscribe to the undiscriminating criticism that universal banks by holding shares in non-banks reduce, to their own benefit, the independence and the scope of action of those companies in which participations are held'. Nor did the Commission find that banks acted to impair competition in non-bank markets by fostering mergers, although 'the Commission does not rule out that banks could pursue such a policy, in the future, in order to increase and stabilise the intrinsic value of their shares' (ibid., 1980, p. 51).[1] The Commission also found 'no evidence that the right to vote proxies had been abused' (Eckstein, 1980, p. 475).

The only substantive change that either commission recommended (in addition to disclosure of the directors' affiliations) is a limitation on the percentage of equity shares that a bank can own – 25 per cent by the Gessler Commission and 5 per cent by the Monopoly Commission. Eckstein (1980, pp. 478–9) objects to the Gessler Com-

---

[1] However, the brewing industry is an exception that is recognised as a special case.

mission's 25 per cent ceiling because 'such a limitation might in fact distort competition between small and medium credit institutions and large credit institutions, because while smaller banks own parts of non-banks in relatively few cases, when they do so their share is relatively great'.[1] Despite these recommendations, neither detailed investigation of the West German universal banking system found evidence of detrimental concentration.

Nor is there any theoretical reason for concern about bank ownership or control of equity shares in a particular business. Consider the extreme situation of a bank owning 100 per cent of the shares of a company. This situation gives the company no particular advantage over its competitors unless the bank were willing to benefit consumers of the company's products at the expense of the bank's stockholders and, to a lesser degree, the company's competitors. This result would occur were the bank to make below-market-rate loans to its subsidiary. The bank would incur an opportunity cost equal to the loss of net profit from not lending to an outside party. If the subsidiary then mistakenly believed that it had a lower cost of capital and sold its product at a lower price, the bank's stockholders would be hurt and consumers of the product would benefit.

Neither report of the studies of the West German universal banking system mentions political power. In particular, there appears to be no concern about universal banks' attempting to bar entry into their markets through political channels, nor is any mention of any such actions. The data, which show a large number of all kinds of financial institutions, do not indicate significant entry restrictions.

Specialised provision of financial services, by contrast, does provide examples of the ability of some producers to achieve governmental protection of their markets. Coalition costs constrain most people in democracies from obtaining such protection. But public choice economists and political scientists long have recognised that special interest groups can reduce these costs because such groups are cohesive and concentrated; hence, they can usually get more political results for their members than their numbers would warrant. This may explain why US savings and loan associations, which specialised in home mortgages, were able to obtain favourable tax treatment for a long time, and why the US securities industry has

---

[1] He appears to be in favor of the Monopoly Commission's five percent limitation, but this conclusion is not clearly stated nor is any argument presented in support of any limitation.

been able to prevent repeal of the Glass–Steagall Act's provisions that keep commercial banks from invading their markets.[1] Universal banks, on the other hand, serve such diverse interests that they are not likely to achieve disproportionate political power.

Conclusions – Concentration of Power

The studies of the universal banking system in West Germany are persuasive. They find almost no evidence of concentrations of power within the financial service industry or by universal banks over non-banks. But there might be some reason for concern if a particular bank owned controlling interests in the shares of competitors. The bank then might cartelise the industry. But this concern is no different whether an individual or non-bank corporation were in the position to form a cartel. The anti-trust statutes can address both potential problems; no special limitation on banks is required. In particular, restrictions on the percentage of equity shares a bank may own are detrimental to the interests of smaller banks (as Eckstein points out), limit benefits that direct bank ownership of a business might achieve, and are of no value for limiting concentrations of power.

6 Competition

Pro: Specialised Banking Serves to Enhance Competition and Enlarge Consumer Choice

If universal banks dominate financial markets, there will be fewer independent organisations and less choice for consumers. Banks will tend to provide securities services together with loans. Hence, companies will not have the alternative of getting advice and bids from independent investment bankers, if they are unable to continue as independent enterprises. Investors' choices then will be influenced primarily by the advice that banks tend to give. Because this advice tends to be conservative, as noted earlier, a consequence may be a lower rate of investment in new enterprises and in risky but promising projects.

Another concern is for limitations on credit to smaller firms when universal banks own shares in larger firms. The limitations on owner-

---

[1] See Macey (1984) and Chapter 11 Section V for a more extensive discussion.

ship (25 per cent in West Germany) tend to limit banks' equity interests in smaller firms, to those firms' possible detriment.

In general, the 'full-service' commercial banks tend not to serve some people well. In the US, for example, savings banks, not commercial banks, offered savings accounts to the working poor, and home mortgages were made principally by savings and loan associations, not commercial banks. Sales finance companies made car loans and consumer finance companies made consumer cash loans long before banks were willing to enter those markets. Thus, specialised institutions played important roles in opening and developing new services.

Con: Competition Is Reduced When Banks May Not Offer Some Services and Products

Consumers benefit when more suppliers offer them services and products. Competition and consumer choice can only increase when commercial banks lawfully can offer any service or product that consumers might buy from them. Thus, a corporation could choose between a commercial bank or an investment bank as its underwriter; consumers could purchase insurance from an independent agent, a bank, or a securities broker; cheque accounts could be maintained at securities firms and at banks; and so forth.

Universal banks would dominate the financial markets only if more specialised institutions do not serve the public as well. In this event consumers could still choose among different universal banks. For example, consider an extreme example of five banks and five securities firms in a specialised financial services market. If each bank merged with a securities firm, consumers could still choose among five suppliers, but now they could get their banking and stock transactions from the same firm, if they wished. Further, the mergers would not prevent them from patronising one bank for loans, another for underwriting, and a third for securities trading. Consequently, consumers' choices would not decline were universal banking adopted.

The concern that smaller companies would find credit more difficult to obtain were banks permitted to own equities is inconsistent with economic logic and actual experience. As is discussed above (concentration of power, con), a bank that favoured its wholly owned company over other potential borrowers would simply be transferring funds within the organisation. A bank that favoured companies in which it held less than 100 per cent equity, *ceteris paribus*, would hurt its own shareholders to the benefit of the other shareholders of those companies if it made loans to them at lower rates than it could obtain from other borrowers. Even if banks engaged in such self-damaging lending practices, smaller companies would be served as long as there were no legal bars to entry into the credit market.

The evidence from West Germany indicates that universal banking does not result in limited sources of credit or other financial services. As just noted, West Germany has 3,250 banking companies, including 3,087 universal banks. If one excludes the 2,239 cooperative banks and the 591 savings banks, there still are 257 universal banks that offer their services to business. In addition, many non-banks (such as companies that sell goods on account) offer credit. Lack of competition should not be a concern.

While commercial banks have not served some people well, this problem is usually the consequence of government constraints. Until very recently, US commercial banks could offer deposit services only within states.[1] This constraint increases the risk of lending to geographically concentrated industries, such as farming. Commercial banks were not allowed to make mortgage loans except on properties within a 50 to 100 mile radius of their home offices; national banks' mortgage loans were limited to a percentage of their savings deposits. Both of these restrictions plus a virtual absolution from taxation of savings and loan associations were largely responsible for the growth of those specialised institutions. Interest rate ceilings on loans imposed by state usury laws made bank lending to consumers economically unfeasible; specialised small loan companies arose in accordance with laws that permitted them to charge higher rates of interest. Thus, banks' apparent failure to serve some people and markets has often reflected legally imposed restrictions.

Conclusions – Competition

It is difficult to understand how allowing banks to offer any service and product could make consumers worse off. If it were less costly for consumers to deal with a universal bank (either because the bank enjoyed economies of scale or scope or because consumers' transaction costs were lower), a single bank would absorb the entire

---

[1] In the 1980s several states passed laws that would permit leading companies to own banks in several states, generally within designated regions or on a reciprocal basis, during the following decade.

industry. As long as entry were not legally constrained, however, consumers would benefit even if the bank took advantage of its monopoly position. But the data do not support the existence of such overwhelming economies. A few large banks have not, and do not, dominate banking in West Germany, which has had universal banking since the 1800s. There, many universal banks and many specialised institutions offer their services to the public. Nor would universal banks benefit from favouring companies in which they have equity interests. With respect to competition, then, removal of all restraints on the products and services that banks can offer and the assets and liabilities that they hold would best serve consumers.

7 Abusive Practices

Pro: Specialised Banking Would Avoid Abusive Practices, Such as Tie-In Sales and Favouritism

If a bank could offer any product or service, consumers might be forced to purchase all their requirements from that bank, and not from other suppliers. For example, a person who wants a mortgage might be required to buy homeowner's insurance, mortgage life insurance, and possibly car insurance from the bank. If the potential mortgagor refused to do so, the bank might deny the loan. Similarly, a business borrower might have to give the bank an equity share in the business to get a loan. Or, the bank might insist that it be named the underwriter for a corporate borrower's shares. Many other examples of tie-in sales could be enumerated. Consumers thus would lose choices and other suppliers of financial services (for example, insurance agents and investment bankers) would suffer an unfair competitive situation.

Favouritism might occur when a universal bank could control or influence the decisions of companies that purchase financial services. As Eckstein (1980, p. 478) reports, 'a strong minority of the [West German Gessler] Commission argued that credit institutions with shareholdings in non-banks exert a greater degree of influence than, and hence have a competitive advantage over, those which are without such ownership. An essential motive for acquiring stock in non-banks is the possibility of acquiring access to the usual banking business of the non-banks, particularly consortium activities'.

Con: Tie-In Sales Are Not Abusive, and Universal Banks Do Not Force Corporations in Which They Have an Interest to Purchase Bank Services at Higher Than Competitive Prices

A consumer's joint purchase of services and products, even when the seller requires it (tie-in sale), is rarely, if ever, an abusive practice – one that is detrimental to the consumer. The consumer is no worse off by having the opportunity to purchase things together instead of having to purchase them separately. Even if a bank can require joint purchases that the consumer does not want, the consumer is no worse off, because the bank could have used this power to make the consumer pay more for the bank's service alone. Thus, a monopoly supplier of mortgages could make a home-owner who could not buy a home without a mortgage pay the supplier the entire net value of home owning. (The only exception to this conclusion is the unlikely situation, explored more fully later, in which a bank's tie-in sales extend its monopoly power to an artificially tied product by forcing independent suppliers out of business and those suppliers then cannot re-enter the market.)

To illustrate, consider a consumer who wants a mortgage loan and homeowner's insurance. A bank requires the consumer to buy both products from it, and offers a package deal with an annual price of $6,000. If that consumer believes that he or she could get a mortgage for only $4,500 and home-owner's insurance from an independent insurance agent at less than $1,500, say, $1,400, the tie-in package would appear to cost $100 a year more than individual purchases. There are only three reasons for the consumer's taking the bank's package. First, it may turn out that he or she cannot obtain a mortgage alone for less than $4,600. Second, the cost to the consumer of making two transactions rather than only one exceeds the possible savings in price. Thus, the consumer would take the bank's offer if the cost of shopping and separate purchases were more than the present value of $100 annually. Third, the consumer is ignorant of the possibilities and simply takes the bank's package without considering alternatives. But a bank could overcharge the ignorant consumer without selling a joint product. Indeed, the bank could exploit fully its market power and the consumer's ignorance without joint sales.

Without legal barriers to entry, extension of a bank's monopoly over some product to an artificially tied product is unlikely to occur.[1] Even if only universal banks provide some set of products (perhaps because only universal banks can offer consumers significant savings in transaction costs), competition among these banks is the same as competition among, say, insurance agents. A monopoly bank also could not successfully charge consumers monopoly prices for artificially tied products unless it could prevent all other firms from supplying those products. But a wide range of non-bank firms produce all financial services other than demand deposits. Hence, a monopoly bank could not prevent entry, except with government help. For example, insurance agents sell many varieties of insurance. They would not be forced to leave the industry if banks formed a cartel, tied car insurance to mortgages, and sold the insurance below the insurance agents' marginal cost. But unless the banks' cost of providing the insurance was lower than the insurance agents' cost, the banks would lose from this strategy. If the bank cartel then attempted to raise the price for car insurance above the agents' marginal cost, the insurance agents would have incentives to offer that product to mortgagors and others. Hence, this attempt at monopolisation would fail unless banks were willing to subsidise consumers. Consumers then would benefit at the expense of the banks' shareholders.

The minority of the West German (Gessler) Commission on Banking Structure alludes to a competitive advantage universal banks might have in dealing with companies in which they own stock and which shares they vote. But consumers should embrace this advantage, with one exception. If the bank's advantage derives from its knowledge of the company, so that it can provide better or less expensive underwriting, insurance protection, and banking services, then the related company's shareholders benefit. The exception would occur if a bank used its position as shareholder and proxy-holder to make the company take the bank's services even though the cost were greater than other institutions would charge. This possibility raises no problems if the bank owns the entire company. But if not, then the non-bank shareholders' wealth would be diminished. However, this situation is no different than if any shareholder or director of a corporation were able to get that corporation to

---

[1] An artificially tied product is one that does not bear a necessary relationship to the primary product. For example, a mortgage may be granted only if the mortgagor purchases automobile insurance from the lender. In contrast, home owner's insurance and a mortgage are not artificially tied, because the two generally must be purchased at the same time, although not necessarily from the same supplier.

overpay for any product or service. Both are frauds on the other shareholders, and both situations are actionable in civil law and may be illegal.

In fact, the Gessler Commission found that banks holding shares in non-banks did not reduce the non-banks' freedom of action (Krümmel, 1980, p. 51). Krümmel also reports that the Gessler Commission found no evidence supporting the allegation that universal banks used their position as shareholders and proxy-voters to deny access by those companies to the banks' competitors for financial services. He reports: '[o]n the contrary, the Commission found that banking services suitable for such a strategy (underwriting business, large-scale credits) are carried out for the group of customers with substantial negotiating power. Experience shows that the freedom of these big customers to choose the best offer is not curtailed by the influence accruing from participations [of universal banks in those companies' affairs]' (ibid., p. 52). Indeed, the Commission found that universal banks generally 'offer their services [to the companies in which they have ownership shares] on the same terms as non-participating banks' (Eckstein, 1980, p. 478).

Conclusions – Abusive Practices

Both economic theory and evidence are inconsistent with the belief that universal banks can impose tie-in sales on consumers that are detrimental to the consumers' welfare. On the contrary, economies can result from services purchased together rather than separately. While the imposition of higher-priced banking products on corporations that universal banks influence or control but do not completely own, would be an abuse, the reports of the West German experience indicate that this has not occurred. In any event, this would be a fraudulent practice, which is not limited to financial services. Hence, there is no need for special limitations on banks.

8 Conflicts of Interest

Pro: Specialised Banking Would Give Rise to Fewer Conflict-of-Interest Situations

Universal banking offers many avenues for conflicts of interest. As delineated by Saunders (1985c), these include:

(a) conflict between the investment banker's promotional role and the commercial banker's obligation to provide disinterested advice;

(b)   using the bank's securities department or affiliate to issue new securities to repay unprofitable loans[1];
(c)   placing unsold securities in the bank's trust accounts;
(d)   making bank loans to support the price of a security that is underwritten by the bank or its securities affiliate;
(e)   making imprudent loans to issuers of securities that the bank or its securities affiliate underwrites;
(f)   direct lending by a bank to its securities affiliate; and
(g)   informational advantages regarding competitors.

In general, concerns about conflict of interest rest on the belief that banks cannot objectively advise their clients on optimal means of financing and on investments if the banks have an interest in securities because of the underwriting activities of ownership of securities. The West German Gessler Commission (1979) investigated somewhat similar charges, though ones not as specific with respect to particular misdeeds. The Commission was charged with investigating the question of whether 'the interests of universal banks conducting all customary banking services and, in quite a number of cases, also holding shares in non-banks, exercising proxy rights on other shares, and holding supervisory board memberships conflict with the interests of their customers' (Krümmel, 1980, p. 35).

Specialised institutions are also subject to conflict of interest abuses. But because of their limited lines of business, there is less opportunity for specialised institutions to abuse their positions. Furthermore, commercial banks occupy a special position in the economy with respect to the stability of the financial system and the degree of trust that people place in them. Hence, it is important that banks be shielded from even suspicions of conflicts of interest.

Con: The Evidence Does Not Support Fears of Conflicts of Interest, and, in Any Event, More Conflict-of-Interest Situations Are Likely If Universal Banking Were Not Permitted

Possible conflicts of interest are present in almost all business situations except those in which a firm offers its services entirely as a

---

[1] Most US banks used wholly owned affiliates for their securities activities because the law prior to 1927 forbade national banks from engaging in this activity and because affiliates allowed banks to offer securities services nationwide.

broker or advice giver or entirely as an order taker. For example, a securities dealer who is asked advice or who makes unsolicited suggestions faces the conflict of recommending a security that the customer should buy but which the dealer does not hold against recommending a security that the dealer holds and wants to sell. A securities underwriter benefits from selling securities in which the underwriter has taken a position. A banker who does not do underwritings has an incentive to recommend loans rather than stock issues to customers who seek to expand their capital. Bankers have incentives to recommend that customers use underwriters who keep large accounts with the bankers. One can go on and on; the possibilities are almost endless.

A brief examination of each of the potential conflicts that Saunders (1985c) specifies reveals that we cannot avoid conflicts of interest by preventing banks from engaging in securities or other activities of the banker is so inclined and is not concerned about the bank's reputation, and if the banker's customers were blind to the possibilities. Furthermore, many of the possible conflicts specified either do not disadvantage consumers or would occur only if the bank were operated contrary to the interests of its shareholders. These following situations, which mirror the list presented earlier, illustrate these conclusions:

(a) a commercial banker can suggest that the customer either borrow from the bank rather than float debentures or securities, or recommend a particular underwriter in return for large, non-interest-bearing deposits and recommendations of customers to the bank by the underwriter;

(b) the bank that wants an unprofitable loan repaid can suggest (disinterestedly, of course) that the customer issue securities; there is no need for a bank to be an underwriter – indeed, the advice (which presumably is against the best interests of the customer and of purchasers of the securities) would be more readily accepted if the bank could appear to be disinterested;

(c) it is illegal for fiduciary to use trust assets for the benefit of the fiduciary; in fact, when US banks were permitted to underwrite and hold corporate securities, they had rules forbidding transactions between the bank's securities affiliates and the trusts it administered;

(d) a bank that makes imprudent loans to support securities that it underwrites is acting contrary to the interests of its shareholders, because the bank gets only a portion of the gain from underwriting while losing the entire amount of loss from defaulted loans;

(e)   similarly, a bank that made imprudent loans to issuers of securities it underwrites would not be acting in a self-serving manner;

(f)   banks that make direct loans to their securities affiliates are simply transferring funds within the organisation; this practice, which was common in the US before the passage of the Glass–Steagall Act, is the economic equivalent of the bank directly purchasing securities; there is no conflict of interest;

(g)   while a bank could gain and use informational advantages obtained from its other banking contacts with customers by engaging in securities operations, we should consider this possibility an operational advantage of universal banking that benefits the bank's customers and the economy; the only conflict of interest issue is the use of confidential information obtained from banking inquiries in ways that the customer did not contemplate, such as the sale or purchase of the customer's securities for the bank's own account or disclosure of the information to the customer's competitors; this misuse of inside information, however, is not restricted to securities transactions directly undertaken by a bank.

In any event, little evidence supports the actual occurrence of the conflict-of-interest possibilities in the pre-Glass–Steagall period in the US, as Chapter 4 reports in detail. The Monopoly Commission (1976) considered the extent to which conflicts of interest are a problem for West German universal banks. Eckstein (1980, p. 479) reports that 'the Commission did not object to the fact that credit institutions had extensive information available to them. But it did object to banks' using this knowledge for the acquisition of participations. Compared to other potential purchasers, credit institutions have an informational advantage which cannot be offset.' Eckstein does not say whether this conclusion reflects actual events or solely the possibility that banks might use their 'inside' information to purchase and sell shares.

The Gessler Commission (1979), however, did research the question. Krümmel (1980, p. 52) reports that

the Commission disagrees with the criticism that banks benefit from an information lead due to their participations that enables them, in the case of economic difficulties of the companies in question, to sell off their shares and to withdraw or recover credits earlier than others. Such information leads exist, however. But, more than any other bank, a bank holding shares cannot exploit them without ruining its reputation in the long run. To judge from experience, banks holding shares are rather more inclined to come to the aid of ailing companies in which participations are held.

Specialised firms also face similar conflicts of interest. Investment bankers advise clients on takeover and merger possibilities, methods of raising capital, decisions about management buy-outs *versus* bank loans *versus* equity or debt issues, and so forth. Sender (1987, p. 85), for example, reports that in 1987 Staley Continental sued its investment banker, 'alleging that Drexel Burham Lambert had tried to pressure its management into a leveraged buyout, then thwarted a 4-million-share common stock offering by selling its own Staley shares to depress the price'. Sender also quotes James Goerter, Goldman Sachs's co-head of investment banking, as saying '[t]here are enormous potential conflicts of interest when you act as principal' (ibid., p. 86). Sender (ibid., p. 90, emphasis in original) gives this example:

> For instance, a client may seek an opinion on the merits of selling a manufacturing division to a leveraged buyout specialist or to another public company, versus spinning it off in a public offering. But the implications for the investment banker's bottom line vary substantially with each option. It can be far more lucrative for the *banker* to advocate an LBO (and to take a stake in it) than to push for a public offering that may be in the best interest of the *client*.

Research presumably done for the benefit of clients presents investment houses with another conflict of interest. Sender (ibid., p. 95) quotes the CEO of a giant money management firm (Capital Guardian): 'I am absolutely sure you do not issue negative research on investment banking clients if there is any chance of doing financing in the near future'.

Security dealers' customers face the possibility that their broker may recommend purchase of a security in which the broker's firm has an indirect interest (a direct interest should be disclosed), such as expectations of future business, or sale of a security when a client of the broker's firm is considering a take-over. Commercial bankers are more likely to suggest loans than stock issues, and direct placements on which they can give advice for a fee, rather than public offerings in which they cannot participate. Consumer finance companies are unlikely to suggest that their clients can get loans at lower rates at commercial banks, and so forth.

Although conflicts of interest are a potential problem for virtually any multiproduct or multiservice organisation, such problems are more severe for specialised institutions than for universal banks. This conclusion follows from considering the benefits and costs to companies and their employees of actions that are contrary to the interests of customers (the essential reason for concern about conflicts of interest).

Consider first the position of a *company*. If it instructs its employees to act so as to benefit the company at the expense of its customers, it will face a cost of expected customer dissatisfaction, which equals the value of business lost times the probability that customers will learn or otherwise come to believe that the company has 'cheated' them. Larger companies, ongoing companies, and companies that produce a wide range of products and services generally have the most to lose (relative to expected benefits), for two reasons. First, larger, more complex companies tend to have more formal systems to control and monitor employees' actions. These companies would find it more difficult to direct employees to act in illegal or unethical ways, because they must fear that an employee with strong moral convictions will 'blow the whistle'. Smaller companies can give employees oral instructions and more effectively weed out potential whistle blowers. Second, the greater the range of products and services provided, the greater the potential cost of the entire company being seen as acting contrary to the interests of its customers in one branch or division. Possible losses in many if not all of its other products probably would more than offset the gains from conflict of interest in one product. Universal banks, then, which tend to be large, multiproduct firms, are less likely than specialised firms to direct employees to engage in conflicts of interest.

Now consider the benefits and costs to *employees* of acting contrary to the interest of customers. Assume first that the employer wants to 'cheat' its customers. Its employees might receive direct rewards in the form of commissions, or indirect ones in the form of promotions and salary raises. Universal banks ordinarily do not pay employee commissions because most of their operations are not amenable to this reward structure. Indeed, this is one reason that commercial banks find it difficult to compete for sales and executive talent with investment banks and securities brokers and dealers.

Assume now that the employer does not want its customers 'cheated'. A universal bank more readily can prevent employees from acting against customers' interests (for example by churning accounts) than can a small organisation, because larger, more formal organisations can afford and must have good systems of internal control. Universal banks (and banks generally) also tend to use formal systems of employee evaluation, in part because they tend to be large organisations. Even if a bank wants employees to take actions that benefit the bank at the expense of its customers, a direct measure of gains from such actions is unlikely to find inclusion in the bank's personnel information and reward system, if for no other reason than fear that outsiders will discover the practice. Thus, employees of a universal bank must hope that their actions defrauding customers on behalf of the bank will be recognised informally and rewarded. Against this hope, is the expectation that if such an action is disclosed, 'offending' employees will be castigated and not protected, as the bank seeks to protect its image.

Conclusions – Conflicts of Interest

Conflict of interest possibilities are present in almost all business arrangements. The public's protection against being victimised is competition among suppliers of services and suppliers' concerns for their reputations. With respect to the banking structure, consumer-damaging conflict-of-interest situations are likely to be fewer for universal banks than for specialised financial service firms. Universal banks are less likely to subject their customers to situations that are contrary to the customers' interests, because these banks have more products to sell (and hence have more to lose than other suppliers), and have more control over their employees. Consequently, if one regards conflict of interest as an important problem, then one must also favour allowing banks to offer all kinds of services.

II SUMMARY AND OVERALL CONCLUSIONS

I have now delineated eight possible advantages and disadvantages of specialised compared to universal banking. From this analysis, I draw the eight conclusions.

1   Financial stability is more likely under universal banking than specialised banking, principally because universal banks are more diversified and therefore can better withstand the effects of unexpected economic changes. But specialised institutions offer the benefits of desirable experimentation, because the authorities may be overly concerned for the failure of very large universal banks. The authorities can largely alleviate the detrimental effects of failures, though, by requiring all depository financial institutions to hold adequate capital and by the authorities following an expeditious reorganisation (closure) policy. In any event, systemic collapse is not a function of financial market structure, but of actions that the central bank takes or does not take.

2   Specialised banking offers government greater opportunities to direct resources, but misallocations and inefficiencies that commonly follow such efforts overcome the benefit.

3   Economies of scale are not likely to be achieved through specialisation, while economies of scope may be foregone from preventing banks from offering an unconstrained range of products and services.

4   Economic development is likely to be enhanced if banks can offer companies a full range of financing alternatives, including more efficient monitoring than can be achieved by individual shareholders. A cost of universal banking may be a less active market for corporate shares; but it is not clear whether this outcome is a consequence of universal banking or is undesirable.

5   Concentration of power has not been a consequence of universal banking. As long as antitrust laws prevent banks (and others) from cartelising an industry, there is no reason for concern about bank ownership of non-banks. There is reason to believe, however, that specialisation is conducive to the development of coalitions that acquire the political power to transfer resources to their members from other people.

6   Universal banking does not reduce competition. Indeed, consumers can only benefit when banks enjoy the right to offer any service or product, as this policy expands consumer choice.

Specialised institutions, though, also can provide alternatives that consumers favor.

7 Tie-in sales are not abusive practices. The only relevant abuse attributed to universal banks is the possibility that the banks might force companies in which they invest to take the banks' services at higher-than-market prices, to the detriment of the companies' other stockholders. This abuse has not occurred in West Germany.

8 There have been charges of conflicts of interest against banks in the US that engaged in securities operations prior to the passage of the Glass–Steagall Act in 1933. A detailed examination of the record shows that almost all these charges are unsupported. A large scale study of West German banks (Gessler Commission) examined possible conflicts of interest in universal banks. That study found no evidence of actions detrimental to the interests of consumers. Furthermore, one expects to find abusive conflicts of interest (which are possible in almost all business and interpersonal situations) to occur at smaller, specialised institutions than at large, diverse, bureaucratic institutions such as universal banks.

The overall conclusion, then, is that universal banking can provide considerable benefits and pose few problems for the economy. This is not to conclude that specialised providers of financial services should not or would not also exist. Experience and logic indicate that these companies can do many things better than can universal banks. In particular, specialised firms are more likely to handle many important aspects of investment banking. Take-overs, leveraged buyouts, mergers, spin-offs, and other capital restructurings often must be completed quickly and imaginatively. As Eccles and Crane (1988) describe, these 'deals' commonly involve very well paid specialists willing to work very long hours during a concentrated time period. Commercial banks, which tend to be bureaucratically organised, often are not well suited to this kind of activity.

Persons and companies not designated as 'banks' also provide a wide range and considerable volume of financial services in countries characterised by universal or specialised banking. People make and hold loans of all kinds to businesses and other persons. Retailers, such as department stores and petrol companies, provide a considerable volume of consumer credit. Businesses provide credit to other businesses in the form of accounts and notes receivable. Both individual investors and businesses purchase and hold securities. Many securities transactions, particularly including securities not listed on a stock exchange, occur without the aid of banks or brokers. Ownership claims on businesses similarly are often issued without the aid of an investment banker. Thus, the adoption of universal banking is unlikely to result in these organisations dominating financial services, as the experience of West Germany demonstrates.

11 Other Reasons for Glass–Steagall

One might wonder why and how Congress agreed to separate investment and commercial banking, considering the paucity of supporting evidence and the weight of evidence to the contrary showing that commercial banks did not fail because of their securities operations or holdings, did not engage in securities-related abusive practices, and were not guilty of conflicts of interest that damage consumers. While the restraint-on-competition, rent-seeking theory probably explains why Congress enacted the legislation and why it has not repealed it, the theory does not explain why passage came when it did. In particular, why was the law not enacted earlier, before commercial banks, through their securities affiliates, came close to dominating the securities business?

Historians have documented the story well, although they mistakenly took Senator Glass's and Counsel Pecora's descriptions of bank failures and abuses at face value. The historians' narratives are nevertheless valuable for their documentation of the atmosphere and beliefs held at the time of the Act. What emerges is a series of factors that contributed to the passage of the Glass–Steagall Act: (i) Senator Glass's strongly and persistently held beliefs about how the banking system should operate and his concerns about stock market speculation (or stock gambling, as he repeatedly put it); (ii) publicity surrounding the failure in 1930 of the Bank of United States, which had dozens of affiliates; (iii) the 1930s banking crisis during which over 9,000 banks failed and the banking system was closed down in several states and then nationally; (iv) Senator Glass's misstatements about the findings of hearings he conducted; (v) extremely damaging publicity from the Pecora Hearings revealing what appeared to be terrible abuses by the most prominent proponent of securities operations, Charles Mitchell of the National City Bank and Company; and (vi) the self-interest of commercial and investment bankers.[1]

---

[1] The description and analysis in this chapter relies on Perkins (1971), Carosso (1970a), Kennedy (1973), and Kelly (1987), among others, and my reading of the *Congressional Record* and the Senate Committee on Banking Currency hearings and reports preceding the Act.

I SENATOR GLASS'S BELIEFS

Senator Glass undoubtedly was the most respected and powerful politician on matters related to banking. As a member of the US House of Representatives he was a major sponsor of the legislation creating the Federal Reserve System in 1913, which he considered to be 'the crowning achievement of his political career' (Perkins, 1971, p. 498). He served as Secretary of the Treasury during the First World War, and, after 1920, as a US senator from Virginia. Although a Democrat when the Senate majority was Republican, he chaired the special subcommittee of the Senate Banking Committee that conducted hearings in 1931 and 1932 on the 'Operation of the National and Federal Reserve Banking Systems', discussed in Chapters 2 and 3. He participated in the Pecora Hearings (1933 and 1934) and was co-sponsor of the Banking Act of 1932 and the Banking Act of 1933.

The apparent failure of the banking system after the 1929 crash was, as Perkins (ibid., p. 498) puts it, 'a bitter blow to the proud architect of the existing banking system', which Glass believed would have been perfect if only the evils of stock speculation had not contaminated it. He believed strongly in the 'real bills' or commercial loan theory, which was in favour in the late 1800s, when he received his formal education, but which leading economists already discredited. The theory holds that commercial banks exist to meet the short-run credit needs of commercial establishments. Banks meet these needs with self-liquidating loans backed by real goods (or bills). Glass well expressed the role of the Federal Reserve in this theory. As he explained to the Senate (*Congressional Record*, 1932, p. 9884): 'The whole purpose of the act was to enable a member bank of the system, when it should have depleted its own liquid and ready resources in responding to the requirements of commerce and agriculture and industry, to take its eligible paper to its Federal reserve bank and get additional funds. And for what purpose? To respond further to the demands of commerce and industry'.

Glass (and his principal long-term adviser, Professor H. Parker Willis of Columbia University) believed that 'the intent of Congress [was] to provide against the use of Federal reserve facilities, directly or indirectly, in stock-market speculative operations' (*Congressional Record*, 1932, p. 9884).[1] He believed strongly, indeed passionately,

---

[1] See Willis and Chapman (1934) for Willis's views.

that securities speculation, engaged in and fuelled by banks misusing their borrowing privileges at the federal reserve banks, was responsible for the country's grave economic condition. Furthermore, as Perkins (1971, p. 503) observes, '[t]he security affiliate, because it was in the forefront of the retailing approach to security distribution, was now being cited as the chief stimulant to "excessive competition" '.

The hearings that Glass conducted in 1931 (Glass Subcommittee Hearings), however, focused almost entirely on bank *lending* to securities brokers and traders, and on what Glass contended was 'use of the Federal Reserves facilities for stock speculation purposes' (Glass Subcommittee Hearings, 1931, p. 272). The data that the subcommittee staff gathered related mostly to loans. While the report described securities affiliates and speculated about bank safety in general, no data or testimony on banks' securities holdings were gathered. Indeed, only a small portion of the record concerned banks' securities affiliates, and most of the data reported involved loans from commercial banks to their affiliates. The affiliates appear to have been important only as an additional symbol of the destructive role stock market 'speculation' allegedly played in corrupting banking and the economy.

II THE FAILURE OF THE BANK OF UNITED STATES

The Bank of United States failed in 1930, causing considerable distress among thousands of small depositors who had relied on it, perhaps because its name mislead them into thinking it was an instrumentality of the federal government.[1] The bank had dozens of affiliates. But none of the affiliates was engaged in securities underwriting or distribution (other than of the bank's own stock), and the bank failed because of overexpansion requiring very high cash payments, concentration in real estate loans and holdings, unsecured loans to bank officers, and fraud. Even so, in Part VII of the Glass Subcommittee Hearings (1931, p. 1068) the bank appears as an example (indeed, the only example) of the evils of securities affiliates: 'In New York State, where most of the large securities affiliates are to be found, sentiment on the subject was aroused

---

[1] The bank was not allowed to use the title, 'Bank of *the* United States', in an attempt to avoid its being misidentified.

among bankers, as well as the general public, by the effects of the stock market deflation in 1929–30, and later by the collapse of the Bank of United States, with its 59 different affiliates'. It is notable that when the Superintendent of Banking for New York, John Broderick, testified before Senator Glass (ibid., pp. 271–83), the committee did not question him about the Bank of United States.[1] Nevertheless, it soon became as an example (usually the only example) of the evils of securities affiliates.

In a long speech to the Senate explaining the sections of the 1932 version of the Glass–Steagall Act that relate to affiliates, for instance, Senator Walcott cited the Bank of United States 'as a typical case of the excessive abuse of affiliates' (*Congressional Record*, 1932, p. 9905; quoted by the Securities Industry Association, 1985, p. 18). But this is the only case he mentions, and his use of this example is very curious. He precedes the quoted statement by saying: 'Many affiliates operate very much as a high-grade private banking house would do in the business of buying and selling securities'. Then he describes the Bank of United States's practice of using affiliates to hold real estate that they purchased 'at close to the top of the market. The whole thing was getting overloaded and top-heavy; they were pyramiding; they were financing by shoe-string operations; and *of course it was inevitable that this great structure of innumerable affiliates should collapse*'. (The emphasised portion of Walcott's speech is the only portion dealing with the Bank of United States quoted by the Securities Industry Association, 1985, p. 18, other than the phrase quoted earlier.)

III THE 1903s BANKING CRISIS

As the number of bank failures increased dramatically, from 642 in 1929 to 1,345 in 1930, and 2,298 in 1931, and the nation's financial system appeared to be on the verge of collapse, Glass introduced a bill on 21 January 1932 presenting the recommendations of the Banking and Currency subcommittee he chaired. (He introduced a bill in 1931 following hearings he had conducted, which called for the immediate examination of banks' securities affiliates and their separ-

---

[1] The Annual Reports of the Superintendent of Banks of the State of New York for 1929, 1930, and 1931 do not include any charges or information on specific problems with or abuses by securities affiliates.

ation in five years; the bill was not voted on.) The 1932 bill provided for increased capitalisation requirements for national banks, structural changes to the Federal Reserve System, greatly expanded branch banking authority for national banks, a federal 'liquidating corporation' that would purchase the assets of closed banks to aid depositors, increased supervision over chain and group banking, and supervision of bank affiliates. Banking groups intensely opposed the bill, Glass held further hearings, he proposed the complete separation of securities affiliates from national banks, and the bill was not submitted to the Senate.

Perkins (1971, p. 518) says that 'Glass was instrumental in formulating the Democratic platform for the 1932 campaign', which called for '[t]he severance of affiliated companies from, and the divorce of the investment banking business from, commercial banks'. As the depression worsened and the banks continued to fail, various commentators increasingly depicted securities speculation as a prime cause. Perkins (ibid., pp. 518–19) reported that, in a speech 'generally agreed to have been one of the most effective . . . of the whole campaign, Glass explained how "with insatiable avarice, great banking institutions, through their lawless affiliates" had unloaded billions of dollars of worthless securities on the American public'.

Perkins (ibid., 1971, p. 520) concludes: 'The November elections, then, in my opinion, virtually sealed the fate of the affiliate system and the union of the two banking functions that had grown to such proportions within that system. Thereafter, any chance of a compromise calling simply for examination and regulation by the government was remote'. The Senate passed the Glass bill during the 'lame duck' session of the 72nd Congress, but only after a filibuster by opponents of the branch banking provisions (especially Huey Long) forced an amendment limiting national bank branching to states that permitted their own banks to branch (Kennedy, 1973, p. 73). The House, however, failed to enact the bill, because it became embroiled in a debate over deposit insurance.

On 14 February 1933, the governor of Michigan closed the state's banks for eight days. Two groups of banks dominated Michigan banking: the Guardian Detroit Union Group and the Detroit Bankers Company. Both groups suffered severe losses in asset values, which they concealed with funds and loan transfers among the associated banks. Securities affiliates and security transactions or holdings played no role in their problems.[1] Rumours spread that the government would devalue the dollar and there was a run on gold, which depleted the reserves of commercial and the federal reserve banks (Wigmore, 1987). President Roosevelt declared a national bank holiday between 6 and 9 March. Understandably, newspapers and politicians perceived this situation as a crisis calling for legislation and the identification and punishment of those responsible.

IV MIS-STATEMENTS BY SENATOR GLASS AND DAMAGING PUBLICITY FROM THE PECORA HEARINGS

In May 1932, Senator Glass reported inaccurately to the Senate: 'The committee ascertained in a more or less definite way – we think quite a definite way – that one of the greatest contributions to the unprecedented disaster which has caused this almost incurable depression was made by these bank affiliates' (*Congressional Record*, 1932, p. 9887). Glass repeatedly restated this theme during the presidential campaign. His great stature as the nation's expert on banking and the father of the Federal Reserve probably gave the charge against security affiliates considerable credence.

On 21 February 1933, just after the Michigan bank holiday, Charles Mitchell, chairman of the National City Bank and National City Company, testified at the Pecora Hearings. Kennedy (1973, p. 104) observes: 'during those nine days when the Senate committee turned its investigation of stock exchange practices to the National City Bank, the commercial bankers suffered great damage at the worst possible time'. Mitchell resigned his chairmanships on 23 February 1933. On 6 March 1933, two days after President Roosevelt's inauguration and his declaration of the Bank Holiday, the new chairman of the National City Bank, James Perkins, spoke to the president about the bank's situation. The following day the bank's board of directors voted to work towards the separation of the National City Company from the National City Bank.[2] On 13 March 1933, National City Bank received a licence from the Treasury Department to reopen for business.

Winthrop Aldrich, Albert Wiggin's successor at Chase National

---

[1] See Kennedy, 1973, chapter IV; Pecora Hearings, 1933 and 1934, parts 9, 10, 11, and 12; and SEP Report, 1934, chapter IV.
[2] Cleveland and Huertas (1985) p. 197.

Bank, followed a similar course after a conference with the new president. He announced that Chase Securities Company would separate from the bank, adding: 'It is impossible to consider the events which took place during the past ten years without being forced to the conclusion that intimate connection between commercial banking and investment banking almost inevitably leads to abuses' (quoted by Perkins, 1971, p. 523). As Chapter 8 reports, he also called for the separation of deposit and investment banking by private banks, such as Chase's rival, J. P. Morgan.

A contemporary professional economist (Preston, 1933, p. 604) describes well the role of the Pecora Hearings and the decline of stock values in the passage of the Glass–Steagall Act:

> The investment division was a very profitable unit of the bank when stocks and bonds were booming. Moreover, it made many friends for the bank. But the heavy losses subsequently suffered by bank clients caused a strong revulsion of feeling against the bank. Banks opposed the divorce of security affiliates when this was first incorporated in the Glass bill and urged regulation instead. In more recent months, there was no effective opposition because security selling has ceased to be profitable and some of the larger banks had already taken steps to eliminate their security affiliates.

V THE SELF-INTEREST OF MANY COMMERCIAL AND INVESTMENT BANKERS

Thus, at the time of its passage, the Glass–Steagall Act benefited many commercial and investment bankers. As Chapter 8 notes, commercial bankers were able to dispose of affiliates and operations that were no longer profitable, and the Act removed private banks that chose the investment banking route as competitors for deposits. Carosso (1970b, p. 428) reports that '[m]ost of the private banking partnerships, about two-thirds according to one estimate, chose to remain in the securities business'. These and other investment bankers (including several firms formed by former managers of commercial bank investment affiliates) then had considerably less competition for the drastically diminished underwriting and securities transaction business.

In 1935 some senators proposed weakening the constraints of the

Glass–Steagall Act in the light of the slow recovery of the economy. Although Senator Glass supported the changes, he had done his previous work against the banks too well. The Congress would not undo, even partially, the separation of commercial and investment banking.

The now specialised investment bankers and commercial bankers formed a symbiotic relationship in the post-Glass–Steagall years. As Carosso (ibid., p. 432) notes: 'Separation of deposit and investment banking also brought about a drastic reduction in the capital available to float new security offerings. . . . More than ever before, security houses had to depend upon commercial bank loans for assistance in syndicating issues'. Although some bankers (the National City Bank, in particular) attempted to get the law changed, most apparently found the evolving relationships satisfactory – at least as long as restraints on entry in banking were effective and the securities market was not robust. Thus, at least until the post-1950s recovery of the securities market, most commercial bankers saw few benefits from upsetting the division of the market for banking and underwriting services. By then many, if not most, institutions had well-vested interests, and the myths surrounding the reasons for the Glass–Steagall Act separation had become well entrenched.

Appendix: Securities Activities of Banking Organisations Permissible Under Federal Law[1]

I INVESTMENT ADVISORY SERVICES

A Portfolio Investment Advice

Regulation Y of the Federal Reserve Board (the Board) authorises bank holding companies to provide portfolio investment advice, including real estate consulting (but not to a real estate developer), subject to observance of standards of care and conduct applicable to fiduciaries. 12 C.F.R. § 225.25(b)(4)(iii) (1987). National banks provide similar services under their trust powers.

B Financial Advice

Regulation Y authorises bank holding companies to provide financial advice to state and local governments such as with respect to matters such as the issuance of their securities. 12 C.F.R. § 225.25(b)(4)(v) (1987). In addition, the Board has approved by order the activity of providing advice in connection with financing transactions for unaffiliated financial and non-financial institutions and advice regarding the structuring of and arranging for loan syndications, interest rate 'swaps' and 'caps', and similar transactions. Signet Banking Corp., 73 Fed. Res. Bull. 59 (1987); 'Sovran Fin. Corp.', 73 *Fed. Res. Bull.* 744 (1987). The Board also has approved by order the provision of financial advice to Canadian governments. Bank of Nova Scotia, 74 *Fed. Res. Bull.* 249 (1988). National banks have similar authority under their general banking powers to provide financial advice. 12 U.S.C. § 24 (Seventh) (1982 & Supp. IV 1986).

C Economic Information and Advice

Regulation Y also authorises bank holding companies to furnish 'general economic information and advice, general economic statistical forecasting,

---

Reprinted with permission from Isaac and Fein (1988), pp. 323–46.
[1] It should be noted that the permissibility of certain of the activities described herein may be affected by ongoing litigation, agency interpretations, and legislative changes in the law.

services and industry studies'. 12 C.F.R. § 225.25(b)(4)(iv) (1987). National banks have similar authority under their general banking powers.

D   Foreign Exchange Advice

Regulation Y authorises bank holding companies to provide advice with respect to foreign exchange transactions. 12 C.F.R. § 225.25(b)(17) (1987). National banks have similar authority under their general banking powers.

E   Consumer Financial Counseling

Regulation Y authorises bank holding companies to provide 'advice, educational courses, and instructional materials to consumers on individual financial management matters, including . . . general investment management'. In providing such services, a bank holding company may not provide advice on specific investments or provide portfolio management. *Id.* If the counseling company also provides discount securities brokerage services, the brokerage and counseling services must be provided by different personnel and in separate offices or in separate and distinctly marked areas. *Id.* National banks have similar authority under their general banking powers.

F   Investment Adviser to Investment Company

Regulation Y authorises bank holding companies to serve as investment advisers (as defined in § 2(a)(20) of the Investment Company Act of 1940, 15 U.S.C. § 80a–2(a)(20) (1976), to both open-end and closed-end investment companies registered under that act, and to sponsor, organise, and manage a closed-end company, subject to restrictions in the Board's interpretive ruling on investment adviser activities. 12 C.F.R. §§ 225.25(b)(4)(ii), 225.125 (1987). The Supreme Court upheld this activity in *Board of Governors* of *the Fed. Reserve Sys.* v. *Investment Co. Inst.*, 450 U.S. 46 (1981). National banks also may serve as investment advisers to investment companies. 'Decision of the Comptroller of the Currency Concerning an Application by American National Bank of Austin, Texas, to Establish an Operating Subsidiary to Provide Investment Advice' (Sept. 2, 1983), reprinted in [1983–1984 Transfer Binder] *Fed. Banking L. Rep.* (CCH) ¶ 99, 723. National banks are subject to the more stringent prohibitions of section 16 of the Glass–Steagall Act and may not sponsor or organise closed-end investment companies. 12 U.S.C. § 24(Seventh).

G   Investment Adviser to REIT

Regulation Y authorises bank holding companies to serve as the advisory company for a mortgage or real estate investment trust. 12 C.F.R. § 225.25(b)(4)(i) (1987). National banks have similar authority under their general banking powers.

H   Merger and Acquisition Advice

National banks are permitted to offer advice and assistance on corporate mergers and acquisitions, including planning, intermediary, research, and counseling services. Letter from the Assistant Director of the Legal Advisory Services Division (May 25, 1982). Recent interpretations from the Comptroller of the Currency's Office indicate that a national bank may act as a 'finder' in bringing together buyers and sellers for a fee, but may not participate in subsequent negotiations. Letter from the Deputy Comptroller for the Northeastern District (May 25, 1984). Although under Regulation Y such services are subject to treatment as impermissible management consulting, except with respect to advice to depository institutions, 12 C.F.R. §§ 225.25(b)(4) n.2(D),225.25(b)(11) (1987), the Board by order has permitted bank holding companies to provide financial feasibility studies and valuations of companies for acquisition and merger transactions and other purposes, such as divestitures, tender offers, bankruptcy reorganisation, employee stock ownership trusts, and charitable trusts. 'Security Pac. Corp.', 71 *Fed. Res. Bull.* 118 (1985); see also Signet Banking Corp., 73 *Fed. Res. Bull.* 59 (1987) (fairness opinions in mergers and acquisitions for nonfinancial institutions; advice in connection with merger, acquisition, and financing transactions for nonfinancial institutions).

I   Management Consulting to Depository Institutions

Regulation Y authorises bank holding companies to provide management consulting advice to nonaffiliated bank and nonbank depository institutions, including advice on international banking, foreign exchange transactions, and investments. 12 CFR. §§ 225.25(b)(11), 225.131 (1987).

J   Stock Quotation Services

The Board has approved by order the activity of providing an on-line stock quotation and financial data base service for customers such as stock exchanges, brokerage firms, and financial institutions. 'Citicorp', 72 *Fed. Res. Bull.* 497 (1986).

K   FCM Advice

Bank holding companies acting as futures commission merchants are permitted to offer advice to a limited extent. See ACTIVITIES WITH RESPECT TO COMMODITIES, *infra* pt. IX.

L   Arranging Real Estate Equity Financing

Regulation Y authorises bank holding companies to act 'as intermediaries for the financing of commercial or industrial income-producing real estate by arranging for the transfer of title, control, and risk of such a real estate project to one or more investors, if . . . the financing arranged exceeds $1 million, subject to conditions designed to avoid any interest by the bank holding company in projects financed'. 12 C.F.R. § 225.25(b)(14) (1987).

II BROKERAGE ACTIVITIES

A Discount Brokerage

The Supreme Court has ruled that discount brokerage services are permissible for bank holding companies under the Glass–Steagall Act, and that such activities are specifically included on the list of permissible nonbanking activities in Regulation Y. *Securities Indus. Ass'n v. Board of Governors of the Fed. Reserve Sys.*, 468 U.S. 207 (1984); *see also* 12 C.F.R. § 225.25(b)(15) (1987). Discount brokerage activities also have been held permissible for national banks. *Securities Indus. Ass'n. v. Comptroller of the Currency*, 577 F. Supp. 252 (D.D.C. 1983) *aff'd*, 758 F.2d 739 (D.C. Cir. 1985), *aff'd in part and rev'd in part sub nom. Clarke v. Securities Indus. Ass'n*, 107 S. Ct. 750 (1987). A discount brokerage office operated by a national bank is not a branch for purposes of the geographic restrictions of the McFadden Act. *Clarke v. Securities Indus. Ass'n*, 107 S. Ct. 750 (1987). Thus, a national bank may operate discount brokerage offices at any location nationwide.

B Full-Service Brokerage Activities

Regulation Y specifically provides that a bank holding company providing discount brokerage services may not provide investment advice or research services. 12 C.F.R. § 225.25(b)(15) (1987) The Board initially carved out a limited exception to this prohibition for institutional and high net worth customers. 'National Westminster Bank PLC', 72 *Fed. Res. Bull.* 584 (1986) (NatWest); see also 'Manufacturers Hanover Corp.', 73 *Fed. Res. Bull* 930 (1987); 'J. P. Morgan & Co.', 73 *Fed. Res. Bull* 810 (1987). The Board's NatWest order was upheld in *Securities Indus. Ass'n v. Board of Governors of the Fed. Reserve Sys.*, 821 F.2d 810 (D.C. Cir. 1987), *cert. denied*, 56 U.S.L.W. 3459 (U.S. Jan. 11, 1988) (No. 87–562). In *Bank of New England Corp.* the Board is expected for the first time to approve the combined offering of securities brokerage and investment advisory services by a bank holding company. *See* 'Application of Bank of New England Corp.', 52 *Fed. Reg. 44,934 (1987) (Board approval anticipated in May of 1988). The Comptroller's Office has allowed a national bank to offer combined discount brokerage and investment advisory services to retail customers, 'OCC Interpretive Letter No. 386', [Current] Fed. Banking L. Rep.* (CCH) ¶ 85,610 (June 19, 1987), and to purchase on the order of customers shares of mutual funds for which the bank acts as investment adviser, 'OCC Interpretive Letter NO. 403', [Current] *Fed. Banking L. Rep.* (CCH) ¶ 85,627 (Dec. 9, 1987).

C   Margin Lending and Incidental Activities

Regulation Y authorises bank holding companies to provide, in conjunction with discount brokerage services, related securities credit activities and incidental activities such as offering custodial services, individual retirement accounts, and cash management services. 12 C.F.R. § 225.25(b)(15) (1987). National banks are permitted to provide similar incidental services under their general banking powers.

D   Gold, Silver, and Coins

The Board by order has authorised bank holding companies to engage in the purchase and sale of gold and silver bullion and coins, but not platinum and palladium, for the account of customers. 'First Interstate Bancorp', 71 *Fed. Res. Bull.* 467 (1985); 'Standard and Chartered Banking Group Ltd.', 38 *Fed. Reg'.* 27,552 (1973). National banks are permitted to buy and sell coins and bullion under 12 U.S.C. § 24 (Seventh).

E   Money Orders, Travellers Cheques and Savings Bonds

Regulation Y authorises bank holding companies to sell money orders and similar consumer-type instruments having a face value of not over $1,000, travelers' checks, and U.S. savings bonds. 12 C.F.R. § 225.25(b)(12) (1987). The Board has authorised by order the sale of money orders having a face value of not over $10,000. 'BankAmerica', 70 *Fed. Res. Bull.* 364 (1984).

F   Sale of Notes of Parent

The Comptroller's Office has issued a letter permitting a national bank to sell on commission notes of its parent bank holding company to the bank's sophisticated and institutional customers. 'OCC No Objection Letter No. 87-3', [Current] *Fed. Banking L. Rep.* (CCH) ¶ 84,032 (Mar. 24, 1987). The Board has indicated that notes issued by a bank holding company should not be sold on the premises of subsidiary banks. 'Securities Activities', 1 *Fed. Res. Reg. Serv. No. 4–867*, –867.1.

G   Foreign Exchange Transactions

Regulation Y authorises bank holding companies to provide 'transactional services with respect to foreign exchange by arranging for "swaps" among customers with complementary foreign exchange exposures and for the execution of foreign exchange transactions', subject to conditions including that the company does not itself execute foreign exchange transactions or take positions for its own account. 12 C.F.R. § 225.25(b)(17) (1987).

H   Options on Money Market Securities

The Board by order has authorised bank holding companies to act as a broker with respect to options on United States government securities, money market instruments, foreign currency, and bullion. 'Citicorp', 70 *Fed. Res. Bull.* 591 (1985); 'Fidelcor', 70 *Fed. Res. Bull.* 368 (1984); 'Security Pac. Corp.', 69 *Fed. Res. Bull.* 742 (1983). National Banks are authorised to provide similar services under their general banking powers.

I   Stock Exchange Membership

Discount brokerage subsidiaries of banks and bank holding companies may maintain memberships and seats on various national and regional securities exchanges, 'BankAmerica Corp.', 69 *Fed. Res. Bull.* 105, 106 (1983), and may lease exchange seats to client lessees. 'OCC Interpretive Letter No. 380', [Current] *Fed. Banking L. Rep.* (CCH) ¶ 85,604 (Dec. 29, 1986).

J   Securities Lending

The Comptroller has permitted a national bank to engage in securities lending and borrowing as part of its brokerage business. *See* 'OCC Interpretive Letter No. 380', [Current] *Fed. Banking L. Rep.* (CCH) ¶ 85, 604 (Dec. 29, 1986); 'OCC Banking Circular No. 196', [1984–1985 Transfer Binder] *Fed. Banking L. Rep.* (CCH) ¶ 86,248 (May 7, 1985).

K   Mutual Funds

Banks and bank holding companies may purchase and sell shares of mutual funds or unit investment trusts (UIT's) as agent for their customers. See MUTUAL FUND ACTIVITIES, *infra*, pt. IV.

L   Sweep Arrangements

Banks and bank holding companies are authorised to offer 'sweep' services in connection wtih discount brokerage services in which idle customer deposits exceeding a predetermined amount are swept into money market mutual funds or other investments. 'BankAmerica Corp.', 69 *Fed. Res. Bull.* 105, 108 (1983).

M   Leasing of Space to Broker

The Board has allowed a state member bank to lease space in its lobby to a discount brokerage firm and to receive a percentage of the firm's gross revenues in addition to rent. Letter from William W. Wiles to Donald W. Smith (Dec. 18, 1986). The Board required the brokerage firm, in addition to other restrictions, to conduct its operations separately from those of the bank, have no common employees with the bank, and provide no investment advice on the bank's premises. *Id.* The Comptroller has allowed a national bank to enter into a similar percentage lease arrangement with a full-service brokerage firm and, unlike the Board, has allowed the bank and broker to share common employees. Letter from Richard V. Fitzgerald, Chief Counsel, OCC (INVEST program) (June 4, 1985).

N   Riskless Principal Transactions

National bank brokers may purchase and sell securities in 'riskless principal' transactions in which the broker, after receiving a customer's order to buy or sell a security, buys or sells the security to offset a contemporaneous sale to or purchase from the customer. 'OCC Interpretive Letter No. 371', [Current] *Fed. Banking L. Rep.* (CCH) ¶ 85,541 (June 13, 1986). The Board has permitted riskless principal transactions only in limited circumstances. 'BankAmerica Corp.', 69 *Fed. Res. Bull.* 105, 116 n.55 (1983); Letter from the Board's Deputy General Counsel to Fred F. Bagwell, Vice President, Federal Reserve Bank of Richmond (June 24, 1986).

O   Acting as Specialist

The Comptroller has permitted a national bank to act as the specialist in Deutsche mark options on the Philadelphia Stock Exchange through a joint venture with a securities firm. Letter from the Deputy Comptroller for Multinational Banking to H. Helmut Loring, Bank of America (Jan. 11, 1984). The Board has denied an application by a bank holding company to act as the specialist in options on French francs traded on the Philadelphia Stock Exchange. 'Compagnie Financiere de Suez, Banque Indosuez', 72 *Fed. Res. Bull.* 141 (1986).

P   Municipal Securities Brokers' Broker

The Board by order has authorised a bank holding company subsidiary to act as a municipal securities brokers' broker and thereby provide brokerage services to other registered securities brokers and dealers, including dealer banks, consisting of acting as an undisclosed agent in the purchase and sale of muncipal securities, including revenue bonds, for the account of customers. 'Independent Banker Fin. Corp.', 71 *Fed. Res. Bull.* 651 (1985).

Q   Options Trading System

The Board by order has authorised a bank holding company to establish and operate a proprietary system for trading over-the-counter put and call options on United States Treasure securities by government securities dealers and other institutions that wish to trade in options on Treasury securities without disclosing their identity to other market participants. 'Security Pac. Corp.', 73 *Fed. Res. Bull.* 815 (1987). This activity was affected by the Competitive Bank Equality Act of 1987 (CEBA) moratorium on the operation of a 'nondealer marketplace in options'. Pub. L. No. 100–86, § 201(b)(2)(C), 101 Stat. 552, 582 (codified at 12 U.S.C.A. § 1841 note (West Supp. 1987); see Board Order of Feb. 4, 1988, vacating its Aug. 5 order.

III   UNDERWRITING AND DEALING ACTIVITIES

A   Government and Bank Eligible Securities

National and state member banks are specifically authorised by the Glass–Steagall Act to underwrite and deal in obligations of the United States, general obligations of states and their political subdivision, and certain specified government guaranteed obligations, and certain money market instruments such as certificates of deposit and bankers acceptances ('bank eligible securities'). 12 U.S.C. § 24(Seventh) (1982 & Supp. IV 1986). Regulation Y authorises bank holding companies to underwrite and deal in bank eligible securities subject to the same limitations that would apply to a member bank engaging in such activity. 12 C.F.R. § 225.25(b)(16) (1987)

B   Bank Ineligible Securities

The Board by order has authorised bank holding companies to underwrite and deal in, to a limited extent, certain securities not eligible to be underwritten by banks, including commercial paper, municipal revenue bonds, mortgage-backed securities, and consumer-receivable-backed securities. 'Citicorp/J. P. Morgan & Co/Bankers Trust N.Y. Corp.', 73 *Fed. Res. Bull.* 473 (1987); 'Chemical N.Y. Corp.', 73 *Fed. Res. Bull.* 731 (1987). The Board requires bank holding companies, in order to avoid being 'engaged principally' in such activities in violation of § 20 of the Glass–Steagall Act, to limit the gross revenues derived from such activities to 5% of an underwriting subsidiary's total gross revenues (the Board indicated that this limit may be raised to 10% after reasonable experience with the activity) and to limit their market share in each type of security to 5% of the total domestic market. 'Citicorp/J. P. Morgan & Co./Bankers Trust N.Y. Corp.', 73 *Fed. Res. Bull.* 473, 485 (1987). The Board also imposed a number of other conditions on the conduct of the activity, including prohibitions on management interlocks, underwriting of affiliates' securities, and extensions of credit to issuers. *Id.* at 503–04. The Board's orders were upheld, with the exception of the 5% market limitation, in *Securities Indus. Ass'n v. Board of Governors of the Fed. Reserve Sys.*, 839 F.2d 47 (2d Cir. 1988), *petition for cert. filed*, 56 U.S.L.W. 3667 (U.S. Mar. 12, 1988). In addition, the moratorium imposed by CEBA prevented bank holding companies from engaging in such activities until after March 1, 1988. 12 U.S.C.A. § 1841 (*West Supp.* 1988). Although of limited effect, it is noteworthy that the Chief Counsel of the Comptroller of the Currency has opined that a national bank affiliate would not be engaged principally in unlawful securities activities if it derived 25% of its business from such activities. 'OCC Interpretive Letter No. 383', [Current] *Fed. Banking L. Rep.* (CCH) ¶ 85,607 (Jan. 29, 1987).

C   FDIC-Insured State Non-member Banks

FDIC insured state non-member banks may establish 'bona fide' subsidiaries that engage in underwriting of investment quality equity and other securities without limitations as to gross revenues or market share. 12 C.F.R. § 337.4

(1987). The FDIC's regulation defines a 'bona fide' subsidiary to mean a subsidiary that is physically separate and distinct in its operation of the bank, shares no common officers, and satisfies other requirements designed to insure its separation from the bank. *Id.* § 337.4(a)(2). The FDIC's regulation is premised on the inapplicability of the Glass–Steagall Act to affiliations between nonmember banks and securities firms. The moratorium in the CEBA applied § 20 of the Glass–Steagall Act to such affiliations until March 1, 1988. 12 U.S.C.A. § 1828 (*West Supp.* 1988). The FDIC's regulation was upheld in *Investment Co. Inst. v. FDIC*, 815 F.2d 1540 (D.C. Cir. 1987), *cert. denied*, 56 U.S.L.W. 3206 (U.S. Oct. 6, 1987).

D   Private Placements

The Board, the Comptroller, and the FDIC have interpreted the Glass–Steagall Act to allow banks to engage in the private placement of securities, including commerical paper and corporate equities. Federal Reserve Board Staff, *Commercial Bank Private Placement Activities*, June 27, 1977; COMPTROLLER OF THE CURRENCY, FDIC, FEDERAL RESERVE BOARD, COMMERCIAL BANK PRIVATE PLACEMENT ACTIVITIES (1978). The private placement of commercial paper by a state member bank was upheld in *Securities Indus. Ass'n. v. Board of Governors of the Fed. Reserve Sys.*, 807 F.2d 1052 (D.C. Cir. 1986), *cert denied*, 107 S. Ct. 3228 (1987). In addition, the Board has approved applications by bank holding companies to engage in the private placement of commercial paper subject to limitations on extensions of credit to issuers and other restrictions. 'Banker Trust N.Y. Corp.', 73 *Fed. Res. Bull.* 138 (1987). The Comptroller of the Currency has allowed national banks to issue standby letters of credit to support commercial paper and industrial revenue bonds privately placed by such banks. [1983–1984 Transfer Binder] *Fed. Banking L. Rep.* (CCH) ¶ 85,449 (1984); [1981–1982 Transfer Binder] *Fed. Banking L. Rep.* (CCH) ¶ 85,293 (1981).

E   Issuance of Notes

A bank holding company may issue commercial paper and short-term notes on an ongoing basis provided that such notes are not sold on bank premises and the aggregate principal amount of such notes does not exceed 25% of the issuer's total assets. 'Acquisition of Non-bank Interests – Selling Demand Notes', 1 *Fed. Res. Reg. Serv.*, 4–303 (April 2, 1982); 'Securities Activities', 1 Fed. Res. Reg. Serv., 4–867, 60 *Fed. Res. Bull.* 36 (1974); 12 C.F.R. § 250.221 (1987). The Comptroller has issued a no objection letter allowing a national bank to sell notes of its parent to the bank's sophisticated and institutional customers. 'No Objection Letter No. 87–3', [Current] *Fed. Banking L. Rep.* (CCH) ' 84,032 (Mar. 24, 1987).

F   Retail Repurchase Agreements

Banks may issue retail repurchase agreements (Repos) under which a bank transfers United States government securities or a fractional interest in a pool of such securities to a customer in exchange for cash under an agreement to repurchase the securities at a future date. 'Repurchase Agreements – Policy on Issuance Of', 1 *Fed. Res. Reg. Serv.* No. 3–1579 (April 13, 1982).

G   Commercial Paper Sweep Arrangements

The Board has allowed a bank holding company to sweep bank deposits into commercial paper issued by the parent, the proceeds of which are used by a non-bank subsidiary to originate or purchase loans that are resold in forty-five to ninety days. Letter from James McAfee, Associate Secretary Federal Reserve Board, to Jerome W. Evans, Senior Vice President and Controller, Equitable bank, N.A. (June 9, 1987); see also 1 *Fed. Res. Reg. Serv.* No. 4–318.1 (Nov. 4, 1982).

IV   MUTUAL FUND ACTIVITIES

A   Private Label Funds

Banks frequently arrange with an independent distributor to organise an open-end investment company (mutual fund) for which the bank will act as investment adviser and which will be marketed by the distributor to the bank's customers. *See supra* section IF. The Comptroller's Office has allowed a national bank subsidiary to recommend and sell to brokerage customers shares of mutual funds for which the subsidiary acts as investment adviser. 'OCC Interpretive Letter No. 403', [Current] *Fed. Banking L. Rep.* (CCH) ¶ 85,627 (Dec. 9, 1987). The Board's investment adviser interpretation states that bank employees should not recommend that a customer purchase shares of any investment company for which an affiliate serves as investment advisor and imposes limitations on bank holding companies with respect to the purchase of fund shares for trust accounts, sharing of a similar name by the adviser and fund, the sale of customer lists to the distributor, and other restrictions. 12 C.F.R. § 225.125 (1987).

B   Shareholder Services

A number of banking organisations provide shareholder services with respect to mutual funds they advise, including answering customer inquiries about the funds, providing personnel and facilities to establish and maintain shareholder accounts and records, assisting shareholders in purchase and redemption transactions, transmitting proxies, and providing monthly statements. 'Banks are Offering More Fund Services', *Wall St. J.*, Feb. 19, 1988, at 31, col. 1.

C   Brokerage of Mutual Funds

Discount brokerage subsidiaries of banks and bank holding companies may purchase and sell shares of mutual funds or UIT's as agent for their customers and may receive a fee from the fund for brokerage and related administrative services, subject to regulatory restrictions including a prohibition on advertising or promotion of any specific fund. Letter from Michael Bradfield, General Counsel, Federal Reserve Board, to Bruce B. Nolte, Vice President, Sovran Investment Corp. (June 27, 1986); OCC Interpretive Letter No. 363 (May 23, 1986). As noted in section IV-C, *supra*, the Comptroller has permitted a subsidiary of a national bank to recommend, purchase and sell, for brokerage customers, shares of a mutual fund it advises.

D Closed-End Funds

A bank holding company may organise, sponsor, and manage a closed-end investment company, 12 C.F.R. § 225.25(b)(4) (1987), and an open-end investment company that issues shares only infrequently. 'Bayerische Vereinsbank AG', 73 *Fed. Res. Bull.* 155, 157 (1987); *Board of Governors of the Fed. Reserve Sys.* v. *Investment Co. Inst.*, 450 U.S. 46 (1981).

E Nonmember Bank Mutual Funds

Regulations of the FDIC allow insured state non-member banks to organise, sponsor, and distribute mutual funds through 'bona fide' subsidiaries that must be operated and maintained separate from the bank. 12 C.F.R. § 337.4 (1987). The FDIC's regulation is premised on the inapplicability of the Glass–Steagall Act to affiliations between nonmember banks and securities firms. 49 *Fed. Reg. 46,722*, 46,723–25 (1984). As noted above, the moratorium enacted by the CEBA covered such affiliations under Glass–Steagall until March 1, 1988.

F Commingling of IRA Funds

National banks are permitted to establish common trust funds for individual retirement accounts (IRA's). *Investment Co. Inst.* v. *Clarke*, 793 F.2d 220 (9th Cir.) *cert. denied*, 107 S. Ct. 422 (1986); *Investment Co. Inst.* v. *Conover*, 790 F.2d 925 (D.C. Cir.), *cert. denied*, 107 S. Ct. 421 (1986); *Investment Co. Inst.* v. *Clarke*, 789 F.2d 175 (2d Cir.) *cert. denied*, 107 S. Ct. 422 (1986).

G Section 4(c)(7) Mutual Fund

A bank holding company may organise, manage, and control an open-end investment company that is not engaged in any business other than investing in securities which do not include more than 5% of the outstanding voting shares of any company. 12 U.S.C. § 1843(c)(7) (1982). Although the current position of the Board's staff is that this provision is intended to be used by a bank holding company only for its own investments, the Board's General Counsel and the Solicitor General advised the Supreme Court in their brief in *Board of Governors of the Federal Reserve System* v. *Investment Co. Institute*, 450 U.S. 46 (1981), that § 4(c)(7) permits a bank holding company to operate an investment company in which other investors have an interest.

Brief for Petitioner at 14–15, *Board of Governors of the Fed. Reserve Sys.* v. *Investment Co. Inst.*, 450 U.S. 46 (1981) (No. 79–927).

H   Section 4(c)(8) Mutual Fund

In 1987, the Chase Manhattan Corporation filed an application to sponsor, distribute, and advise funds through a nonbanking subsidiary which, it argued, would not be 'engaged principally' in underwriting or distribution of securities for purposes of § 20 of Glass–Steagall. Chase withdrew the application, however, apparently in response to the Board staff's conclusion that, by organising the funds, Chase would control them and thus be 'engaged principally' in unlawful securities activities. See 1 *Fed. Res. Reg. Serv.* 4–270.3 (Board ruling of Dec. 14, 1982). The Comptroller of the Currency has interpreted § 20 to permit a national bank to be affiliated with a company that organises, sponsors, and manages mutual funds. 'Comptroller of the Currency Decision to Charter Dreyfus National Bank & Trust Co.', *News Release 83–09* (Feb. 7, 1983); 'Comptroller of the Currency Decision to Charter J. & W. Seligman Trust Co.', N.A., *News Release 83–06* (Feb. 2, 1983).

V   INVESTMENT AND TRADING ACTIVITIES

A   Investment Securities

The Glass Steagall Act specifically authorises national and member banks to purchase for their own account investment securities under limitations prescribed by the Comptroller of the Currency, provided that in no event may the total amount of investment securities of any one obligor held by a bank exceed 10% of the bank's capital and surplus. 12 U.S.C. § 24(Seventh) (1982 & Supp. IV 1986). The Comptroller has defined the term 'investment security' to mean a 'marketable obligation in the form of a bond, note, or debenture which is commonly regarded as an investment security' and is not predominantly speculative in nature. 12 C.F.R. § 1.3 (1987). Bank holding companies are authorised to make similar investments. 12 U.S.C. § 1843(c)(5) (1982).

B   Bank Eligible Mutual Funds

National and state member banks are permitted to purchase for their own account shares of open-end investment companies whose portfolios consist solely of securities eligible for bank investment. 'Banking Practices', 1 *Fed. Res. Reg. Serv. No. 3–416.14*, at 3–224.18 (May 1985); *OCC Banking Bulletin No. 83–58 (Dec. 15, 1982)*.

C   Five Percent Investments

A bank holding company may acquire, as a passive investment, voting securities of a company that represents 5% or less of the outstanding shares of any class of voting securities of the company. 12 U.S.C. § 1843(c)(6) (1982); 12 C.F.R. §§ 225.22(c)(5), 225.137 (1987).

D   Non-voting Equity Investments

Bank holding companies may make non-voting equity investments in securities firms provided that the investments do not result in control of the securities firm. In reviewing the proposed investment by The Sumitomo Bank, Ltd., in Goldman, Sachs & Co., the Board established a framework for such investments under which, inter alia, the investment, including subordinated debt, may not exceed 24.9% of the target firm's capital, the companies may not share common management officials, the amount of business between them will not increase and will be maintained on an arms-length basis with no customer referrals, and the investor will enhance its capital position by an amount that will substantially offset the funds invested. Letter from William W. Wiles to John L. Carr (Nov. 25, 1986). The Board stated that passive, noncontrolling investments structured within this framework do not raise any Glass–Steagall issues. *Id.*

E   DPC Acquisitions

Bank holding companies may acquire voting securities in the ordinary course of collecting a debt previously contracted (DPC) in good faith, without prior Board approval, if the shares are divested within two years of acquisition or longer if the Board grants an extension. 12 U.S.C. § 1843(c)(2) (1982); 12 C.F.R. § 225.22(c)(1) (1987). National banks similarly may acquire stock DPC and may exchange real estate acquired DPC for preferred stock. OCC Interpretive Letter No 395 (Aug. 24, 1987) (LEXIS, Banking library, OCC file).

F   Financial Futures and Options

National and state member banks are authorised to purchase and sell for their own account financial options and futures on securities that are permissible investments for member banks. 12 C.F.R. § 255.142 (1987); 'OCC Interpretive Letter No. 260', [1983–1984 Transfer Binder] *Fed. Banking L. Rep.* (CCH) ¶ 85,424 (June 27, 1983); *OCC Banking Circular 79*, April 19, 1983; 'Financial Contracts', 1 *Fed. Res. Reg. Serv. No. 3–1535 at 3–478.6 (Dec. 1985).*

G   Arbitrage of Financial Futures

The Comptroller has allowed national banks to engage in the arbitrage of financial futures contracts against other financial futures contracts on bank eligible securities. 'OCC No Objection Letter No. 86–13', [Current] *Fed. Banking L. Rep. (CCH)* ¶ 84,019 (Aug. 8, 1986). The Board has denied an application by a bank holding company to buy and sell foreign currency futures for its own account through pit arbitrage. 'Citicorp', 68 *Fed. Res. Bull.* 776, 779–80 (1982).

H   Options on Foreign Currency and Eurodollar Deposits

The Comptroller has permitted national banks to buy and sell for the account of the bank foreign currency and Eurodollar time deposits and options on such instruments and to act as a market maker for such options on United States stock exchanges subject to certain conditions to limit the bank's liability from its exchange activities. 'OCC Interpretive Letter No. 384', [Current] *Fed. Banking L. Rep* (CCH) ¶ 85,608 (May 19, 1987).

I   Community Development Investments

Regulation Y authorises a bank holding company to make 'equity and debt investments in corporations or projects designed primarily to promote community welfare, such as the economic rehabilitation and development of low-income areas by providing housing, services or jobs for residents'. 12 C.F.R. § 225.25(b)(6) (1987).

J   Small Business Investment Corporations

The Small Business Investment Act authorises national banks to own 100% of the voting stock of a small business investment company. Bank holding companies are permitted to make similar investments under § 4(c)(5) of the BHCA, subject to certain limitations. 'Acquisition of Non-bank Interest-SBIC', 1 *Fed. Res. Reg. Serv. No. 4–175*, at 4.56.1 (Sept. 1961); 'Acquisition of Nonbank Interests', 1 *Fed. Res. Reg. Serv. No. 4–296*, at 4–94 (Nov. 1982).

K   New York Investment Company

The Board by order has approved the operation by a bank holding company of a New York investment company chartered under article XII of the New York banking Law provided that the company does not engage in certain activities authorised for such companies, such as underwriting securities. 'European-American Bancorp', 63 *Fed. Res. Bull.* 595 (1977).

L   Shares Held in Fiduciary Capacity

Bank holding companies are permitted to hold shares in good faith in a fiduciary capacity. 12 U.S.C. § 1843(c)(4) (1982); 12 C.F.R. § 225.22(c)(3) (1987).

M   Loan Participations

Commercial banks have traditionally bought and sold loans and participations in loans pursuant to their general authority to discount and negotiate promissory notes. 12 U.S.C. § 24(Seventh) (1982 & Supp. IV 1986).

N Securities Borrowing and Lending

Banks may borrow and lend their own investment and trading account securities as well as customers' securities held in custody, trust, or pension accounts to cover securities short sales and option and arbitrage positions. 'Securities Lending – Supervisory Policy Statement', 1 *Fed. Res. Reg. Serv. No. 3–1579.5, at 3–498–7 (May 6, 1985).*

O Debt-for-Equity Swaps

A bank holding company may acquire up to 100% of the shares of a foreign public sector company and up to 40% of the shares of a foreign private sector nonfinancial company if the shares are acquired from a foreign government by conversion of sovereign debt obligations, the proceeds of which are used to purchase the shares. In addition, the bank holding company may not acquire more than 25% of the shares of a private sector company unless another shareholder(s) holds a larger block of voting shares and complies with restrictions on extension of credit and director interlocks. 12 C.F.R. § 211.5(f) (1987), *as amended by* 53 Fed. Reg. 5358 (1988). Such shares may be held by an insured bank under certain circumstances approved by the Board and may be held for no more than fifteen years.

VI SECURITISATION OF ASSETS

The Comptroller has authorised national banks to issue and sell mortgage-backed securities and certificates evidencing ownership interests in other pooled assets of the bank. 'OCC Interpretive Letter No. 388', [Current] *Fed. Banking L. Rep.* (CCH) ¶ 85,612 (June 16, 1987) (citing prior OCC rulings, including 'OCC Interpretive Letter No. 362', [Current] *Fed. Banking Law Rep.* (CCH) ¶ 85,532 (May 22, 1986) (national bank subsidiary may issue, underwrite, and deal in collateralised mortgage obligations). The Comptroller concluded that this activity is authorised under the National Bank Act and does not involve the sale of a 'security' within the meaning of Glass–Steagall. *Id.* In most cases, the bank arranges for the distribution of asset-backed securities through an investment bank, but some banks have sold such securities directly to the public or established bank holding company subsidiaries to distribute such securities. The Securities Industry Association has challenged the Comptroller's interpretation under the Glass–Steagall Act. See *Securities Indus. Ass'n. v. Clarke*, No. 87–4504, slip op. (S.D.N.Y. filed June 25, 1987).

The Federal Financial Institutions Examination Council (FFIEC) has ruled that sales of securitised assets will be treated as a sale of assets without recourse to the bank for call report purposes, even if the bank retains a residual interest in an escrow account established to absorb loan losses. FFIEC Press Release of Nov. 21, 1986.

Sales of securitised assets when the bank retains an interest are treated as deposits subject to reserve requirements under the Board's Regulation D. 12 C.F.R. § 204.2(a)(1)(vii) (1987). Sales of mortgage-backed securities are not treated as reservable deposits if the bank retains no more than a 10% interest in the pooled assets. *Id.* § 204.2(a)(2)(ix).

In Congress, some argued that the moratorium in the CEBA covered the sale of securitised assets. See 133 *Cong. Rec.* E3446 (daily ed. Aug. 20, 1987) (statements of Rep. Schumer). Another view is that this activity was authorised in writing prior to March 5, 1987, and thus was not subject to the moratorium. See 133 *Cong. Rec.* E3602 (daily ed. Sept. 17, 1987) (statement of Rep. Barnard).

VII JOINT VENTURES

The Board has permitted bank holding companies to engage in joint ventures with securities firms under limited circumstances. In 'Amsterdam-Rotterdam Bank, N.V.', 70 *Fed. Res. Bull.* 835 (1984), the Board approved a joint venture between a foreign-based bank holding company and a United States company whose subsidiaries engaged in sponsoring mutual funds. *Id.* at 835–36. The joint venture engaged in investment advisory and discretionary portfolio management services, primarily for foreign clients with respect to United States securities. *Id.* at 835.

In 'Independent Bankers Financial Corp.', 71 *Fed. Res. Bull.* 651, 652 (1985), the Board approved a joint venture between a securities brokerage subsidiary of a bank holding company and a wholly-owned subsidiary of a foreign securities company for the purpose of engaging in municipal securities brokerage services to other registered securities brokers and dealers and acting as undisclosed agent in the purchase and sale of municipal securities for the account of its customers. *Id.* at 652. In both cases, the Board imposed extensive conditions designed to maintain a separation among the joint ventures, the securities firms, and the bank holding companies. *Id.* at 653–54; 'Amsterdam-Rotterdam Bank, N.V.', 70 *Fed. Res. Bull.* 835, 836 (1984).

In 'Chemical New York Corp.', 73 *Fed. Res. Bull.* 362 (1987), the Board approved a joint venture between eleven bank holding companies and sixteen investment banking companies to act as an interdealer broker of United States government securities for primary dealers. The Board concluded that the arrangement did not raise significant concerns in view of the wide dispersion of ownership and limited activities of the joint venture. *Id.*

The Comptroller of the Currency has permitted a national bank to act as the specialist in Deutsche mark options on the Philadelphia Stock Exchange through a joint venture with a securities firm. Letter from the Deputy Comptroller for Multinational Banking to H. Helmut Loring, Bank of America (Jan. 11, 1984).

VII NEW DEPOSIT INSTRUMENTS

A Market Index Account

In 1987, The Chase Manhattan Corporation introduced a new deposit account that ties returns to the stock market. The so-called 'Market Index

Invest Account' is a time deposit account that bears interest based on a portion of the increases in the Standard & Poor's 500 Composite Stock Price Index and is offered with maturities of three, six, nine, or twelve months with either a guaranteed minimum interest rate or no guaranteed return. The principal and guaranteed return are insured by the FDIC. The Investment Company Institute has challenged the new account as the issuance and sale of securities in violation of § 16 of the Glass–Steagall Act. *Investment Co. Inst. v. Chase Manhattan Bank*, No. 87–1093, slip op. (D.D.C. Apr. 21, 1987). The Commodity Futures Trading Commission has issued a proposed regulatory framework affecting 'hybrid' commodity related instruments under the Commodity Exchange Act. 53 *Fed. Reg.* 2510 (Jan. 28, 1988); 52 *Fed. Reg.* 47,022 (Dec. 11, 1987).

B Deposit Participations

The Comptroller's Office has authorised a national bank to sell to depositors participation interests in FDIC-insured certificates of deposit (CD's) issued by other banks which the bank will purchase from pooled deposits. 'OCC Interpretive Letter No. 385', [Current] *Fed. Banking L. Rep* (CCH) ¶ 85,609 (June 19, 1987). As described in the OCC letter, the FDIC does not insure the participation certificate, although the underlying CD is FDIC-insured. The Comptroller's Office noted that no court has yet addressed whether the antifraud provisions of the securities laws cover participation certificates in deposits and advised the bank to seek the SEC's views on this point. The Supreme Court held that a bank CD issued by a federally regulated bank was not a security under the securities laws in view of the pervasive system of federal bank regulation and FDIC insurance in *Marine Bank v. Weaver*, 455 U.S. 551, 556–59 (1982). On the other hand, a lower court held that bank CD's marketed by Merrill Lynch are securities covered by the securities laws in *Gary Plastics Packing Corp. v. Merrill Lynch, Pierce, Fenner & Smith, Inc.*, 756 F.2d 230, 240–42 (2d Cir. 1985).

IX ACTIVITIES WITH RESPECT TO COMMODITIES

A Futures Commission Merchant

Regulation Y authorises bank holding companies to act as futures commission merchants (FCM's) for nonaffiliated persons in the execution and clearance on major commodity exchanges of futures contracts and options on futures contracts for gold and silver bullion, foreign exchange, government securities, certificates of deposit, and other money market instruments that a bank may buy or sell in the cash market for its own account, if the activity is conducted through a separately incorporated subsidiary of the bank holding company and complies with other requirements in the regulation, including a restriction against trading for a holding company's own account except for hedging. 12 C.F.R. § 225.25(b)(18) (1987). The Board by order has authorised bank holding companies to engage in executing and clearing futures contracts on a municipal bond index, 'Bankers Trust New York Corp. (BT

Futures Corp.)', 71 *Fed. Res. Bull.* 111 (1985), and on stock indexes and options on such futures contracts. 'J. P. Morgan & Co.', 71 *Fed. Res. Bull.* 251 (1985). National banks may engage in similar activities. See 'OCC Interpretive Letter No. 380', [Current] *Fed. Banking L. Rep.* (CCH) ¶ 85,604 (Dec. 29, 1986); 'OCC Interpretive Letter No. 365', [Current] *Fed. Banking L. Rep.* (CCH) ¶ 85,535 (Aug. 11, 1986); 'OCC Interpretive Letter No. 357', [Current] *Fed. Banking L. Rep.* (CCH) ¶ 85,527 (Feb. 26, 1986); 'OCC Interpretive Letter No. 356', [Current] *Fed. Banking L. Rep.* (CCH) ¶ 85,526 (Jan. 7, 1986).

B   Advice on Financial Futures and Options

Regulation Y authorises bank holding companies acting as FCM's to provide investment advice to financially sophisticated customers with respect to the purchase and sale of futures contracts and options on futures contracts for commodities and instruments with respect to which FCM activities are authorised under Regulation Y, provided that a company may not trade for its own account other than to hedge. 12 C.F.R. § 225.25(b)(19) (1987). The Board by order has authorised bank holding companies to provide advice with respect to stock index futures and options on such futures. 'Citicorp', 73 *Fed. Res. Bull.* 220 (1987). National banks may engage in similar activities. See 'OCC Interpretive Letter No. 365', [Current] *Fed. Banking L. Rep.* (CCH) ¶ 85,535 (Aug. 11, 1986).

C   Futures on Agricultural Commodities

The Comptroller has permitted national banks to execute transactions in futures contracts for agricultural commodities on behalf of loan customers for the sole purpose of hedging risks associated with the customers' loans from the bank. 'OCC Interpretive Letter No. 356', [Current] *Fed. Bank L. Rep.* (CCH) ¶ 85,526 (Jan. 7, 1986). The Board has denied an application by a bank holding company to engage in trading of physical commodities futures on a foreign futures exchange. 'Bankers Int'l Corp.', 67 *Fed. Res. Bull.* 364 (1981).

D   Commodity and Price Index Swaps

The Comptroller has authorised national banks to act as principal in commodity price index swaps with customers in which the bank would act as intermediary between two counterparties to a matched transaction. 'OCC No Objection Letter No. 87-5', [Current] *Fed. Banking L. Rep.* (CCH) ¶ 84,034 (July 20, 1987). The Board has authorised bank holding companies to conduct commodity swaps through export trading subsidiaries. Letter from the Board to Citicorp (July 2, 1987).

E   FCM Margin Financing

The Comptroller has allowed national banks to provide margin financing to FCM customers who trade in securities and securities options. 'OCC

Interpretive Letter No. 380', [Current] *Fed. Banking L. Rep.* (CCH) ¶ 85,604 (Dec. 29, 1986).

F   Commodities Exchange Membership

The Comptroller has permitted subsidiaries of national banks to hold memberships on securities and commodities exchanges and to lease exchange seats to customers as an incident to permissible brokerage activities. 'OCC Interpretive Letter No. 380', [Current] *Fed. Banking L. Rep.* (CCH) ¶ 85,604 (Dec. 29, 1986).

X   SECURITIES ACTIVITIES ABROAD

A   Branches

The Board's Regulation K authorises United States member banks to establish branches in foreign countries that may engage in the following securities activities:

1   *Investments*

a. Investments in the securities of the central bank, clearing houses, government entities, and government sponsored development banks of the country in which the foreign branch is located,

b. Other debt securities eligible to meet local reserve or similar requirements, and

c. Shares of professional societies, schools and the like necessary to the business of the branch, provided that the total investments may not exceed 1% of total deposits of the bank's branches in that country. 12 C.F.R. § 211.3(b)(2) (1987).

2   *Government Obligations*

Underwriting, distributing, buying, and selling obligations of:

a. the national government of the country in which the branch is located;

b. an agency or instrumentally of the national government; and

c. a municipality or other local or regional governmental entity of the country, provided that no member bank may hold such obligations for its own account in an aggregate amount not exceeding 10% of the bank's capital and surplus. 12 C.F.R. ¶ 211.3(b)(3) (1987).

B   Edge and Agreement Corporations

The Board's Regulation K also authorises the formation of corporations, pursuant to § 25(a) of the Federal Reserve Act, 12 U.S.C. § 611 (1982), which may engage in the following securities activities:

1 Fiduciary and Investment Advisory

a. Holding securities in safekeeping for, or buying and selling securities upon the order and for the account and risk of customers provided such services for U.S. persons must be with respect to foreign securities only. 12 C.F.R. § 211.4(e)(7)(i) (1987).

b. Acting as paying agent for securities issued by foreign governments. *Id.* § 211.4(e)(7)(ii).

c. Acting as trustee, registrar, conversion agent, or paying agent with respect to any class of securities issued to finance foreign activities and distributed solely outside of the United States. *Id.* § 211.4(e)(7)(iii).

d. Conducting private placement activities, except that the Edge corporation may not otherwise engage in the business of underwriting, distributing, or buying or selling securities in the United States. *Id.* § 211.4(e)(7)(iv).

e. Acting as investment or financial adviser by providing portfolio investment advice and portfolio management with respect to securities, other financial instruments, real property interests and other investment assets, and by providing advice on mergers and acquisitions, provided such services for U.S. persons may be with respect to foreign assets only. *Id.* § 211.4(e)(7)(v).

f. Providing general economic information and advice, general economic statistical forecasting services and industry studies, provided such services for U.S. persons may be with respect to foreign economies and industries only. *Id.* § 211.4(e)(7)(vi).

C Subsidiaries

The Board's Regulation K authorises domestic banking organisations to engage in the following securities activities abroad through subsidiaries:

1 Investment Advice

Providing investment, financial, or economic advisory services. 12 C.F.R. § 211.5(d)(8) (1987).

2 Mutual Fund Activities

Managing a mutual fund if the fund's shares are not sold or distributed in the United States or to United States residents and the fund does not exercise managerial control over the firms in which it invests. 12 C.F.R. § 211.5(d)(11) (1987).

3 Underwriting and Dealing

Underwriting, distributing, and dealing in debt and equity securities outside the United States, 'provided that no underwriting commitment by a subsidiary of an investor for shares of an issuer may exceed $2 million or represent 20% of the capital and surplus or voting shares of an issuer unless the underwriter is covered by binding commitments from subunderwriters or other purchasers'. 12 C.F.R. § 211.5(d)(13) (1987).

4 Section 4(c)(8) Activities

Activities that the Board has determined by regulation to be closely related to banking. 12 C.F.R. § 211.5(d)(15) (1987).

5 Other Activities

With the Board's specific approval, banking organisations may engage in other activities that the Board determines are usual in connection with the transaction of the business of banking or other financial operations abroad and consistent with the Federal Reserve Act or the Bank Holding Company Act. 12 C.F.R. § 211.5(d)(16) (1987). Other activities approved by the Board include:

a. Acting as a broker on foreign futures exchanges with respect to gold bullion, foreign government bonds, Eurodollars, and sterling deposit interest rate futures. 'Citibank Overseas Inv. Corp.', 68 *Fed. Res. Bull.* 671 (1982).

b. Acting as an FCM on non-United States exchanges. 'J. P. Morgan & Co.', 71 *Fed. Res. Bull.* 251 (1985).

D Joint Ventures

A bank or bank holding company may invest in a foreign joint venture with a securities firm, provided that not more than 10% of the joint venture's consolidated assets or revenues may be attributable to activities not listed as permissible for a subsidiary. 12 C.F.R. § 211.5(b)(1)(i) (B) (1987).

E Portfolio Investments

A bank or bank holding company may make portfolio investments (investments in up to 20% of the voting shares of a nonfinancial company and including securities held in trading or dealing accounts) in a foreign organisation if the total direct and indirect portfolio investments in foreign organisations engaged in activities not permissible for joint ventures does not at any time exceed 100% of the investor's capital and surplus. 12 C.F.R. § 211.5(b)(1)(i)(C) (1987).

F Debt-for-Equity Swaps

A bank or bank holding company may acquire shares of foreign companies through the conversion of sovereign debt obligations. 12 C.F.R. § 211.5(f) (1987); see also supra Part V(0).

G Debts Previously Contracted

A bank or bank holding company may hold shares acquired to prevent a loss upon a debt previously contracted in good faith but such shares must be disposed of no later than two years after acquisition, unless the Board authorises retention for a longer period. 12 C.F.R. § 211.5(e) (1987).

XI   UNITED STATES SECURITIES ACTIVITIES OF FOREIGN BANKING ORGANISATIONS

A   Direct Activities

A foreign organisation that controls a bank, branch, agency, or commercial lending company in the United States generally may engage in securities activities in the United States only to the same extent as a domestic bank holding company under § 4 of the BHCA. 12 U.S.C. §§ 1841(h), 3106(a) (1982); 12 C.F.R. § 211.23(f) (1987).

B   Grandfathered Activities

The International Banking Act (IBA) grandfathered non-banking activities of foreign banks conducted on or before July 26, 1978. 12 U.S.C. § 3106(c) (1982). Such activities may continue to be conducted by the foreign bank unless the Board determines that termination of such activities is necessary to prevent undue concentration of resources, decreased or unfair competition, conflicts of interest, or unsound banking practices in the United States. The CEBA amended the IBA to provide that such grandfather rights will be terminated two years after the date on which a foreign bank becomes a bank holding company by acquiring control of a bank in the United States. 12 U.S.C. § 3106(c)(2) (1982).

C   Foreign Activities

Foreign banking organisations may engage in securities activities of any kind outside of the United States. 12 C.F.R. § 211.23(f) (1987).

Bibliography

Bacon (Representative, US Congress) (1933) 'Extension of Remarks – H. R. 5480', *Congressional Record*, 73rd Congress 1st Session, 75 Part 4, 22 May, 1933, pp. 3949–65.

Beatty, Randolph P. and Jay R. Ritter (1985) 'Investment Banking, Reputation, and the Underpricing of Initial Public Offerings', *Journal of Financial Economics*, vol. 15, pp. 213–32.

Beneviste, Lawrence M. and Paul A. Spindt (1988) 'Bringing New Issues to Market: A Theory of Underwriting', *Finance and Economics Discussion Series*, 39, Division of Research and Statistics, Federal Reserve Board, Washington, DC (August).

Benston, George J. (1973) *Bank Examination*, Monograph Series in Finance and Economics (formerly *The Bulletin*, Salomon Brothers Center for the Study of Financial Institutions, Graduate School of Business Administration, New York University).

Benston, George J. (1977) 'Graduated Rate Ceilings and Operating Costs by Size of Consumer Cash Loans', *Journal of Finance*, vol. 32 (June), pp. 695–707.

Benston, George J. (1982) 'Why Did Congress Pass New Financial Service Laws in the 1930s? An Alternative Opinion', *Economic Review* (Federal Reserve Bank of Atlanta), vol. 67 (April), pp. 7–10.

Benston, George J. (1985) *An Analysis of the Causes of Savings and Loan Failures*, Monograph 1985–4/5, Monograph Series in Finance and Economics (Salomon Brothers Center for the Study of Financial Institutions, Graduate School of Business Administration, New York University).

Benston, George J., Robert A. Eisenbeis, Paul M. Horvitz, Edward J. Kane, and George G. Kaufman (1986) *Perspectives on Safe & Sound Banking: Past, Present, and Future* (Cambridge, MA: MIT Press).

Benston, George J., Gerald A. Hanweck and David B. Humphrey (1982) 'Scale Economies in Banking: A Restructuring and Reassessment', *Journal of Money, Credit, and Banking*, vol. 14 (November, Part I), pp. 435–56.

Benston, George J. and George G. Kaufman (1988) *Risk and Solvency Regulation of Depository Institutions: Past Policies and Current Options*, Monograph 1988–1, Monograph Series in Finance and Economics (Salomon Brothers Center for the Study of Financial Institutions, Graduate School of Business Administration, New York University); a shorter version appears in Haraf and Kushmeider (eds) 1988, pp. 63–99.

Boyd, John H. and Stanley L. Graham (1988) 'The Profitability and Risk Effects of Allowing Bank Holding Companies to Merge with Other Financial Firms: A Simulation Study', *Quarterly Review* (Federal Reserve Bank of Minneapolis), Spring, pp. 3–20.

Brewer, Elijah III (1988) 'A Note on the Relationship between Bank Holding Company Risk and Nonbank Activity', Federal Reserve Bank of Chicago, Occasional Paper SM88–5.

Brewer, Elijah III, Diana Fortier, and Christine Pavel (1988) 'Bank Risk From Nonbank Activities', *Economic Perspectives* (Federal Reserve Bank of Chicago), July/August, pp. 14–26.

Brunner, Karl (ed) (1975) *Government Credit Allocation* (San Francisco: Institute for Contemporary Studies).

Cable, John (1985) 'Capital Market Information and Industrial Performance: The Role of West German Banks', *The Economic Journal*, vol. 95 (March), pp. 118–32.

Carosso, Vincent (1970a) *Investment Banking in America: A History* (Cambridge, MA: Harvard University Press).

Carosso, Vincent (1970b) 'Washington and Wall Street: The New Deal and Investment Bankers, 1933–1940', *Business History Review*, vol. 64, pp. 425–45.

Citicorp (1985) *Memorandum of Citicorp in Response to Request for Information Concerning Activities of the National City Company*, a portion of an 'Application of Citicorp for CSI to Engage, to a Limited Extent, in Underwriting and Dealing in Certain Investment Securities' to the Board of Governors of the Federal Reserve System (6 November).

Cleveland, Harold van B. and Thomas F. Huertas (1985) *Citibank, 1812–1970* (Cambridge, MA: Harvard University Press).

Congressional Record (1933) *Proceedings and Debates of the First Session of the Seventy-Second Congress*, volume 75-part 9, 2 May 1932 to 17 May 1932, pp. 9357–10494 (Washington: US Government Printing Office).

Congressional Record (1932) *Proceedings and Debates of the First Session of the Seventy-Third Congress*, volume 77-part 4, 12 May 1933 to 25 May 1933, pp. 3295–4326 (Washington: US Government Printing Office).

Corregan, E. Gerald (1987) 'A Framework for Reform of the Financial System', *Quarterly Review* (Federal Reserve Bank of New York) (Summer), pp. 1–8.

Eccles, Robert G. and Dwight B. Crane (1988) *Doing Deals: Investment Banks at Work* (Cambridge, MA: Harvard Business School Press).

Eckstein, Wolfram (1980) 'The Role of Banks in Corporate Concentration in West Germany', *Zeitschrift fur die gesamte Staatswissenschaft (ZgS)*, vol. 136, pp. 465–82.

Edwards, George W. (1942) 'The Myth of the Security Affiliate', *Journal of the American Statistical Association*, vol. 37, pp. 225–32.

Eisemann, Peter C. (1976) 'Diversification and Congeneric Banking Holding Company', *Journal of Bank Research*, vol 12 (Summer), pp. 68–77.

Eisenbeis, Robert A. and Larry D. Wall (1984) 'Bank Holding Company and Diversification', *Proceedings of a Conference on Bank Structure and Competition* (Chicago: Federal Reserve Bank of Chicago), pp. 340–67.

Farrar, Donald E. (1981) 'Commercial Banks, Trust Departments and Concentration of Power: A Legacy of Glass–Steagall', Capital Market Working Papers 5, Directorate of Economic and Policy Analysis, US Securities and Exchange Commission.

Federal Reserve Committee (1933) *225 Bank Suspensions: Case Histories from Examiners' Reports*, Material prepared for the information of the Federal Reserve System by the Federal Reserve Committee on Branch, Group, and Chain Banking.

Fein, Melanie L. (1986) 'The Separation of Banking and Commerce in American Banking History', Appendix A to the *Statement by Paul A. Volcker, Chairman, Board of Governors of the Federal Reserve System*, before the Subcommittee on Commerce, Consumer & Monetary Affairs of the Committee on Government Operations of the United States House of Representatives (June) A–1 – A–13.

First National City Bank (1970) *Brief for Respondent First National City Bank*, Investment Company Institute v. Camp, in the Supreme Court of the United States, October Term.

Fischer, Thomas G., William H. Gram, George G. Kaufman, and Larry R. Mote (1984) 'The Securities Activities of Commercial Banks: A Legal and Economic Analysis', *Tennessee Law Review*, vol. 51, pp. 467–518.

Flannery, Mark J. (1985) 'An Economic Evaluation of Bank Securities Activities Before 1933', in Walter (ed.) (1985), pp. 67–87.

Flannery, Mark. J. (1988) 'Payments System Risk and Public Policy', in Haraf and Kushmeider (eds) (1988) pp. 261–87.

Flynn, John T. (1930) *Investment Trusts Gone Wrong!* (New York: New Republic).

Franke, Hans-Hermann and Michael Hudson (1984) *Banking and Finance in West Germany* (New York: St Martins Press).

Gerschenkron, Alexander (1962) *Economic Backwardness in Historical Perspective* (Cambridge, MA: Belknop Press of Harvard University Press).

Gessler Commission (1979) (Commission on Banking Structure, Studienkommission), *Grundsatzfragen der Kreditwirtschaft*, Schriftenreihe des Bundesministeriums der Finanzen, no. 28, Bonn.

Giddy, Ian H. (1985) 'Is Equity Underwriting Risky for Commercial Bank Affiliates?', in Walter (ed.) (1985), pp. 145–69.

Glass Subcommittee Hearings (1931) *Operation of the National and Federal Reserve Banking Systems*, Hearings before a Subcommittee of the Committee on Banking and Currency, United States Senate, 71st Congress, 3rd Session, Parts 1 through 6 and VII.

Glass Subcommittee Hearings (1932) *Operation of the National and Federal Reserve Banking Systems: Hearings on S. 4115 Before the Senate Committee on Banking and Currency*, 72nd Congress, 1st Session.

Glass Subcommittee Report (1932) *Operation of the National and Federal Reserve Banking Systems. Report No. 584 to accompany S. 4412* (22 April).

Golembe Associates (1982) *Commercial Banking and the Glass–Steagall Act* (Washington, DC: American Bankers Association).

Hamilton, James D. (1987) 'Monetary Factors in the Great Depression', *Journal of Monetary Economics*, vol. 19, pp. 145–69.

Haraf, William S. and Rose Marie Kushmeider (eds) (1988) *Restructuring Banking and Financial Services in America* (Washington, DC: American Enterprise Institute).

Hayes, Samuel L., III, A. Michael Spence, and David Van Praag Marks (1983) *Competition in the Investment Banking Industry* (Cambridge, MA: Harvard University Press).

Heggestad, Arnold (1975) 'Riskiness of Investments in Nonbank Activities by Bank Holding Companies', *Journal of Economics and Business*, vol. 27 (Spring), pp. 219–23.

Herman, Edward S. (1980) 'Commerical Bank Trust Departments', in *Abuse on Wall Street: Conflicts of Interest in the Securities Markets*, A Twentieth Century Fund Report (Westport, CN: Quorum Books), pp. 23–157.

Huertas, Thomas F. and John L. Silverman (1986) 'Charles E. Mitchell: Scapegoat of the Crash?', *Journal of Business History*, vol. 60 (Spring), pp. 81–103.

Hunter, William C. and Stephen G. Timme (1986) 'Technical Change, Organisational Form, and the Structure of Bank Production', *Journal of Money, Credit, and Banking*, vol. 18 (May), pp. 152–66.

Investment Company Institute (1979) *Misadventures in Banking: Bank Promotion of Pooled Investment Funds* (Washington, DC: Investment Company Institute).

Investment Company Institute (undated) *Proposed Bank Entry Into Mutual Funds: Some Economic Policy Issues* (Washington, DC: Research Department, Investment Company Institute).

Isaac, William M. and Melanie L. Fein (1988) 'Facing the Future – Life Without Glass–Steagall', *Catholic University Law Review*, vol. 37 (Winter), pp. 281–346.

Jaffe, Dwight M. (1975) 'Housing Finance and Mortgage Market Policy', in Brunner (ed.) (1975), pp. 93–122.

James, Christopher (1987) 'Some Evidence on the Uniqueness of Bank Loans', *Journal of Financial Economics*. vol. 19 (December), pp. 217–75.

Jenrette, Richard H. (1984) 'Testimony of Securities Industry Association Presented by Richard H. Jenrette Chairman of the Board of Directors on S. 2181 and S. 2134 Before The Senate Committee on Banking, Housing & Urban Affairs March 7, 1984', *Competitive Equity in the Financial Services Industry*, Hearings before the Committee on Banking, Housing, and Urban Affairs, United States Senate, 98th Congress, 2nd Session, Part III.

Jensen, Michael C. and William H. Meckling (1976) 'Theory of the Firm: Managerial Behavior, Agency Costs, and Capital Structure', *Journal of Financial Economics*, vol. 3, pp. 305–60.

Johnson, Rodney D. and David R. Meinster (1973–4) 'The Analysis of Bank Holding Company Acquisitions: Some Methodological Issues', *Journal of Bank Research*, vol. 4, pp. 58–61.

Kane, Edward J. (1985) *The Gathering Crisis in Deposit Insurance* (Cambridge, MA: MIT Press).

Karmel, Roberta (1980) 'Glass–Steagall: Some Critical Reflections', *Banking Law Journal*, vol. 97, pp. 631–41.

Kaufman, George G. (1988) 'Bank Runs: Causes, Benefits, and Costs', *Cato Journal*, vol. 7 (Winter), pp. 559–87.

Kaufman, George G. and Larry R. Mote (1989) 'Securities Activities of Commercial Banks: The Current Economic and Legal Environment', in *Research in Financial Services: Private and Public Interests*, George G. Kaufman (ed.) (Greenwich, CT: JAI Press), pp. 223–62.

Kelly, Edward J. III (1985a) 'Legislative History of the Glass–Steagall Act', in Walter (ed.) (1985), pp. 41–65.

Kelly, Edward J. III (1985b) 'Conflicts of Interest: A legal View', in Walter (ed.) (1985), pp. 231–54.

Kelly, Edward J. III (1987) 'Statement of Edward J. Kelly III Before the Senate Committee on Banking, Housing and Urban Affairs, in *Modernisation of the Glass–Steagall Act*, Hearing before the Committee on Banking, Housing, and Urban Affairs, United States Senate, 100th Congress, 1st Session, 30 July, pp. 59–67.

Kempf, Uta (1985) *German Bond Markets* (London: Euromoney Publications).

Kennedy, Susan E. (1973) *The Banking Crisis of 1933* (Lexington: University of Kentucky Press).

Knight, Robert E. (1970) 'Correspondent Banking, Part 1: Balances and Services', *Monthly Review* (Federal Reserve Bank of Kansas City) (November), pp. 3–14.

Knight, Robert E. (1976) 'Account Analysis in Correspondent Banking', *Monthly Review* (Federal Reserve Bank of Kansas City) (May), pp. 3–15, 24.

Krümmel, Hans-Jacob (1980) 'German Universal Banking Scrutinised', *Journal of Banking and Finance*, vol. 4, pp. 33–55.

Kwast, Myron L. (1987) 'The Impact of Underwriting and Dealing on Bank Returns and Risk', Financial Studies Section, Board of Governors of the Federal Reserve System (April).

Litan, Robert E. (1987) *What Should Banks Do?* (Washington, DC: The Brookings Institution).

Lucia, Joseph L. (1985) 'The Failure of the Bank of the United States: A Reappraisal', *Explorations in Economic History*, vol. 22, pp. 402–16.

Marcus, Alan J. and Israel Shaked (1984) 'Deposit Insurance Using Option-pricing Estimates', *Journal of Money, Credit and Banking*, vol. 16 (November), pp. 446–60.

Macey, Jonathan R. (1984) 'Special Interest Groups Legislation and the Judicial Function: The Dilemma of Glass–Steagall', *Emory Law Journal*, vol. 33 (Winter), pp. 1–40.

May, A. Wilfred (1934) 'Investment Operations of Commercial Banks', chapter XXIII in Willis and Chapman (1934), pp. 535–47.

Mayer, Thomas A. (1975) 'Credit Allocation – A Critical View', in Brunner (ed.) (1975), pp. 39–92.

Mehle, Roger W. (1975) 'Bank Underwriting of Municipal Revenue Bonds: Preserving Free and Fair Competition', *Syracuse Law Review*, vol. 26 (Fall), pp. 1117–56.

Meinster, David R. and Rodney D. Johnson (1974) 'Bank Holding Companies: Diversification Opportunities in Nonbank Activities', *Eastern Economics Journal*, vol. 1 (October), pp. 316–23.

Meltzer, Allan H. (1975) 'Credit Availability and Economic Decisions' in Brunner (ed.) (1975), pp. 123–50.

Monopoly Commission (Monopolkommission) (1976) Hauptgutachten 1973/1975 *Mehr Wettbewerb ist möglich* (Baden-Baden).

Monopoly Commission (Monopolkommission) (1978) Hauptgutachten 1976/1977 *Fortschreitende Konzentration bei Großunternehmen* (Baden-Baden).

Moore, Terris (1934) 'Security Affiliate Versus Private Investment Banker – A Study in Security Originations', *Harvard Business Review*, vol. 12 (July), pp. 480–2.

Morgan, J. P. and Co. (1984) *Rethinking Glass Steagall* (New York).

Natter, Raymond (1988) 'Glass–Steagall Act Reform: The Next Banking Issue on the Congressional Agenda', *Federal Bar News & Journal*, vol. 35 (May), pp. 185–91.

Neuberger, Hugh and Houston H. Stokes (1974) 'German Banks and German Growth, 1883–1913: An Empirical View', *Journal of Economic History*, vol. 34 (September), pp. 729–30.

Neville, Howard Ralph (1960) *The Detroit Banking Collapse of 1933* (East Lansing: Bureau of Business and Economic Research, Michigan State University).

Note (1983) 'National Banks and the Brokerage Business: The Comptroller's New Reading of the Glass–Steagall Act', *Virginia Law Review*, vol. 69 (October), pp. 1303–49.

Orbe, Lawrence F. III (1983) 'Glass–Steagall: Lest We Forget', *Florida State University Law Review*, vol. 11, pp. 163–95.

Osterweis, Steven (1932) 'Securities Affiliates and Security Operations of Commercial Banks', *Harvard Business Review*, vol. 11 (October), pp. 127–32.

Peach, W. Nelson (1941) *The Security Affiliates of National Banks*, The Johns Hopkins University Studies in Historical and Political Science (Baltimore: The Johns Hopkins Press).

Pecora Hearings (1933 and 1934) US Congress, Senate, *Stock Exchange Practices*, Hearings before the Committee on Banking and Currency United States Senate, 72nd Cong., 2nd Sess. and 73rd Cong., 2nd Sess. on S. Res 84 and S. Res 56 and S. Res 97.

Pecora, Ferdinand (1939) *Wall Street Under Oath: The Story of Our Modern Money Changers* (New York: Simon & Schuster).

Perkins, Edwin J. (1971) 'The Divorce of Commercial and Investment Banking: A History', *The Banking Law Journal*, vol. 88 (June), pp. 483–528.

Pontecorvo, Guilio (1958) 'Investment Banking and Security Speculation in the Late 1920's', *Business History Review*, vol. 32 (Summer), pp. 166–91.

Pozdena, Randall J. (1987) 'Commerce and Banking: The German Case', *FRSF Weekly Letter* (Federal Reserve Bank of San Francisco) (18 December).

Preston, Howard H. (1933) 'The Banking Act of 1933', *American Economic Review*, vol. 23 (December), pp. 587–90.

Pugel, Thomas A. and Lawrence J. White (1985) 'An Analysis of the Competitive Effects of Allowing Commercial Bank Affiliates to Underwrite Corporate Securities', in Walter (ed.) (1985), pp. 93–139.

Ritter, Jay R. (1984) 'Signaling and the Valuation of Unseasoned New Issues: A Comment', *Journal of Finance*, vol. 39, pp. 1231–7.

Rogowski, Robert J. (1978) 'Commercial Banks and Municipal Revenue Bonds', *Banking Law Journal*, vol. 95, pp. 155–72.

Ronn, Ehud I. and Avinash K. Verma (1986) 'Pricing Risk-Adjusted Deposit Insurance: An Option-Based Model', *Journal of Finance*, vol. 41 (September), pp. 871–95.

Santsmeru, Anthony M. and Joseph D. Vinso (1977) 'Estimating the Probability of Failure of Commercial Banks and the Banking System', *Journal of Banking and Finance*, vol. 1 (September), pp. 185–205.

Saunders, Anthony (1985a) 'Bank Safety and Soundness and the Risks of Corporate Security Activities', in Walter (1985), pp. 171–206.

Saunders, Anthony (1985b) 'Conflicts of Interest: An Economic View', in Walter (ed.) (1985), pp. 297–320.

Saunders, Anthony (1985c) 'Securities Activities of Commercial Banks: The Problem of Conflicts of Interest', *Business Review* (Federal Reserve Bank of Philadelphia) (July-August), pp. 17–27.

Schwartz, Anna (1988) 'Financial Stability and the Federal Safety Net', in Haraf and Kurshmeider (eds) (1988).

SEC Report (1939a) US Securities and Exchange Commission, *Study of Investment Trusts and Investment Companies, Part 2: The Statistical Survey of Investment Trusts and Investment Companies*, House Document No. 70, 76th Congress, 1st Session, 3 January 1939 (Washington, DC: US Government Printing Office).

SEC Report (1939b) US Securities and Exchange Commission, *Study of Investment Trusts and Investment Companies: Commingled or Common Trust Funds Administered by Banks and Trust Companies*, House Document No. 476, 76th Congress, 2nd Session, 23 September 1939 (Washington, DC: US Government Printing Office).

SEC Report (1940) US Securities and Exchange Commission, *Study of Investment Trusts and Investment Companies: Part 3, Chapters 1 and II, Abuses and Deficiencies in the Organization and Operation of Investment Trusts and Investment Companies*, House Document No. 279, 76th Congress, 1st Session, 3 May 1939 (Washington, DC: US Government Printing Office).

SEC Report (1942) US Securities and Exchange Commission, *Study of Investment Trusts and Investment Companies: Part 3, Chapter VII, Abuses and Deficiencies in the Organization and Operation of Investment Trusts and Investment Companies* House Document No. 136, 77th Congress, 1st Session, 26 February 1941 (Washington, DC: US Government Printing Office).

Securities Industry Association (1985) *Questioning Expanded Bank Powers: A case for maintaining the fundamental separation between the banking and securities industries* (New York, NY and Washington, DC) (September).

Securities Industry Association (1987) *Statement of Securities Industry Association Before the Senate Committee on Banking, Housing, and Urban Affairs*, 8 December (duplicated) (Washington, DC).

Seligman, Joel (1982) *The Transformation of Wall Street* (Boston: Houghton Mifflin).

Sender, Henny (1987) 'The Client Comes Second', *Institutional Investor* (March), pp. 84–98.

SEP Report (1934) *Stock Exchange Practices, Report of the Committee on Banking and Currency*, pursuant to S. Res. 84 (72nd Congress) and S. Res. 56 and S. Res. 97 (73rd Congress) (Washington, DC: US Government Printing Office).

Silver, David (1987) *Written Statement of the Investment Company Institute Before the Senate Committee on Banking, Housing and Urban Affairs* (23 January).

Smirlock, Michael and Jess Yawitz (1985) 'Asset Returns, Discount Rate Change, and Market Efficiency', *Journal of Finance*, vol. 40 (September), pp. 1141–58.

Staff of the Board of Governors of the Federal Reserve System (1984) *A Review and Evaluation of Federal Margin Regulations* (December).

Stover, Roger D. (1982) 'A Reexamination of Bank Holding Company Acquisitions', *Journal of Research*, vol. 12 (Summer), pp. 101–8.

Swary, Itzhak (1986) 'Stock Market Reaction to Regulatory Action in the Continental Illinois Crisis', *Journal of Business*, vol. 59, pp. 451–73.

Tallman, Ellis (1988) 'Some Unanswered Questions about Bank Panics', *Economic Review* (Federal Reserve Bank of Atlanta) (November/December), pp. 2–21.

US Congress, Senate, Banking Committee (1982) Subcommittee on Securities, *Securities Activities of Depository Institutions*, 97th Cong., 2 Sess. (February).

US Department of the Treasury (1975) 'Public Policy Aspects of Bank Securities Activities: An Issue Paper', in *Securities Activities of Commercial Banks*, Hearings before the Subcommittee on Securities of the Committee on Banking, Housing and Urban Affairs, United States Senate, 94th Congress, 1st Session, pp. 22–87.

United States Presidential Task Force on Market Mechanisms (Brady Commission) (1988) *Report of the Presidential Task Force on Market Mechanisms: Submitted to the President of the United States, the Secretary of the Treasury, and the Chairman of the Federal Reserve Board* (Washington, DC: Treasury Department).

Wall, Larry D. (1987) 'Has Bank Holding Companies' Diversification Affected Their Risk of Failure?', *Journal of Economics and Business*, vol. 39, pp. 313–26.

Wall, Larry D. and Robert A. Eisenbeis (1984) 'Risk Considerations in Deregulating Bank Activities', *Economic Review* (Federal Reserve Bank of Atlanta) (May), pp. 6–19.

Walter, Ingo (ed.) (1985) *Deregulating Wall Street: Commercial Bank Penetration of the Corporate Securities Market* (New York: John Wiley).

Werner, Morris R. (1933) *Little Napoleons and Dummy Directors. Being the Narrative of the Bank of United States* (New York and London: Harper & Brothers).

Westerfield, Ray B. (1933) 'The Banking Act of 1933', *Journal of Political Economy*, vol. 31 (December), pp. 721–49.

White, Eugene N. (1983) *The Regulation and Reform of the American Banking System, 1900–1929* (Princeton: Princeton University Press).

White, Eugene N. (1986) 'Before the Glass–Steagall Act: An Analysis of the Investment Banking Activities of National Banks', *Explorations in Economic History*, vol. 23, pp. 33–55.

Wigmore, Barrie A. (1987) 'Was the Bank Holiday of 1933 a Run of the Dollar Rather Than the Banks?', *Journal of Economic History*, vol. 47 (September), pp. 739–55.

Willis, H. Parker (1934) 'The Banking Act of 1933 – An Appraisal', *American Economic Review*, vol. 24, pp. 101–10.

Willis, H. Parker and John M. Chapman (1934) *The Banking Situation* (New York: Columbia University Press).

Index

Abbreviations used in the index are consistent with those in the text.